Virginia State Parks

A Complete Outdoor Recreation Guide
for
Campers, Boaters, Anglers, Hikers
and Outdoor Lovers
by
Bill Bailey

In Cooperation with the Virginia
Department of Conservation & Recreation

Glovebox Guidebooks of America

To our readers: Travel outdoors entails some unavoidable risks. Know your limitations, be prepared, be alert, use good judgment, think safety and enjoy Virginia's terrific outdoors. Be bold!

Special thanks to Joe Elton and Gary Waugh and to all the staff at all the parks. Virginia has some of the finest parks---and staff---in the nation!

Copyright ©1996 by Glovebox Guidebooks of America/Bill Bailey

Cover design by Dan Jacalone
Cover photo courtesy of the Virginia Dept. Conservation & Recreation
Editor, Bill Cornish
Managing Editor, Penny Weber-Bailey

Published by   **Glovebox Guidebooks of America**

1112 Washburn Place East
Saginaw, Michigan 48602-2977
(800) 289-4843 or (517) 792-8363

Library of Congress, CIP

Bailey, William L., 1952-

Virginia State Parks Guidebook
(A Glovebox Guidebooks of America publication)
ISBN 1-881139-14-X

Printed in the United States of America

10 9 8 7 6 5 4 3 2 1

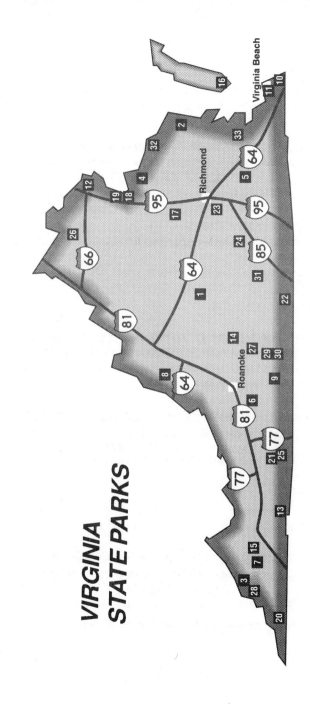

VIRGINIA
STATE PARKS

Richmond

Roanoke

Virginia Beach

Contents

State parks and recreation areas

Foreword

For more than 25 years, Virginia has proudly used the slogan *"Virginia is for Lovers."* It has been a centerpiece of our tourism promotion. Virginians also have bragging rights when it comes to climate, location and diverse natural attractions. Beautiful mountains carrying the Appalachian Trail, the Chesapeake Bay, the world's largest estuary, sun drenched Atlantic beaches and historically significant tidal rivers are home to a multitude of creatures big and small and offer exciting recreational opportunities for families and individuals.

It's hard to argue with the statement that "Virginia has it all"---soaring mountains, majestic rivers, sparkling shorelines and rich history. And perhaps no group of properties so thoroughly captures the natural and cultural majesty and diversity of Virginia as does her state park system.

This easy to read *Glovebox Guidebook to Virginia's State Parks* is your handy guide to many of the mysteries and adventures that often allude the casual visitor. It also provides all the information needed to ensure your visit is a convenient and carefree one. Your most memorable outdoor adventures await you in Virginia.

Humpback whales and loggerhead turtles are frequently seen from the pristine beaches at False Cape State Park in southern Virginia Beach. In 1607, the brave men and women of the Virginia Company, who established the first permanent settlement in our nation, first touched soil on this continent on the shores of the Chesapeake Bay on what is now First Landing/Seashore State Park. The sights and sounds they experienced almost 400 years ago can be enjoyed today.

On June 15, 1936, Virginia became the first state to open an entire state park system on the same day when it opened its six original parks. The log cabins and lodges built by the Civilian Conservation Corps still serve as popular overnight accommodations for park visitors. Today, Virginia has 30 of the finest state parks in the country. I love Virginia's state parks and I think you and your family will too---just give them a try.

I'm often asked what you can do in the parks. Let me make a few suggestions and share some of my favorite experiences:

Horseback riding or hiking at Grayson Highlands where ponies run free, or at Hungry Mother where lake fishing is terrific.

Bike, hike or ride horseback along the New River Trail, a 57-mile section of abandoned rail line that hugs the New River which offers excellent fishing and scenic canoeing, rafting and kayaking.

Add some relaxation to that business meeting, or a special setting to a family reunion by using one of our conference centers, Cedar Crest (at Twin Lakes State Park) or Hemlock Haven (at Hungry Mother State Park).

Virginia's state parks offers access to the state's four largest lakes. The serious and casual sportsmen alike enjoy both the boating and variety of fish species at Claytor Lake, Smith Mountain Lake and Lake Anna. They can also enjoy the state's largest impoundment, Buggs Island Lake, from either Staunton River or Occoneechee State Park.

Douthat Lake is stocked with rainbow and brown trout and Staunton River offers excellent striped bass angling.

William Jennings Bryan called Natural Tunnel "the eighth wonder of the world" and our chairlift takes visitors down to the tunnel floor. Children of all ages enjoy both the tunnel and our railroad museum. I sighted eagles at six parks last year (Caledon, Chippokes Plantation, Mason Neck, Belle Isle, James River and Lake Anna) and saw many different raptors and migrating songbirds during the Annual Birding Festival at Kiptopeke on the Eastern Shore.

I watched spellbound children and adults mesmerized by the authenticity of sights and sounds during Civil War battle reenactments at Sailor's Creek and Staunton River Battlefield.

What could be better for the soul than the sights, sounds, smells and adventures captured in the natural environment of our state parks? I hope you and your family will take time this year to visit Virginia's wonderful state parks. Whether you're just passing through or looking for a special outdoor adventure don't miss our parks...*they're a natural.*

Joe Elton, Director
Virginia State Parks

Introduction

Beginning with six parks in 1936, the Virginia state parks system has grown to 43 parks, including historical state parks, peaceful natural areas and a linear multi-use trail.

These one-of-a-kind open spaces and wonderful family places are charming and rustic, sometimes modern, often wild—always friendly and exciting places—for unlimited recreation activities for every family member. Almost everything you can look for in the outdoors is in Virginia.

The parks hold the promise of exciting discoveries for people with all types of outdoor interests. You may visit a Civil War battlefield or a stone tower where musket balls were made. Visit General George Washington's gristmill or travel to Chippokes Plantation, one of Virginia's oldest working plantations. Travel to Chesapeake Bay, enjoy sparkling coastal beaches or head to the rugged Virginia Appalachian Mountains in the west. Hike the famous Appalachian Trail or an educational self-guided trail. See the natural phenomenon at Fairy Stone or a natural tunnel carved through a mountain. You can also visit any of 24 modern visitor centers.

Virginia state parks reflect the incredible diversity of natural and cultural resources of the state. Other natural treasures you'll discover include pristine coastal lands, salt marshes, natural history information, museums, camping sites—or comfy cabins or lodges, lots of fishing opportunities, hiking or biking, interesting history, unique geological formations, Victorian mansions, swimming, and cabins to rent.

Virginia has some of the finest state parks and natural areas in the country. This is your comprehensive guide to enjoying each and every one of them.

General fees and services

Most parks have a day-use parking fee of $1.50 to $2.50 depending on the time of year and day of the week. Fees are collected on weekends from April to Memorial Day, then daily to the Labor Day weekend, and again on weekends through October. First Landing/Seashore State Park collects day-use parking fees year-round. An annual parking pass is available.

Boat launching and rentals

Fees for boat launching vary. An annual parking/boat launching pass is available which is good at all state parks except Leesylvania State Park.

Most of the boat rental concessions operate from Memorial Day weekend to Labor Day weekend, offering rowboats, paddleboats and canoes by the hour or day.

Fishing

The Commonwealth's state parks offer access to the state's four largest lakes as well as several major rivers, the Chesapeake Bay and Atlantic Ocean. Smaller manmade lakes in a number of parks are excellent fisheries for largemouth bass, trout, crappies, panfish and bream.

Historic sites

Admission to historic sites (Chippokes, George Washington's Grist Mill, Shot Tower and Southwest Virginia Museum are reasonable. There are special rates for children under 12 years old (6 years and under are free).

Swimming

Swimming pools and guarded beaches generally operate from Memorial Day weekend to Labor Day weekend for a fee. Children under 3 years are free and there are special rates for children 12 and under. Discount or annual swimming tickets are offered at some units.

Camping

Nineteen Virginia state parks have campgrounds totaling 1,500 sites. Some of the campgrounds have electrical/water hookups, which tend to be larger sites, able to accommodate recreational vehicles. Many campgrounds have tent sites and group campgrounds. Developed group campgrounds have picnic tables and access to a bathhouse. Most campsites have a picnic table and fire ring. Camping fees vary depending on the park and type of site (primitive, hook-ups, etc.).

Primitive hike-in camping is offered at False Cape and Sky Meadows. Primitive drive-in camping is available at Smith Mountain and Occoneechee. The maximum camping period is 14 days in any 30-day period. Advance registration can be made at each park or by calling (800) 933-PARK between 9 a.m. and 4 p.m. weekdays.

Cabins

Seven parks have a total of 140 climate controlled cabins. The parks include Claytor Lake, Douthat, Fairy Stone, Hungry Mother, Seashore, Staunton River and Westmoreland state parks. Some cabins are cinder block and many are hand-hewn log cabins nestled deep in the woods, along ridges or near lakes. Most cabins are rented on a weekly basis; however, two-night minimum stays are offered on a limited basis (nightly reservations must be made at least one month in advance). Cabins are typically available from March 1 to early December. Reservations go on sale on Sept. 1 of each year. To make a reservation call *(800) 933-PARK* from 9 a.m. - 4 p.m. weekdays; in the Richmond area, call (804) 225-3867.

One-room cabins have a combined dining and living room with a kitchen and shower-bath. They can accommodate two persons.

One-bedroom cabins have a combined dining and living room (a maximum of two extra beds are available at an additional cost), bedroom, kitche shower bath. A total of four people can stay in the one-bedroo

Two-bedroom cabins have a combined dining and living two extra beds are available at an additional charge), and shower-bath. They accommodate four p occupancy of six.

Douthat State Park Lodge has six bedrooms, two bathrooms (one with tub and one with a shower) and can accommodate 13 persons with a maximum occupancy of 15 persons. The lodge is rented only as a unit; individual rooms are not available.

Westmoreland overnight cabins are rustic and available Memorial Day through Labor Day. They can be rented for as short as two nights and a maximum of two consecutive weeks. They accommodate four people and are furnished with four single bunk beds. Pillows, linens and towels are not provided, nor are a kitchen or bathroom. Guests have free use of showers and bathrooms at the nearby campground. Reservations must be made through the park directly; call (804) 493-8821. The cabin cancellation fee is $10.

Trails

Hiking, biking and bridle trails criss-cross the state parks, giving visitors a chance to explore hardwood forests, coastal marshes, meadows, mountains and shorelines. The Appalachian Trail can be accessed from Grayson Highland and Sky Meadows state parks.

Environmental education

Just about every park has seasonal outdoor education programs; many also have year-round learning opportunities for school, scout, church and civic groups. Most programs start at the visitor center or amphitheaters and teach about natural and cultural history. A variety of special events and guided hikes are also popular in the parks.

Meeting

s might be the perfect place for
conference. Hungry Mother's
eting and dining spaces for up
meeting spaces and outdoor

ing is available Memorial
nd hour-long guided trail

and
models.
oom (a maximum
wo bedrooms, kitchen
rsons with a maximum

Picnic shelters

Many parks have picnic shelters and gazebos for rent. Most are perfect for family reunions, offering nearby rest rooms, water and grills. Shelters can be reserved by the half-day or full day by calling the individual units. Pocahontas' dining halls can be rented by the full day.

Pets

Pets are welcome in many campgrounds, some cabins and most everywhere else is the state parks. When outside they must be on a six foot leash. Individual parks have their own rules regarding pets.

Alcoholic beverages

The display and use of alcoholic beverages is prohibited.

Park accessibility

Virginia is making the units as barrier-free as possible for the convenience of persons with disabilities. The state park system encourages people with special needs to contact the park you are visiting for more information.

For more information

All fees and services are subject to change. Check with the State Parks Reservation Center or any state park for the latest prices, programs and activities. *Call (800) 933-PARK.*

1 Bear Creek Lake State Park
Land: 326 acres Water: 40-acre lake

Bear Creek is in the middle of the Piedmont. Between the mountains to the west and the coastal plains to the east, the Piedmont is characterized by gently rolling hills amid a mixture of pines, cedars and hardwoods. Quiet Bear Creek is known for quality facilities and a friendly staff like the larger parks, without the crowds.

The 16,242-acre Cumberland State Forest almost completely surrounds Bear Creek, also offering a broad menu of outdoor recreation including four natural areas, sporting clay range, one picnic shelter, significant hiking trails, four lakes, hunting, fishing and scenic areas. The state forest is managed for multiple-use purposes including watershed protection, timber production, recreation and research. State forests, like Cumberland, are self-supportive; income is received from the sale of forest products and hunting stamp sales. Also in the state forest is a marker commemorating the Revolutionary War hero Jesse Thomas.

The focal point of the state park is the lake, which is surrounded by an updated campground, five hiking trails, natural areas, swimming beach, boat ramp and shoreline fishing. The park also provides access to the Willis River Trail, a 16-mile trail that winds through the Cumberland Forest.

Bear Creek was constructed in 1938 by the Virginia Department of Agriculture through the State Forestry Division. Although the park was built during the closing days of the Great Depression, it was not built by members of the Civilian Conservation Corps, who built so many parks across the nation. The men that built the park were simply carpenters, farmers and unskilled laborers seeking jobs. They built two pavilions, six fireplaces and many of the buildings still used at the forested park.

The tract was turned over to the Division of State Parks in 1940 and operated for day use until 1962, when the campground was opened and the name changed to Bear Creek Lake State Park.

Seventy-five percent of the park's use during the summer is on Friday, Saturday and Sunday.

Information and Activities

Bear Creek Lake State Park
Route 1, P.O. Box 253
Cumberland, VA 23040
(804)492-4410

Directions: 4.5 miles northwest of Cumberland. From Route 60, travel west on Route 622 and south on Route 629 to the park entrance. Bear Creek is less than one hour from Richmond. The office has a small reception area and a 20-foot-by-20-foot deck attached.

The lightly used park is surrounded by agricultural lands, pastures and scattered woodlots. A significant part of the tract is river bottom. The only public use at James River park is permitted hunting and fishing. Special use permits can be obtained from the Bear Creek park manager.

Campground: Forty out of the 58 sites have full hook-ups. All of the sites

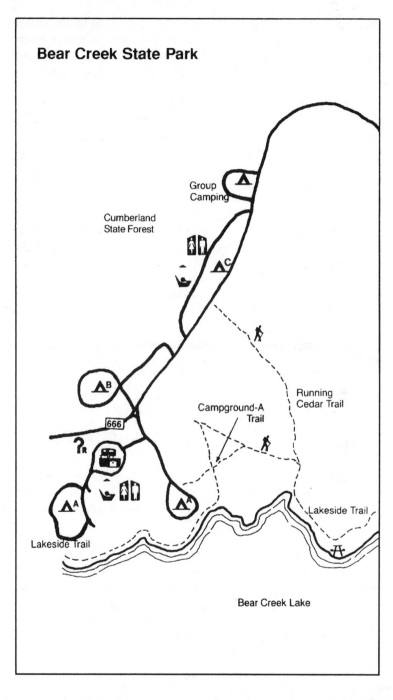

Bear Creek State Park

Group
Camping

Cumberland
State Forest

Running
Cedar Trail

Campground-A
Trail

666

Lakeside Trail

Lakeside Trail

Bear Creek Lake

are along a hard-surfaced road. Also along the road are some wonderful Civilian Conservation Corps pavilions with twin fieldstone fireplaces and timber-frame construction. Shelter No. 3 is particularly attractive with its bulky peeled-bark log construction, stone floor and handsome roof line.

Loop A, sites 1-17, offers some cozy sites near the water. Site 10, which is back in the woods a few yards, would make a terrific tent site. Sites 12 and 14 are very close to the water along a flat bank several feet above the surface. Site 17 is large enough for a medium-sized RV rig and right on the safe-feeling lake. Bring your canoe and launch it from this grand campsite. A block showerhouse serves this loop.

Sites in the 20s are high above the lake and shady. Some of these small sites are outlined by timbers and are on a rounded peninsula offering a water view. Site 21 features a wonderful water view in two directions and a winding trail that takes campers down to the shimmering lakeshore. Site 22, also near the water, is perfect for a small RV rig or tent.

Sites in the B loop, 1-14, have flat gravel pads, fire rings and picnic tables. Site 6 is slightly oversized in this small loop and has a view of a densely wooded valley. Site 9 is also oversized, but close to the road. Site 20 is oversized, offering a side yard-like area for additional camping gear or chairs. There is no showerhouse in the B loop.

Sites in the C loop are shady and served by a showerhouse that is outfitted with a drinking fountain and bulletin board. Site 5 is large and next to the showerhouse. Site 6 receives some midday sunlight. Sites 8 and 10 are oversized, kidney-shaped, above a private wooded hollow. Some of the sites in this small loop are separated by a wall of vegetation and spaced out better than the other loops. Some are also oversized in the back of the sites, ideal for large rigs or campers with boats and extra equipment.

Group camping is offered at Bear Creek; call the park manager for details.

Fishing: Local anglers swear by live bait from the shoreline, boat or handicapped accessible fishing pier. Panfishing is good near the culverts. When the water warms, try fishing near the dam. The lake has two underwater structure areas that were made from Christmas trees. The biggest and best structure is marked by an orange post at the end of the 24-

foot-long fishing pier.

If you catch a grass carp at Bear Lake, please return the fish to the water unharmed. They are here purposely to rid the lake of undesirable vegetation. The carp is a large fish weighing up to 25 pounds. You'll recognize them by their large mirror-like scales. Usually prolific breeders, the carp in the lake are sterile. Therefore the lake has only a limited number of the grazing fish.

The lake also has northern pike, crappie, largemouth bass, channel catfish and sunfish.

Mobile anglers might also want to try the Willis River, where the occasional gar can be taken, or the Appomattox River, a major tributary to the James River.

Boating: From a tiny tan shed canoes, paddleboats and rowboats are rented by the day or hour. The park's single-lane boat launching ramp is at the breast of the dam. Only electric powered boats are permitted on the lake. Boats are rented during the summer only.

Hiking: Five trails totaling seven miles criss-cross the mostly wooded park. The Lost Barr Trail, at the west end of the lake, is an interpretive trail with 10 signs along its 1.5-mile length. The easy trail offers hikers an opportunity to learn about lakeshore ecology and general natural history.

You'll also learn that foxes walk on tip-toes, deer on toenails and raccoons and skunks on long hind legs. Toe-walkers include predatory animals like dogs and cats. Stealthy and quiet, toe-walkers step lightly on padded toes. Toe-nail walkers like deer, sheep and cows have learned to run on hoofs or toe-nails. Many can run fast and outmaneuver toe-walkers. Neither quiet nor fast, humans are flatfooted. Along with raccoons and skunks, we have long hind feet or hands and walk on the whole of the foot. Along the trail you'll find a sign that depicts the many types of feet the animal kingdom has.

The 16-mile Willis River Trail can be accessed from a trailhead with parking. The Willis River Trail is a route through the Cumberland State Forest through striking hardwoods and past many scenic overlooks. Most of the trail was originally cleared in 1986 from the swinging bridge over the Willis

River to Winston Lake. There are plans to extend the trail all the way to the Appomattox courthouse where Lee surrendered. The extension would require the permission of private landowners and more resources than are presently available. There is no camping along the Willis River Trail.

Day-use areas: The best equipped day-use areas are near the beach where play apparatus, shady picnic tables and pavilions are located.

Beach: Outlined by a split-rail fence, the cove-side beach is sandy and served by a gravel parking lot, pavilion, small playground, nearby boat rental, day-use areas and changing house. The water is divided into three patrolled sections and the beach is about 125 yards long. One of the sections is in shallow water and meant for use by toddlers and small children. Bring your volleyball to play on the sand court only steps from the water. The beach is open Memorial Day weekend to Labor Day.

The food concession is a few steps above the beach past a grassy area. The gray vertically-sided building has a large deck and brightly colored umbrella tables. The walk-up-style concession serves chicken fingers, chips, soft drinks, shrimp boats, fish fillets, curly fries, onion rings, hamburgers and sandwiches. They also sell batteries, inflatable toys, T-shirts, insect repellent, goggles, sunscreen, towels, water jugs, hats and swim passes.

Also at the concession stand is an air hose that can be used to inflate floating toys and inner tubes. A three-sided kiosk on the deck offers information about the park, natural history and neighboring attractions. The modern bathhouse, which is connected to the food concession by a broad wooden deck, has showers, toilets and metal lockers.

Nature: The rolling hills of the region are prime habitat for songbirds, turkey, pheasant, raccoon, deer, quail, reptiles and amphibians. The natural areas are diverse, including bottomland hardwoods on an alluvial flood-plain, granite rock quarries, abandoned fields, managed open spaces and forests with clay soil.

Some areas have shrubby pines, black oaks, hickory, ash and hackberry. This diversity increases visitors' chances to see wildlife significantly.

Wildflowers of note include jack-in-the-pulpit and pink lady's slippers. The

Bear Creek archery range is especially popular before hunting season.

Cumberland Forest includes four pristine natural areas: Willis River, Rock Quarry, Red Cedar and Turkey Ridge. Each has hiking trails and interesting natural features.

One of the best interpretive programs offered at the park is canoe trips on the Willis River. Some programs and special events are offered during the summer, depending on staff availability.

Hunting: Abundant populations of deer and turkey make the surrounding forest lands popular with hunters, especially bow hunters. Call the park manager for hunting seasons, regulations and details. Hunters might be interested in the sporting clay range in the nearby Cumberland State Forest. It is open Wednesday - Sunday.

Archery range: Bear Creek has the only archery range in the Virginia State Parks system. There is a small fee to use the range that is open 8 a.m. - 4 p.m. October to April and 8 a.m. - 7 p.m. May to September.

Shooters should inspect all equipment for damage before shooting. Follow the numerical order of targets, shoot only designated targets, make sure the shooting lane is clear before firing, only one shooter should fire at a time, and other shooters and spectators must remain behind the shooting station. Shooters are asked not to use crossbows or broadhead arrows. Persons under 15 years old must be supervised by an adult. A small brochure rack contains this and other information about the range. Call (804) 492-4121 for additional information.

The range consists of 10 excelsior bale targets with assorted big-game paper faces. Each target is identified one to 10 with three-inch by three-inch red and white target number signs. Also along each shooting lane are three suggested shooting stations. These are clearly identified with different colored signs (stakes). Generally, the shot distances are as follows: green, short range; orange, medium range; and yellow, long range. A scoring system can be developed using these stations.

All of the targets are in the woods and simulate typical shots encountered while hunting.

Insiders tips: The nearby Bear Creek Market at the entrance to the park has fishing, camping, ice, baits and gasoline. Visit one of only two gravestones in the Cumberland State Forest that carries an epitaph written by Charles Dickens. He wrote the inscription for Charles Irving Thornton in 1842.

2 Belle Isle State Park

Land: 733 acres   Water: Rappahannock River/creeks

Heavily wooded and rural, Belle Isle State Park, in the Tidewater region, is the first park to be purchased with funds from the 1992 Parks and Recreation Facilities Bond. It was purchased in 1993. The pastoral park is bordered by the Rappahannock River and flat agricultural fields that roll off into the distance. Many of the farm fields are actually inside park boundaries, and portions of them will be gradually developed over the next few years.

The master plan calls for controlled development over a 20-year period. New roads and other infrastructure improvements are under way. During the next few years the park will gain a rustic campground, boat launch on Deep Creek, 12 cabins, swimming pool, group camping area, additional trails, fully restored residence for groups, enhanced day-use areas and more.

Belle Isle is rich in native and colonial history. Inhabited by members of the Powhattan Tribe, the area was visited by American Indians on a seasonal basis, attracted to the area by the variety of food, materials for tools and shelter, and clay for pottery and pipe making. These early people lived peacefully, growing corn and tobacco.

In 1692, John Bertrand settled in the area, one of the first of several colonial plantation owners. The park continues to be farmed today using many conservation methods that reduce field runoff into neighboring creeks and rivers that flow into the Chesapeake Bay watershed.

Belle Isle is a park with a lot of potential.

Information and Activities

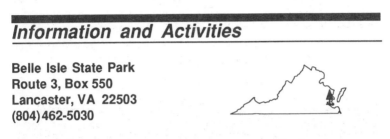

Belle Isle State Park
Route 3, Box 550
Lancaster, VA 22503
(804) 462-5030

Directions: Off Route 683 near Lively. The park office is a single-story, white frame house with a red brick chimney. Swimming is not permitted in the park.

Hiking: Trails are still being developed in the park. Two trails are color coded and ready for use. Watch House Trail (.5 mile) is blazed in red and connects the park office to the Rappahannock River across wetlands and fields. The Neck Fields Trail (1.2 miles) runs parallel to the river.

Fishing: Shoreline anglers report fair to good fishing for croakers, spots and a few trout and rockfish. Bloodworms and peelers are the recommended live bait. A small L-shaped wooden fishing pier is behind the Pollard Environmental Education Center. Anglers also wade off the lightly wooded shoreline in this tract of the park.

Boating: Canoeing the Rappahannock River or the Deep and Mulberry creeks is relaxing, offering a chance to observe a variety of habitats. The park also offers guided canoe trips during the summer.

The powerful Rappahannock River is like the James and Potomac: All are intertwined with the colorful early history of the country and state. John Smith sailed up the river near Fredericksburg in the early 1600s, seeding small villages that sprang up along the way.

President George Washington, a river expert in his own right (legend holds George once threw a silver dollar across the Rappahannock), once told Congress that if measures weren't taken to improve the navigation of the Rappahannock below the falls at Fredericksburg, a day would come when upstart seaports like New York might overshadow the region.

The Rappahannock River was the de facto border between the Union and the Confederacy. Along its banks four major battles were fought during the Civil War. The bloody battles of Spotsylvania Courthouse, Chancelorsville, Fredericksburg and the Wilderness resulted in the deaths of more than 100,000 Americans between December 1862 and May 1864.

After murdering President Lincoln, John Wilkes Booth fled south through Maryland, across the Potomac near what is now the Route 301 bridge, and entered Virginia through King George County to cross the Rappahannock to Port Royal, where he was shot in a burning barn near the village. By the way, isn't it about time we cleared Dr. Richard Mudd's name for treating Booth's wounds on that fateful day?

A canal built near it from Fredericksburg to Waterloo in 1829. The manmade river was meant to expedite moving the Rappahannock River raw materials from the interior to the coast and to return finished products from the coast to markets inland. The canal has 47 locks, 20 dams and was never finished due to the competition of railroad delivery and expansion. Parts of the canal can still be seen.

Paddlers can explore many sections of the Rappahannock River, finding quiet parts like those near Belle Isle, or wilderness, riffle and rapids in other stretches. One of the best sections is Remington to Kellys Ford, great for beginning and intermediate boaters with moderate rapids.

Day-use areas: Tables, grills and open spaces are on the water west of the park office. The best picnic areas are behind the Pollard Environmental Education Center, east of the park office along the river. Many shady spots with terrific scenic water views are on this mowed point of land. Other picnic tables are grouped under the canopy of huge trees. Across the river are some old boats and crab houses and moorings.

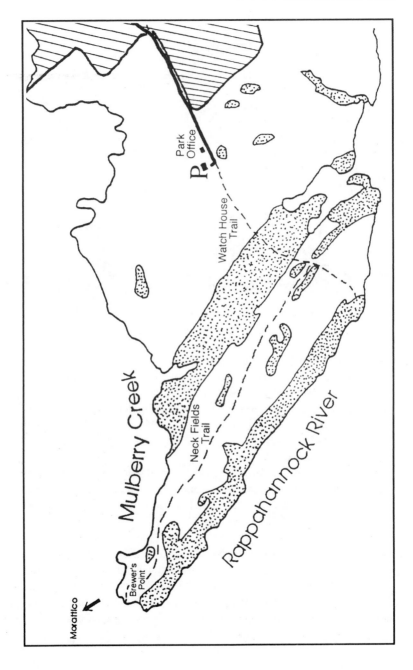

The park is rapidly developing new recreational facilities.

Conference center: On the water, the small cement block conference center (it reminds you of a ranch-style house), called a "conference shelter," can seat up to 40 people. It's heated and air-conditioned and the kitchen is equipped. A bay window offers a view of the water. The low building can be rented by groups and is surrounded by picnic tables and open spaces along the uneven shoreline.

The tidy building is available for half-days or full-day rentals. The center has a wonderful water view and is only steps away from the Pollard Environmental Education Center, and a few yards from a splendid view of lush agricultural fields.

Nature: Diverse habitats offer good numbers of wildflowers, mammals and birds to view. From tidal wetlands interspersed with farmlands and upland forests, many species are found including deer, fox, raccoon, osprey, bald eagles, opossum, woodchuck and wild turkey. Much of the park's careful development has been designed to not disturb nesting bald eagles.

Wildflowers include the cardinal flower, black-eyed Susan, Carolina elephant's foot, goldenrod, aster, hog peanuts, boneset, narrow leaf mint, several types of sedge and grasses, and many others. Spring is the best time to view Belle Isle wildflowers.

Tree types include sweet gum, red maple, southern red oak, Virginia pine, willow or black oak, and nine kinds of shrubs including holly, alder, dogwood, blueberry, winged sumac and others.

Environmental education: Teaching the teacher how to conduct outdoor education lessons is the primary focus of the park's small staff. School groups can then visit the gently rolling park, hike the trails and learn about general ecology principles from their classroom teacher. Teachers may use the park's various equipment at no charge.

The overnight residents' quarters is a Williamsburg-style house that can sleep 25 in five bedrooms. Groups may rent the facility for one or more nights and use the remainder of the park as an outdoor classroom. Groups need to bring their own sleeping bags and most other overnight equipment, supplies and food.

The two-story house is called the Garland and Peggy Pollard Environmental Education Center and its front yard is outlined by a colonial-style picket fence, gate, boxwood hedges and a red stone walkway. The backyard is about three mowed acres along the lazy Rappahannock River. The front steps to the huge house are of slate, the back has a patio, and the roof is covered with shake shingles and moss. Windows with shutters are three-over-three and the fireplace has raised panels and cove moldings. The classic house is the perfect place for youths and other organized groups to use while learning about nature in the park.

The park staff plans to restore the formal garden and hedgerows at the rear of the house. Near the house are plenty of metal-legged picnic tables, tin trash barrels and large trees. Some of the tables are extended and accessible for people with disabilities. An interpretive building is in the long-range master plan.

Insiders tip: Your organized group would love the overnight Pollard center in this quiet, rural park.

3 Breaks Interstate Park
Land: 4,500 acres Water: Lakes and whitewater river

Breaks Interstate has the largest canyon east of the Mississippi River, stretching more than five miles and reaching more than 1,600 feet deep. It is sometimes called the Grand Canyon of the South. The canyon's sheer rock walls and lush mountains covered with forests and thick stands of rhododendron make it one of the most scenic places in America.

The name "breaks" was derived from a break in Pine Mountain created by the grinding, cutting action of Russell Fork of the Big Sandy River as it slowly carved a five-mile gorge through the sandstone, on its way to join the Ohio River.

This area was once covered by a vast sea that left layers of sediments of mud and clay. In ancient times, tremendous forces under the earth's surface pushed these layers of sediment upward in a dramatic mountain-building action. In this area, the thrusted earth created two long mountain ridges with fractures and faults on all four sides of the two new mountains. Over thousands of years, erosive forces wore down the new ridges and created river channels which wore ever deeper hollows and valleys. In such a manner, the grinding, cutting action of the Russell Fork slowly cut the huge gorge through the northern end of Pine Mountain. The crest of Pine Mountain is 2,800 feet above sea level.

The Breaks gained widespread recognition in 1900 when John Fox Jr., author of *"The Trail of the Lonesome Pine,"* wrote in Scribner's Magazine: "There the bass leaps from rushing waters, and there, as nowhere else this side of the Rockies, is the face of nature wild and shy...Somewhere through the green thickness of poplar, oak and maple, the river lashes and boils between gray boulders, eddies and dances and laughs through deep pools or leaps in the waves over long riffles...There the river grinds through, with a roar of freedom that once must the star..." Fox's article inspired the first surge of visitors to the rugged beauty of the Breaks.

It wasn't until 1951, when the first two-lane hard-surfaced Breaks access road was built linking Kentucky and Virginia, that the development of the jointly operated park began in earnest. Breaks Interstate Park was officially dedicated in 1955 and ground was broken two years later for the first three facilities. Today, a park commission operates the unit. The park grounds now include acreage in three counties—Pike County on the Kentucky side and Dickenson and Buchanan counties on the Virginia side. More than $8 million have been spent on land acquisition over the years. Breaks Interstate is one of the finest state parks in the East.

Information and Activities

Breaks Interstate Park
P.O. Box 100
Breaks, VA 24607
(703) 865-4413
(703) 865-4414 - lodge

Directions: Seven miles east of Elkhorn City, Ky. and eight miles north of Haysi, Va., on KY-VA 80. The park is about 202 miles west of Roanoke.

Visitor center: The attractive center, with a vaulted tongue-and-groove ceiling, houses numerous interpretive displays and serves as an information center, comfort station and office for the educational staff.

Educational displays in the center consist of photographs, drawings, relief maps, mounted wildlife (including reptiles and large birds), descriptions, dioramas, geological samples and artifacts. Other exhibits include examples of mining equipment (safety lamps, rescue kits, roof supports, blasting equipment, hard hats, etc.), coal types, fossils, information on animals used in the mines (ponies and goats) and natural history information.

Daniel Boone was on an exploration trip from North Carolina and discovered the Breaks in 1767. Boone carved his name and date on a tree near Sand Lick. In 1771, after exploring Kentucky, Boone crossed back over the Cumberland Mountains near the Breaks and again left his mark on a tree upstream from the Great Water Gap he discovered four years later.

In the Daniel Boone exhibit is a Kentucky long rifle. The American long rifle has also been called the Pennsylvania long rifle, Kentucky long rifle, squirrel rifle and locally known as the "Hawg rifle." This long rifle was made in the mid-1800s by Joseph Glougoucher Co. of Philadelphia. During the early 1800s a rifle cost $2.25 and a very fancy rifle would cost between $11 and $15. A good rifleman could hit the head of a man at 300 yards. The rifle weighs eight pounds, 12 ounces and was carried on the shoulder. Percussion caps, packing rags, lead shot former, ball shot and ramrods are also part of the display.

Other information at the visitor center includes the role of the Breaks in the Civil War and mountain feuding. The Hatfields of Logan County and the McCoys of Pike County fought on opposite sides in the Civil War, and in the 1870s they began a 36 year clan feud that became a legendary horror story. Sixty-five violent murders were attributed to both sides. They eluded justice by intimidating juries, sheriffs and judges. Nine Hatfields were finally convicted of murder in 1889, in a trial that attracted national attention. When Hatfield leader Devil Anse died in 1921, the feud was considered officially over.

In addition, the visitor center has information about moonshiners, building the railroads and pioneer life. In the lobby, a brochure rack contains information about regional attractions and other nearby parks, and a relief model of the mountains and the Breaks area.

Surrounding the visitor center are some outdoor displays including agricultural implements, a grist mill, huge salt kettle (cast in 1860), log cabin and an example of a moonshiner's still complete with worm barrel and kegs. From these outdoor exhibits, guests can look down the valley through the trees and see the amphitheater. Many school groups visit these outdoor amenities.

Restaurant: Fittingly called the Rhododendron Restaurant, the large dining room offers a panoramic view of the rugged mountains that are covered with rhododendron and forests. There is a 20-foot-wide patio that guests can use for an outdoor view of craggy ledges, rolling mountains, and an American flag flapping atop Tower Rock. A vending area, lodge front desk and gift shop are also at the restaurant.

Inside the airy restaurant are a wall of windows, buffet, tasteful floral carpeting and perfectly laid-out tables. The wood tongue-and-groove ceiling is vaulted overhead; a fireplace and brass lights are adjusted for just the right amount of light to dine by. The restaurant serves lunch and dinner and has a kids-only menu. Small dining rooms are also available for private parties or meetings.

Gift shop: Sharing the building with the restaurant is a well-stocked gift shop behind the lodge front desk and check-out counter. Interesting items include a "yard stick," which is actually about a 10-inch length of twig with a tag that says, "This is a yard stick I know this because I found it in my yard ...It can be used to measure things, the depth of a mud puddle; the amount of gasoline in your lawnmower; you can play fetch with your dog; you can even use it to start a fire, but whatever you do, don't put it back into your yard."

Other items in the packed gift shop include candles, T-shirts, caps, wooden crafts, figurines, ash trays, flags, walking sticks, dolls, jewelry, hard candy, textile products, throws, purses, pillows, plaques with sayings printed on them, wind chimes, mugs, post cards, small toiletry items, pocket knives, books and hillbilly backscratchers, which is a corn cob stuck on the end of a two-foot stick. Across the street from the gift shop and restaurant is a small

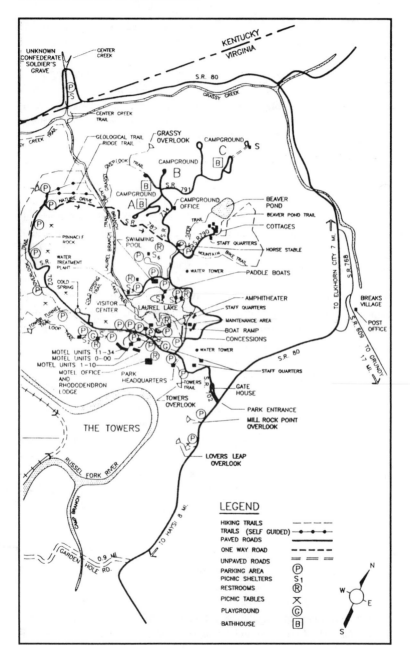

playground.

Campground: The shed-like campground office is 1.3 miles from the entrance of the park and open April through October. An ice machine, firewood, maps and other information are available for campers. Sites at the secluded and wooded, 112-space campground have picnic tables, trash barrels and fire rings. The campground does not take reservations. Full and partial hook-ups are available. A total of three large bathhouses, equipped with hot showers, are located in the many sections of the campground. A gravel trail connects the campground to the swimming pool and Laurel Lake a half-mile away. Breaks Interstate is one of the best furnished campgrounds in the state park system.

Campground A (sites 35-65) is hilly, heavily wooded and has gravel pads. A few sites are pull-throughs. The wood-frame bathhouse has two exterior drinking fountains and two small swings next to it. Sites in the double-spur section are small- to medium-sized. Sites 45, 46 and 47 are at the end of the spur and are some of the best sites in the entire campground. These sites oversized are surrounded by patches of rhododendrons.

Campground B (sites 1-34) is shaded and hilly, and comprised of a loop and a spur. About one-third of the sites are for tents, with the remainder offering hook-ups. A single centrally located bathhouse serves the area. At the end of the loop is the Grassy Overlook Trailhead. Some older play equipment, including four swings, are near the bathhouse. Sites 11-15 have a view of a heavily wooded valley. Most sites in this section are for medium-sized RV rigs, except for pull-through site 17 which can handle a large unit. Site 34 is an interesting site, perched on the rim of ridge, flat and private. Sites 30 and 32 are the most private of the sites in this section.

Campground C (sites 66-138, group overflow sites are 123-138) has two spurs and a long pleasant loop. All of the sites in the mountainside 66-80 spur have full hook-ups and are shady. Sites 73 and 74 are next to each other but on different elevations; they are both terrific sites. Staff says site 72 is popular, but can be windy due to its high elevation. Site 71, notched into the mountainside, is oversized. Site 77 is a pull-through.

Sites in the rest of the C campground are larger than the A and B loops; many can accommodate medium to large trailers and motor homes. In places, the

The scenic overlooks are some of the finest in the country.

difference in elevation between sites can be as much as 100 feet. A small playground is near site 88, and the tan and burgundy bathhouse is close to sites 85 and 86. Some sites, like 91, 97, 16 and 17 get some midday sunlight. Sites 96 and 98 are two of the best sites for large RV rigs. Site 100 is a perfect pull-through site for a medium-sized RV rig.

Motor lodge: Perched on the rim of Breaks gorge, the charming lodge offers overnight guests a spectacular view of The Towers, a vertical rock outcropping. The two-story lodge consists of two buildings offering a total of 34 rooms with individual balconies and breathtaking views. The lodge is in a thicket of rhododendrons and about 1,000 feet directly above Russell Fork of the Big Sandy River. The rooms are modern and motel-like, and the rates are nominal. The lodge is within a short walk of the restaurant, gift shop and visitor center. It's a great vacation value.

Cabins: Four modern split-level fieldstone and wood housekeeping cabins are clinging to the mountainside in a quiet shady area well off the park road. A distant view of the lake is available from the colony of cabins that are open year-round and rented by the week. Each of the peaceful cabins has an outdoor grill and seating. A reddish railing and black lampposts are stationed at the corners of the angular cottages.

Fishing: Licenses are sold at the office during regular business hours. Bluegill and bass are stocked in the lake, but some of the best nearby fishing is in the 1,143-acre Flannagan Reservoir. Anglers can find largemouth bass, catfish, walleye and panfish in the flood controlled lake.

Boating: Next to the swimming pool is the small boat rental that offers pontoon-style pedal boats by the hour and half-hour. The small cove-side boat concession has two wooden docks and is open daily during the summer.

Whitewater: Russell Fork is Virginia's most intense, scenic and dangerous whitewater rivers. One and one-half miles of the gorge's most ferocious water is nationally known and has the reputation of humbling even the most experienced paddler. The water is at its most violent in October after a planned release arranged with the Corps of Engineers during the annual drawdown of the Flannagan Reservoir.

The huge boulders, falls and twists of the river can be accessed from a number of locations. These very technical whitewaters can be extremely dangerous. It is wise to be an experienced paddler and to make your first trip with an expert.

Gentler whitewater rafting tours are operated by at least eight rafting companies. The best trips are during October. Contact the park office for a list of guided rafting operators.

An annual Russell Fork Gorge Race is set for mid-October.

A very narrow winding road accesses the single-lane boat ramp on Laurel Lake. The launch is best for cartop boats, canoes and small fishing boats. Boats with gasoline motors are not permitted on the small Lake. Parking for 10 trailers and tow vehicles is at the top of the hill.

Hiking: Both quiet park roads and 13 trails totaling 12 miles are perfect for hiking. Trails vary from easy walking to moderate to difficult. Maps are available at most of the contact points around the park. The sightseeing and photographic opportunities, solitude and wildlife viewing from the trails are some of the best in the state.

Chestnut Ridge Nature Trail (1 mile) starts near the Stateline Overlook. The self-guided trail has 30 learning stations marked by a trailside post. Each post corresponds with a mention in the brochure that is available at the visitor center. I completed the trail, stopping and reading each write-up in about 1.5 hours.

Along the trail you'll learn about the Shawnee and Cherokee Indians who once stalked the chestnut-dominated virgin forest, competing with natural predators for food. The chestnuts, which provided food and timber, tragically died due to a blight that was introduced from China into the United States in the early 1900s. By the end of the 1930s, all of the chestnut trees in the area had been killed. Fortunately oak and hickory lived on, forming the climax hardwood forest that covers the ridge tops. Both red and white oak flourish and were once used for baskets, cane chairs, split-rail fences, wagon wheels, flooring and split shingles for roofing. Fragrant magnolias (and its cousin, the yellow poplar or tulip tree), rhododendron and mountain laurel are also abundant along the winding trail.

At post 10 are the remains of a chestnut log and the evidence of the fatal disease which swept the country killing every American chestnut in its path. The deadly blight was caused by a parasitic fungus. The fungus spores enter the tree through wounds or insect damage in the bark and kill the tree within a few years. Nearby is Canyon Cliff, rock outcrops that are 300 million years old and scattered open spaces where grasses, shrubs and blackberries thrive.

At station 16, if you listen carefully (and at the right time), you can hear water flow in the rocks. In the mid- to late-summer, the above-ground spring dries up, the water table drops and the spring flows underground. Also in this area is a cliff overhang that once served as a campsite for Indians and a cave carved into the sandstone.

Other features include a place in the rock called crossbreeding, which is a fossilized sand bar among layers of sedimentary rock. The crossbreeding seen at station 20 is the layers that lie at an angle to the main layers of stratified rock. There is also a fossilized log jam, one-time natural bridge, towering hemlocks and delicate partridge berry plant that has tiny red berries in the fall.

At one point along the trail are examples of faults and joints in the rock. Faulting is the movement along a break in the earth's crust. It is a word too frequently used when referring to a fracture in a rock. The main fault of the area is the Pine Mountain Overthrust Fault, about 125 miles long, which forms Pine Mountain. The Russell Fork Fault basically follows another fault upriver from the canyon. Joints and fractures have no motion; faulting has motion. Joints are most often seen in the interior of the Breaks area.

At the end of the loop, learning stations include information about quartz pebbles, a hanging stone, coal mining, lichen and mosses and a mini-geology lesson about rock formation.

Cold Spring Trail (.5 mile) is a moderate hiking trail that follows a stream bed from Cold Spring to the Laurel Branch. It is rocky and wet after heavy rains.

Grassy Creek Trail (.5 mile) is a moderate trail that follows Grassy Creek to its junction with Russell Fork River. It's a steady uphill grade from its intersection with River Trail to the Laurel Branch Trail.

Grassy Overlook Trail (.5 mile) can be accessed from the campground and is an uphill hike to the overlook that faces the Kentucky-Virginia line and as well as Grassy and Center creeks.

Lake Trail (.5 mile) is easy walking along Laurel Lake past wetlands and inlets. This is a good birding and wildlife viewing trail.

Laurel Branch Trail (1.25 miles) follows the stream its entire length. The last half of the trail is rugged and uneven, passing through thickets of mature rhododendrons and interesting rock formations called The Notches.

Overlook Trail (.75 mile) is easy to moderate in difficulty as it meanders along the edge of cliffs offering a continuous view of the canyon. This is the best trail to see the overlooks and gorge during the spring and fall. This trail is for adults; if you take small children, hang on to them.

A busy Breaks Interstate restaurant and gift shop.

Prospector's Trail (1.5 miles) skirts 350 feet beneath the base of the cliffs under some major overlooks. The rocky trail is moderate and features excellent scenery.

Other trails include Ridge Trail (.5 mile), which is a good birding trail; River Trail (1 mile) that is extremely steep and rugged; Tower Trail (.15 mile) and Tower Tunnel Trail (.2 mile) that are lined with blueberry bushes that ripen in July and August.

Mountain biking: Use the trail at your own risk, say the signs.

Day-use areas: Like many Kentucky state parks, Breaks Interstate has more playground equipment than the typical Virginia state park. Often the play apparatus are located near picnic shelters, campgrounds and cabins. Breaks Interstate has some great stone and wood picnic shelters with fireplaces scattered around the park that can be reserved.

The rugged park has more than 200 picnic tables, seven picnic shelters and plenty of open spaces.

Overlooks: A series of protected overlooks on the eastern rim provide safe vantage points for viewing Breaks gorge and other features including Pine Mountain, Russell Fork of the Big Sandy River, Skegg Gap, The Towers, The Chimneys, Tower Tunnel, Clinchfield (CSX) Railroad line, Stateline Tunnel, Potters Flat and Grassy gorge.

The overlooks, which have nearby parking, include Towers Overlook, Pinnacle Overlook, Tower Tunnel Overlook, Clinchfield Overlook, Stateline Overlook (handicapped accessible platform), Lovers Leap Overlook and Mill Rock Point Overlook. The popular viewing sites range in elevation from 700 to 920 feet directly above the river. The lookouts have strong rails, walkways, steps, viewing platforms and informative signs.

The Stateline Overlook is the most interesting of the many roadside viewing points. From the vantage point, you are standing in Virginia and looking at both Virginia and Kentucky. Pine Mountain begins here and runs in a southwesterly direction for about 125 miles. The ribbon-like road below is Kentucky State Route 80, which runs by the park entrance. The main boundary line follows the crest of Pine Mountain. The elevation here is 1,760 feet.

From some of the overlooks, guests can hear the rush of the river rapids, winds plowing between the mountains, and birds of prey floating on the invisible waves of the wind, and thermals along ridges.

Swimming pool: Open Memorial Day to Labor Day, 10 a.m. 6 p.m. weekdays, 10 a.m. - 8 p.m. Saturday and Sunday. There is a small admission. The guarded L-shaped Olympic-size pool features a huge hard-surfaced and grassy sunning area and a redwood and fieldstone bathhouse. Two large parking lots are adjacent to the swimming complex, and the lake can be seen in the distance. Shelter No. 3, which has a large nearby playground, is above the pool and has a popular pavilion for family reunions.

A small kiddy's pool and snack concession are also part of the clean and popular complex.

Nature: The rich deciduous and mixed forest is abundant with flora and

A variety of environmental education programs are conducted at the park. This youth group is near the log cabin and large visitor center.

---

fauna. Each spring, flowering shrubs and wildflowers cover the forest floor including pink lady's slippers, white dogwood, Catawba rhododendron, yellow lady's slippers, ferns, Dutchman's britches, cow vetch, showy orchid, bloodroot, blue bells, dogtooth, flame azaleas, wood lilies, cardinal flower, trillium, mountain laurel, two species of magnolia tree and 60 species of trees. A handy *"Identifying Fall Foliage"* booklet will help you recognize and learn about several common tree species.

The forest floor is also covered with thick patches of moss, ferns and fungi.

The forest that crowned every ridge in the vast region was cut beginning about 1885 and continuing into the 20th century. The sprawling, climax forest boasted trees measuring seven feet thick and towering more than 100 feet above the forest floor. Most of the giants were floated down the Russell Fork through the Breaks gorge downstream to market. Some trees cut in the park were skidded down a hollow on the east side of the gorge and dumped into a logchute hole at the base of The Tower, to begin their downstream journey.

In 1909 the world's largest cement splash dam was built upstream of Breaks Gorge, creating an 85-acre lake. When this lake was filled with logs, the gates were opened, flooding the river and splashing the logs through the five-mile-long gorge. During its first year of use, the dam splashed 40 million board feet of logs through the gorge.

The forests have returned and now are home to wild turkey, gray squirrel, various songbirds, ruffed grouse, raptors, owls and most common mammals. The wetland and lake are excellent habitat for ducks, shorebirds, reptiles and amphibians. Little brown and big brown bats are commonly seen flying in the campground and throughout the park.

Programs: The park has a healthy supply of programs for all ages. Join staff naturalists on a variety of hikes or listen to bluegrass music on a summer evening. Other activities include gospel sings, arts and crafts festival, Christmas tree lighting and youth programs.

Nature drive: Unique to the Virginia state park system is the hard-surfaced, one-way nature drive. On each side of the single lane, is a 20-foot-wide mowed step up against the forest. Mixed deciduous, scattered conifers trees and large rhododendrons line the entire length of the drive. In places the canopy of trees forms a tunnel-like effect. The entrance to the nature drive is about 100 yards from the Stateline Overlook parking area.

Daniel Boone: One of my favorite pioneer figures, Daniel Boone, the famous frontier explorer and hunter, is credited with discovering Breaks gorge. Boone never rested. In 1767, he and two companions departed from their homes in North Carolina along the Yadkin River to explore the frontier known as Kaintuck. Daniel traveled on foot throughout this wilderness searching for a westerly and northerly river route through the mountains into the unsettled blue grass region.

The party forded the headwaters of the northerly flowing New River and crossed the Clinch River, which flows south into the Tennessee River. Leaving the Great Valley of Virginia behind, the trio headed for the Cumberland Mountains, where they found themselves on the headwaters of a stream flowing in a northerly direction. Along this stream they happened upon a salt lick, where they camped and where Boone carved his name in a tree, as mentioned earlier. This salt lick is now called Sand Lick, and is on Russell Fork upstream from Haysi, Va.

Just a short distance downstream on Russell Fork, the explorers discovered the spectacular river gorge. Even these rugged men were stopped by the force of the churning and grinding river that had rocks the size of cabins tossed along its path. No one knows for sure if the group made it through the gorge where the mighty river crashed into rock walls and where rapids drowned out every sound. It is more likely wise old Daniel Boone guided the men onto the eastern rim of the canyon, some 1,000 feet above the river, thus going around the gorge by crossing the tabletop plateau where the present day park facilities are located.

Not much is written about Boone's exploits here, but if he did stand at the Stateline Overlook scanning the rugged line of ridges making up the face of Kaintuck to the north and west, he must have wondered how far he could continue through such a rugged wilderness.

Downstream, Boone and his companions came to the confluence of the Russell Fork and Levisia River, which together form the Big Sandy River. The intrepid trio spent the winter here, returning to their families in the spring of 1768.

Hunting: Deer populations have increased over the years. Call the park office for details.

Insiders tips: The lodge or the cabins are a terrific vacation value. Fall foliage is at its peak during the last half of October. Gospel sings, held Memorial Day, Father's Day and Labor Day weekends, draw thousands to the park.

4 Caledon Natural Area
Land: 2,579 acres Water: Potomac River

The forested slopes, including huge virgin hardwoods that heard the rumble of the Civil War, dip to the edge of the Potomac River. Some of the untouched forests and marshland remain as they were 400 years ago when the first settlers landed and began to explore the wilds of Virginia. These same cathedral-like forests also attract many American bald eagles. Unlike most state parks equipped with pools, beaches, cabins or camping, Caledon is a learning center, an oasis for outdoor education, eagles and reflection.

Caledon Natural Area is a designated National Natural Landmark and celebrated as one of the best places to view bald eagles during the summer. The region has one of the largest concentrations of bald eagles on the East Coast. The natural area maintains about three miles of shoreline along the Potomac River.

Five miles of wooded trails, interpretive bald eagle tours and an interpretive center concentrate on teaching about the area's natural history and bald eagles. The area is one of the best places to view eagles in the East. Tours are offered from mid-June until Labor Day; call for details and reservations (see below). Wildlife viewers can also hike the trails unguided year-round.

In the spring when migrating fish fill the Potomac, up to 60 immature and mature bald eagles return to the area, perching along the cliffs and riverside, and soaring along the river. Viewing the eagles is regulated and guided tours are carefully designed to offer public access without disturbing the huge birds of prey. Tours take about 1.5 hours and there is a small fee. Bring a pair of binoculars.

The tract was donated to the Commonwealth in 1974 by Ann Hopewell Smoot in memory of her late husband. At the time, it was the largest land gift ever given to the state. The former house of Mrs. Smoot is now a busy visitor center.

Information and Activities

Caledon Natural Area
11617 Caledon Road
King George, VA 22485
(540) 663-3861

Directions: From Fredericksburg, take Route 218 east 22 miles. From Route 301, take 206 to 218 about 1.5 miles. There is no camping or swimming at the park. Pets are prohibited on the trails.

Visitor center: The two-story colonial-style house is open 9 a.m. - 5 p.m. Wednesday - Sunday. Visitors can browse the small gift shop (mugs, T-shirts, some jewelry, hummingbird feeders, etc.), view interpretive displays and animal mounts, watch hummingbirds at the feeders or sit on the back wooden deck that overlooks a natural area.

The office is in the visitor center. The recreation area is open 9 a.m. to sunset. Be sure to check your watch against the sundial located in front of the main entrance of the visitor center.

The field behind the visitor center has been allowed to remain in its natural

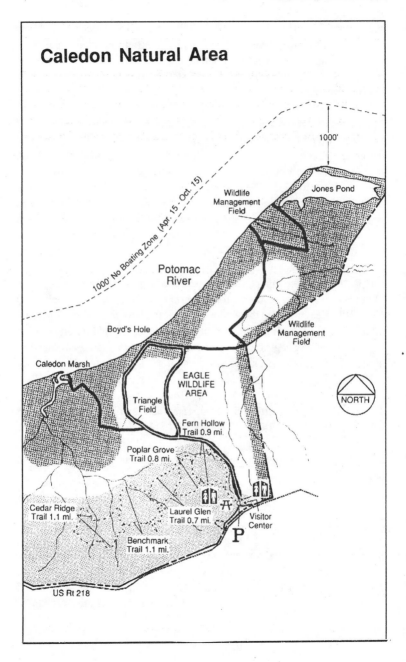

Caledon Natural Area

1000'

Jones Pond

Wildlife Management Field

1000' No Boating Zone (Apr. 15 - Oct. 15)

Potomac River

Boyd's Hole

Wildlife Management Field

Caledon Marsh

EAGLE WILDLIFE AREA

NORTH

Triangle Field

Fern Hollow Trail 0.9 mi.

Poplar Grove Trail 0.8 mi.

Cedar Ridge Trail 1.1 mi.

Laurel Glen Trail 0.7 mi.

Visitor Center

Benchmark Trail 1.1 mi.

P

US Rt 218

state to provide food and cover for wildlife and various plants. Structures have been introduced to enhance the use of the field by many species of wildlife. This type of backyard habitat can be constructed in almost any backyard. In the area are a feeding station, purple martin house and interpretive signs.

The majestic forests that once blanketed the Potomac shoreline inspired Scottish settler John Alexander to name this area Caledon after Caledonia, the great forest of Scotland. Alexander and his sons cleared the land and raised tobacco and grain. They built a two-story house overlooking the Potomac River in 1735. The house was later destroyed by fire. Through the centuries the farms passed from one Alexander generation to the next. Louis Egerton Smoot inherited the land in the early 1900s and built the house that is now the visitor center. The rolling forests criss-crossed by clear streams were donated to the state in 1974.

Eagle tours: The guided tours are seasonal, offered 10 a.m. and 2 p.m. Thursday - Sunday. For more information or to make a reservation call (703) 633-3861. Leaving from the visitor center, a 1.5-hour tour takes visitors by mini-bus to Boyd's Hole or Caledon Marsh, popular eagle foraging areas. In these locations eagles can be seen while they perch, soar overhead or hunt the Potomac River. During the trip, visitors can play eagle trivia games, see a model eagle's nest and learn about the eagle and its habitat.

There is a small fee, with special group rates. Children 6 and under are free with accompanying adult. Wear comfortable clothes and shoes, hat, sunglasses, sunscreen and insect repellent. Also bring a snack and water. Meet inside the visitor center 15 minutes before your scheduled tour is to begin.

Hiking: The natural area has five trails totaling about five miles in length. The trails lead visitors through maturing and old growth forests of oak-beech, hickory and polar-tulip over gently rolling ridges and across creeks. Keen sense, patience and silence will help you locate and observe many plants and animals. Some interpretive signs are along the trails. Trails are dirt and easy to moderate in difficulty. Use caution on the pea-gravel trail that takes you down to the trailheads through the day-use area—it can be slippery.

Cedar Ridge (1.1 miles, blazed in white) has an elevation deviation of 40 to 130 feet and features wooded ridges, ravines and old growth forests.

Benchmark Trail (1.1 miles, blazed in orange) has an interesting stone survey benchmark dated 1754.

Laurel Glen Trail (.7 mile, blazed in yellow) was built in 1987 with elevations from 40 to 100 feet. Great examples of climax growth and a creek bed rich in vegetation and animal life are found along this trail.

Poplar Grove Trail (.8 mile, blazed in blue) was constructed in 1986. The trail is mixed second growth forest, with the fallen remains of massive American chestnut trees killed by blight 40 years ago.

Fern Hollow Trail (.9 mile, blazed in red) was finished in 1986 and has 60-100-foot elevations. The trail is mostly second growth, mature oak-hickory (many huge beeches are also along the dirt trail) with some older climax growth near the bridge. Fern Hollow Trail has a self-guided brochure that is available at the visitor center. Match the brochure to numbered posts along the way.

Eagle watching tips: Eagles fly with a straight-wing profile. Vultures fly with a V-shaped profile. Eagles usually fly point-to-point rather than in circles; vultures often circle. Adult eagles are dark brown with white heads and tails; vultures have naked red heads visible at close range and two-tone blackish wings. Immature eagles have molted white and brown undersides with faint white lines under each wing.

Use binoculars and be patient. Maybe equally important is to visit the park when the great school of migratory fish enter the bay and rivers from late April to October. The James River below Richmond is also a great place to try to spot eagles.

Serious eagle watchers can tell you about observing selfish birds harassing osprey to steal their freshly caught dinner; airborne acrobatics and mating; high-speed dives to the water's surface; and squadrons of the birds flying over the river screaming at the winds. Some eagles' wingspans can reach eight feet. Mostly a fish eater, eagles also hunt rabbit, musket and squirrels. I'm glad I'm not a rabbit—it seems every predator hunts Mr. Cottontail.

Hike by yourself or join an eagle tour.

Nature: The natural area has two major goals. The first is to protect America's symbol, the bald eagle through proper management of important habitat. The second is to bring quality outdoor education by providing controlled access, educational exhibits and interpretive programming. There are about 300 pairs of breeding bald eagles in the Chesapeake Bay region.

The natural area is carefully managed so that both human and eagle guests enjoy their stay. In fact, it is zoned to protect the great birds while also providing an enjoyable and educational opportunity for families and visiting school groups. Bordering Route. 218 and continuing north to the Potomac River for about a mile, the Educational-Recreational Area includes the visitor center, day-use picnic area and hiking trails.

Day-use area: A small picnic area is equipped with rest rooms and grills near the trailheads adjacent to the environmental education center.

Insiders tip: Plan a spring eagle tour. Call ahead for a reservation.

5 Chippokes Plantation State Park

Land: 1,683 acres Water: James River

Pronounced *"CHIP-oaks,"* Chippokes Plantation State Park is one of the oldest working farms in the nation, gracefully combining history and recreation along the south bank of the James River, across from Jamestown Island.

Captain William Powell, a well-known colonial leader, received a land grant of 550 acres along the Chippokes Creek in 1619, making it the earliest recorded land in the region. The fertile plantation and the creek were named for an Indian chief who befriended early English settlers. Under the ownership of Colonel Henry Bishop in 1646, the plantation was expanded to its present boundaries, encompassing 1,683 beautiful acres.

Albert Carroll Jones, in 1854, built the stately brick Chippokes Mansion overlooking the James River. The river-side mansion was stuccoed and painted white to serve as a landmark for passing boat traffic. Near the mansion, along the river and farmlands, the plantation was also known for one of the few legal distilleries in the Commonwealth. There is a fascinating history of liquor, war and huge profits that Jones and the plantation were involved in.

The rolling plantation changed owners several times before it was bought by Thornton Jeffress of Rochester, N.Y. and V.W. Stewart of Wilson, N.C., in 1918. The Stewarts moved to Chippokes and renovated the grounds and compiled a detailed history of the property. Upon her husband's death, Mrs. Stewart, in order to preserve the property, donated Chippokes Plantation to the Commonwealth as a memorial to her husband in 1967. The park opened that year.

Information and Activities

Chippokes Plantation State Park
Route 1, Box 213
Surry, VA 23883
(804) 294-3625

Directions: Chippokes is in Surry County, 5.5 miles east of Surry and 65 miles southeast of Richmond. Access is via Route 10, 1.5 miles east of Surry to Route 634, which leads to the park. The park office is inside the visitor center, which is on a high bank above the James River. From the split-rail fence along the ridge behind the office, visitors can hear the waters lap on the gravel shoreline.

Emergency number: Fire and rescue, 294-5264.

Visitor center: Carefully placed on red brick flooring are a number of free-standing interpretive displays. Information includes narratives of the Chippokes Indians, artifacts and natural history descriptions. The visitor center is open weekends Memorial Day weekend to Labor Day. At one end of the building are a set of soft drink machines and a picnic table.

One of the most interesting displays describes the life of William Berkeley, the "Cavalier governor." He was one of the most colorful and significant in colonial history. Albert Jones, a prosperous farmer who developed extensive apple orchards, stills, and farming, is also profiled. A labeled farm tool exhibit including huge iron wrenches, clippers, horseshoes, wood planes, shears, ship building tools and axes is displayed in a small classroom near the rear of the visitor center. An interesting crank-operated corn sheller and fodder chopper (chopped cornstalks in bulk) are also displayed in the center.

History: Chippokes' first English owner, William Powell, was part of a bold new adventure in a strange new land. In 1607, just across the James River from Chippokes, 104 colonists stepped ashore at Jamestown. Little did they know that this small colony would come to be recognized as the first successful English settlement in America. All of the founders had one thing in common: they were all adventurers willing to gamble for high stakes in a new world. Men had been lured by fantastic stories of the land where the streets were "paved with gold." Reality was quite different, however. Life became a day-to-day struggle for survival. Despite the rich supply of wild game along with the Indians' initial willingness to share their crops, hunger was commonplace.

Political squabbles and disease took their toll. The first men who came to America were not farmers, and had little interest in farming. Thus their first attempt at an agrarian life failed. It wasn't until 1611 that real farming got underway at Jamestown when Captain John Smith insisted that planting, building and discipline take precedence over looking for gold. With the arrival of Lord Delaware, a new governor, more settlers came. Private use of the land was recognized and the area began to thrive and expand. After years of despair and disappointment, Jamestown made a radical change for the better.

In 1612, a young colonist, finding the local Indian tobacco too bitter for his taste, had some precious seeds from the milder, more pleasant tasting tobacco of the West Indies smuggled into the country. Thanks to John Rolfe and his discriminating taste, tobacco cultivation was born. It alone promised an end to poverty and the beginning of prosperity.

In 1619 several important events occurred. A Dutch ship from the West Indies arrived with about 200 black people aboard, the first such ship to arrive in British North America. "That same year a ship sailed from England

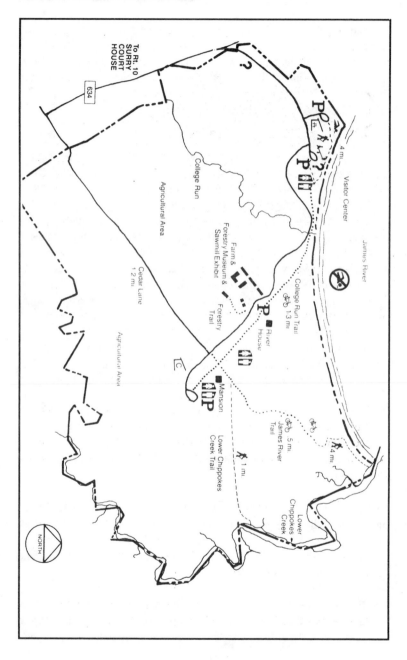

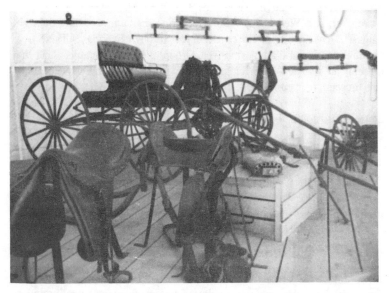

You can easily spend two hours roaming around the farm museum.

with 100 young maids, young and uncorrupted, to make wives of the inhabitants," says the description on the reader board.

The first representative assembly in America was convened in 1619 at Jamestown. Therefore, in that one year, the colony had established family-oriented homesteads, a source of servant labor and a representative governing body, all of which ensured a more permanent society in the wild new land.

Farm museum: Here's your chance to imagine what it might have been like living on a farm in rural Virginia in 1850. The farm and forestry museum, located on plantation lands that are some of the oldest continuously farmed tracts in the country, is endowed with thousands of farming and forestry implements and artifacts. Many of the displays are numbered, with nearby reader boards and cards describing their use and history. The displays are very well-designed, informative and educational for all ages. Many historic photographs are used to interpret Virginia farming life and work styles.

The museum is open on weekends March to May and September to November, and Wednesday - Sunday during the summer (June through August). The facility is closed December through February. There is a nominal parking and admission fee. Group rates are available. Call the museum at (804) 294-3439 for details on special events and other activities. The museum opened in 1990.

Seven white colonial-style farm buildings lined up side by side around a courtyard represent various stages of farm life. The well-maintained buildings contain more than 3,000 interesting objects. They interpret chores like building a farm, preparing the soil, planting, cultivating and harvesting crops. Additional exhibits feature tools used by craftsmen such as the blacksmith, wheelwright, cooper and cobbler. Other displays include farm animals, processing, preserving, small tools and house wares. Many tools on display were hand-forged by our ancestors, who struggled to raise crops, their gardens and their animals by any means possible.

Interestingly, many of the displays depict a succession of tools used for the same job. Visitors can see the evolution and improvements over previous tools, saving time and energy for the farmer. For example in the harvesting of wheat, farmers first used the hand-held sickle, hook and scythe, which cut the wheat. Next, came the hand-held grain cradle, which cut the wheat and swept it to one side. With Cyrus McCormick came the reaper, which allowed the farmer to ride a horse or mule which pulled the reaper. Still later came the grain binder, which bundled the stalks with string for easy handling. And today, of course, farmers cover vast fields with complex, air-conditioned combines. Many rickety hay and crop harvesting machines are displayed.

The well-lighted museum features a number of rare artifacts. One of the oldest items in the collection is an ox-drawn plow called a rooter or bull tongue plow which dates to the early 1600s.

Home lifestyle artifacts include clunky-looking cooking utensils, wood stoves and tub-like old wringer washers. Washing laundry was a major and strenuous chore for farm wives. Clothes were hand-washed in boiling water in wash tubs and wash stands by rubbing them against boards or stirring them with hand agitators. Clothes were then wrung by hand or simple mechanical wringers. The first mechanical washers appeared in 1836—one of the first was called the "Red Dasher." The first electric washing machine was manufactured in 1914—the first laundry soap ad only minutes later.

Farm women were skilled in many important crafts such as spinning, basket making, caning, weaving, candle making, sewing and tailoring. These crafts were as important to the domestic economy as blacksmithing and carpentry were to the general economy.

Women on the farms were also responsible for preserving food, baking and cooking. Many utensils were invented to help with these tasks including Rube Goldberg-like sausage stuffers, food choppers, food hashers (which look like food smashers), mills, grinders and many other devices on display.

Simple as it may seem, brooms and broom making were very important (there were no Hoover vacuums in those days). In the 19th century brooms were made from broom corn, a species grown chiefly in the north, though some Virginia farms produced the fine bushy stock. A broom making machine (on display) was used to press a handful of broom corn to proper shape and sew it in a flat form onto the handle.

Antique and tool buffs will have fun trying to identify tools that the museum curator can't. The board full of small tools is called the "UFO (Unidentified Fascinating Objects) Tools." You can examine them, making guesses as to their possible use. One UFO tool looks like a small hatchet on hormones. Other unique tools look like something from a dental school 200 years ago.

Other tools we don't see or use much today include ice cutting tools. Before modern refrigeration, perishable foods were stored in insulated ice boxes often covered with sawdust. Ice had to be harvested in the dead of winter using specialized tools like jagged ice saws, large tongs, ice forks, ice block movers and hooks. The tools were used to cut, lift and move blocks of ice. Many of these tools are on display near historical photos and narratives recalling the difficult wintry job.

One important harvesting machine is the thresher. American threshing machines evolved from a British thresher invented 1788. In the U.S, Jerome Case began experimenting with a thresher in the 1830s. His improved machine not only beat the precious grain out of the heads, it also separated the straw and chaff. As other generations of the machine appeared in the

The museum has hundreds of examples of old and interesting farm machinery.

19th century, elevators and blowers were installed to control the straw and chaff and keep it away from the back of the machine.

Steam engines were used to power early threshers. Horses were used to move the complex machines from site to site. Threshing machines were used until the 1930s when they started to be replaced on farms by combines. The combines could thresh the grain in the fields as it was harvested, a more economical and practical way of grain harvesting and handling.

Other important farm machines at the museum include the Whitney cotton gin (circa 1790) that separated cotton from seed, a Burr mill that was a hand-cranked or belt-driven device used to grind corn for livestock, corn shellers, fanning mills and grain cradles of various types.

To many, the most important processing machines were stills and equipment to make gin, whiskey and cider. Apple cider, peach and apple brandy and whisky have long been popular farm products. Virginia farmers have grown apple and peach orchards since the colonial days. Many farms had a cider mill, and larger farms or plantations had cider presses that extracted the juice from apples and other fruit. In 1836 apple and peach brandy were highly profitable in Surry County. Chippokes plantation owner Albert Jones operated a licensed still to produce these brandies in the 1860s. He reportedly sold liquor to both the Union and Confederate troops. Tradition holds that the Chippokes plantation was spared destruction during the Civil War because of its peach brandy.

In the back country it was too expensive to ship bulky corn and rye cargo overland. Copper whiskey stills can brew the grains into profitable, high volume, low bulk commodities. Many farms profited, making all types of spirits.

Many hand cultivating tools used by Virginia farmers meant back-breaking work. Some of the tools are called "grubbing hoes," reflecting how hard weeding and cultivation were. One of the colonial farmer's biggest chores was grubbing the quick-growing weeds from the fields before they killed the crops. Various cultivating tools and early crop sprayers which were introduced in the 19th century are displayed.

One large section of the museum is dedicated to peanut growing and teaching visitors about the important of the crop during the formative days of the Commonwealth. Special peanut farming equipment was developed after the Civil War as peanuts became an important crop. Visitors will see crude peanut planters, weeding devices, bulky shellers, one-row diggers, horse-drawn peanut farming vehicles and more. You'll see everything but a jar of peanut butter.

Until the early 20th century, picking peanuts off the vine was done by hand, a tedious and time consuming method. In 1906 the Benthall Machine Company opened a plant in Suffolk to manufacture mechanical pickers. An example of a 1937 model is on display and shows the fan, dragging chain and diamond-shaped wire which removed pods from the vine and stem. The entire harvester was run by a 10-horsepower motor. The plucked peanuts fell into a basket and were then poured into peanut bags held open by a wooden frame. The vine was carted away and used for fodder.

The job of shelling peanuts was done by hand until devices like the Star

Peanut Sheller began to appear in 1900.

Other buildings at the museum describe planting machines, various plows and soil preparation tools, wheelwright's tools, shingle making, the cooper's role in container building, and the job of the carpenter, who was responsible for building anything of wood.

The museum also has a small sales counter, time line wall display, information about tobacco farming and some simple toys and crafts for sale.

Across the road from the pastoral farm museum is the white clapboard-sided River House, a farm house with a small demonstration garden filled with sample plots of crops including soy beans, peanuts, cotton, tobacco and other common crops. Built in 1642, the River House is the oldest structure on the property.

Boating: There is no boating access from the park, but nearby launching ramps offering excellent opportunities to explore and fish the wide James River.

The James River is the longest, largest and most important river in the state. It offers easy paddling on the upper reaches and pleasure craft opportunities near the park.

Fishing: The wide James River has many challenges for the average angler along its total length. From Williamsburg west to James is fresh water, Williamsburg east is brackish water. West of Williamsburg you'll find largemouth bass, rough fish and good-sized catfish. Fishing in front of the park to the Hogg Island Game Area can be slow. Freshwater anglers will want to try the upper reaches of the river for muskie. Best advice is to check with local bait and tackle shops for conditions and hot spots.

Hiking: The park has 3.5 miles of easy biking and hiking trails, about a half mile of which is accessible to people with physical disabilities through the historic area (mansion) and auto farm tour road.

Day-use areas: Picnic areas are scattered around the park, usually near main features like the visitor center, museum or mansion. They have drinking water, charcoal grills and modern rest rooms. Some angular-shaped picnic shelters are available on a reservation or first-come, first-served basis. The areas often have play equipment and well-maintained tables and parking.

A conference shelter with a kitchen is available for a small fee. Educational groups typically use the small shelter.

Swimming pool: Open 10 a.m. - 7 p.m. Thursday - Sunday and holidays, Memorial Day weekend to Labor Day, for a small fee (children 3 years and under are free). A snack bar serves the pool with sandwiches, burgers, hot dogs, corn dogs, beverages, pizza and ice cream. The tidy food concession serves both pool patrons inside and visitors outside.

The main pool is L-shaped with a wide deck and is surrounded by five lifeguard stands. A small curving blue slide and two diving boards (10 feet deep) are open and regulated by the lifeguard staff. An angular wood-frame changing room has showers. Bench seats and lounges are deckside. The pool's diving area is 37 feet by 40 feet and the main pool section is 164 feet by 55 feet wide. The total volume of the pool is 276,000 gallons.

A small children's wading pool (25-feet-by-25-feet) is separate from the main pool and perfect for toddlers and pre-schoolers. The swimming complex and changing house are enclosed by an eight-foot-tall fence.

Mansion: The mansion is open 1 p.m. - 5 p.m. weekends and holidays April to October for a small fee. Spring is a terrific time to visit the gardens surrounding the mansion. During the Christmas season, the mansion is decked in Victorian-period decorations.

The formal gardens around the red brick mansion are accented by azaleas, crepe myrtle, boxwoods, hedges and flower beds. Gravesites and a variety of historic outbuildings surround the stately mansion.

Nature: I've been an active birder for more than 20 years, and I got my closest and best view of two mature and one immature bald eagles from along the ridge line near the day-use area adjacent to the visitor center. The birds had wingspans of nearly seven feet, and on this day were seemingly unperturbed with my presence as they slowly glided along the ridge, switching back and forth to catch air under their wings.

Special events include historic wagon and river house tours, mansion tours (1 p.m. - 5 p.m. weekends and holidays) canoe tours (1 p.m. - 5 p.m. Saturday after July 1 to Labor Day, small fee, to register call 804-294-3625), junior ranger, beach walks and various nature programs. The Pork, Peanut and Pine Festival held on the park grounds is held in mid-July annually. Barbecue pork, peanut pie, homemade foods and hay rides are offered.

Hunting: Limited deer hunts are offered on about 800 acres. Call the park manager for details.

Insiders tips: The park may develop a camping area in the future. Spend a half-day at the farm museum, the other half at the sparkling clean pool.

6 Claytor Lake State Park

Land: 472 acres Water: 4,500-acre, 21-mile-long lake

The unit is on a sweeping bend of long and narrow, deep and cold Claytor Lake that was built in 1939 by the Appalachian Power Company. The dam that forms the lake is on the New River and has four generators with a capacity of 18,750 kilowatts each. Elevations from 5 feet to 1,841 feet offer scenic views, hiking, wildlife viewing opportunities and an interesting backdrop for cruises on the only large excursion boat operated in a Virginia state park.

In early 1944, area residents expressed an interest in developing a state park on the dammed lake. The idea, which was embraced by civic and business leaders, led to fund-raising efforts in three counties—Pulaski, Radford and Blacksburg. The initiative was widely supported, and resulted in the purchase of 437 acres from Appalachian Power.

The land was then given to the state to be evaluated and developed as Claytor Lake State Park. Due to the lack of operating money, the Radford Chamber of Commerce operated the park in 1949-50. The Division of State

Parks took over the operation of the unit in 1951. Eleven years later, an additional 35 acres were purchased and facilities were improved.

The lake and park are named for William Graham Claytor, who was vice president of Appalachian Power and supervised the construction of the power-generating dam. A portrait of Claytor hangs in the Howe House visitor center. Claytor was a Bedford County native and son of a state senator. He was active in encouraging park development and in land acquisition, and eventually made his home on the lake that bears his name.

More than 300,000 people annually visit the park.

Information and Activities

Claytor Lake State Park
Route 1, Box 267
Dublin, VA 24084
(540) 674-5492

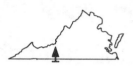

Directions: In Pulaski County, two miles southeast of I-81 (Exit 101), on Route 660 near Dublin.

Emergency number: 911 system.

Visitor center: The Howe House, a beautiful two-story red brick house with a wide gray porch, serves as the visitor center during the summer and a park office year-round. Bricks for the stately house were kiln-dried on the property. Behind the house, down a slope to the rocky lakeshore, is an octagonal-shaped pavilion and a view of the white cruise boat. The gazebo, whose walkway is lined with old-style lampposts, is often used for outdoor weddings.

The first things you notice inside the renovated house are the staircase and creaky wide pine floorboards. A large portion of the house is dedicated to interpreting the lives of the Howe family, lifestyles and artifacts of that era. Haven B. Howe was the builder of the house and born in Pulaski County. The Howe family name is a distinguished one in the history of the settlement of south Virginia. Haven B. Howe's grandfather, Daniel Howe, was a soldier

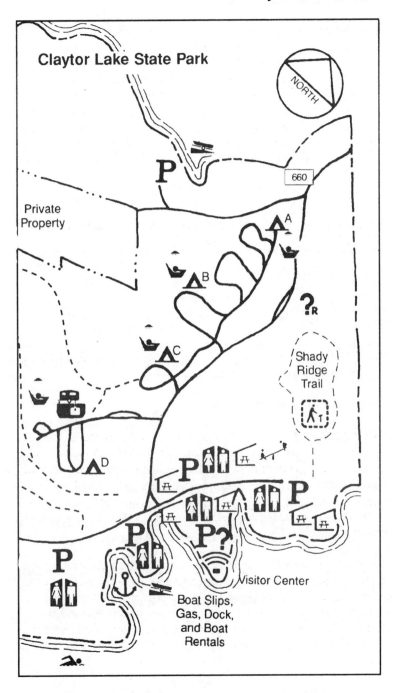

in the Continental Army and fought in the Battle of King's Mountain in North Carolina. After the Revolution he held offices as presiding justice and high sheriff in the present day county. John D. Howe, father of Haven, was born in the county and also served as justice for a number of years. In 1873 Haven married Cathrine McGavock-Cloid in a large double parlor of the Cloid house at Dunkard Bottom.

The Cloid home was a large three-story Victorian structure built by Cathrine's father, David Cloid, in 1847. David was the son of Thomas Cloid, who had purchased a great parcel of the Dunkard Bottomland in the early 1800s. The site of the Cloid house is now under the waters of Claytor Lake, next to the home of Col. William Christian. Haven B. Howe served as a member of Company F of the 14th Virginia Cavalry at the age of 17 in 1864.

During the Civil War, he took part in the Milford Dinwittie Courthouse and Five Forks battles. In Pulaski County, Howe was regarded as a successful cattle farmer, raising pure-blooded white-faced Herford cattle. He served as county supervisor for four years and was a member of the Virginia state legislature as a delegate representing Pulaski and Giles counties.

As evidenced by the remarkable woodworking in the house, Haven B. Howe was a resourceful and creative craftsman, using choice woods from surrounding forests including maple, walnut, birch and pine. He also fashioned most of the furniture his family required.

A prominent citizen in his time, he was also ahead of his time regarding the struggle to halt pollution of the New River by iron ore smelting plants. Although the plant brought prosperity to the area, Howe strived to inform the public of the dangers of dumping mineral waste into the freshwater. In 1911, a year before his death, he was called as a witness by the U.S. War Department to testify on the pollution problem in the New River. Government ships navigating the Ohio River were being damaged by mineral waste channeled into the Ohio by its tributaries, the New River being one of the most polluted. As of Jan. 1, 1912, no ore mud could be dumped into the New River, mandated by a court order. This was the final episode and a fitting legacy for Haven B. Howe, who died in December 1911. A black and white photo of Haven, who has kind-looking eyes and a bushy mustache, is hung above the fireplace.

Also in the visitor center is a Theater Room where stone tools, wildlife and wildflowers are interpreted. Rest rooms are downstairs in the impressive house. The basement of the visitor center is an environmental education center, where various natural history displays are featured.

Cruise boat: Departing daily from Claytor State Park, the 600-foot Pioneer Maid is a nifty double deck, Coast Guard certified boat with an 18-foot beam and two diesel engines. The clean, white boat can accommodate 140 passengers on one fully enclosed carpeted deck that is surrounded by windows for a panoramic view. It's easy to see the wait staff scurry around the patrons serving piping hot, home cooked meals.

The dinner boat departs from the Civil War-era Howe House and features a historical narration along a river-like lake that has been in use for more than 15,000 years. The excursions include luncheon, dinner, moonlight and champagne brunch cruises. One of the most popular weekly cruises is the Friday evening prime rib buffet for a very reasonable price.

Luncheon cruises might feature a colonial buffet, gourmet deli or a buffet of authentic recipes from the kitchen of George Washington and Thomas Jefferson, such as golden Monticello breast of chicken, baked polenta and Virginia baked country ham. Cash bars and private charters for your group are also available. For more information call (800) 419-0378.

Campground: The unit has 132 camping sites, with 44 in the D section having water and electrical hook-ups. This loop opens early in the spring and closes late in the fall, offering large sites appropriate for RV rigs. Bathhouses, with hot showers and laundry sinks, are centrally located in each of the four camping loops. The dump station is near campground D. All of the sites have fire rings and picnic tables. Most of the sites are gravel or gravel and grass.

Loops A, B and C sites are compact and small, ideal for tents and pop-up campers. These three loops are densely wooded and along a hard-surfaced road.

The D loop is preferred, offering a good mix of shade and open, airy sites. Sites in the high 30s and 40s are especially easy for RV rig drivers to maneuver in and out of. Sites 14 and 15 can accommodate huge motor homes

The sandy beach is popular year-round.

_____

or travel trailers. Some of the sites in the teens are pull-throughs. Sites 22-30 are some of the most level pull-through sites in the loop.

Many sites are backed up against a pencil-straight pine plantation where songbirds may be sighted, especially kinglets and finches.

Cabins: The 12 wonderful lakefront cabins are identical and furnished with rustic furniture, fireplace, electric appliances, kitchenware and linens included in the weekly rental. The cabins are cinder block with covered rough-sewn cedar siding and air conditioning. They have two bedrooms and can sleep four, with a maximum capacity of six. One bedroom has a full-sized bed and the other has twin beds. The bathrooms have a shower stall.

Each cabin has a screened porch and a living room with fireplace. Firewood is usually available. The cabins are available from March to December. You may park your boat only steps away from your unit. Bring your fishing rod.

Cabins 1-3 are grouped together and have lampposts and side-yard seating with a terrific view of the tree-lined shore, hills and water. All of the cabins have attractive and large grassy areas surrounding them, ideal for family field games. The cabins are equally nice and in front of a wooded area. Cabin 12, at the end of the spur, has the most privacy.

Many cabin guests enjoy walking along a section of the shoreline in both directions of the colony. Many of the driftwood-choked coves near the cabins are hotbeds for shorebirds and waterfowl.

Fishing: Many anglers fish the shoreline behind the Howe House visitor center and along the many tiny coves that form a jagged shoreline around almost the entire lake. Anglers may also use a wooden fishing dock across a small cove from the Howe House. Two stores just outside the park sell live bait. Striper and muskie anglers gravitate to the upper end of the lake, while walleye fishermen must work hard to find their migratory prey. White bass, especially during spawning, school in large numbers and are easily caught using jigs and crankbaits.

The lake is well-known for a large population of smallmouth bass that can be taken in good numbers in the spring and fall, and much of the summer in deep water.

Local anglers recommend areas near Stewarts Hollow, the mouth of Dublin Hollow, Twin Hollow and the island near Roseberry Cove to be good fishing waters. The oxygen-rich lake is a good to very good fishing.

A kids fishing contest is held on the Saturday following Father's Day each June.

Boating: Hungry boaters can eat a hot dog and soft drink from the snack bar, buy gasoline, rent a boat, moor their craft for the season or buy marina supplies. The marina has three floating mooring docks. A small island is in front of the tan cement block marina that is landscaped with beds of shrubs and annual flowers. Next to the snack window is a large mural of the lake that depicts the names of many of the coves, fish species found in the lake and other landmarks and hollows along the upper and lower lake.

Attached to the marina building is a large elevated deck that offers a relaxing spot to view the busy, lighted docks below. Colorful small sailboats, pontoons and runabouts bob at their mooring stations at the cove-side marina. The boat launch next to the marina complex offers a courtesy dock and mooring cleats. A state game commission-operated ramp is just north of the park. Boats can be rented from a small shed near the two gasoline pumps. Also nearby is a porta-potty dump station.

At a special flat dock designed for sculling boats, rowing enthusiasts use the marina and placid lake as an exercise area. The long, man-powered boats have foot stirrups and skinny oars that propel them at rapid speeds up and down the channel.

Claytor Lake Dam: The dam was built during 1937-39 by the Appalachian Power Company. The massive structure is 135 feet high, 108 feet wide at the base, 1,150 feet long and cost about $11 million to build. Claytor Lake covers about 4,495 acres, reaches a length of 21.6 miles and has 100 miles of rugged and scenic shoreline.

Hiking: Claytor Lake has two hiking trails. The 1.6-mile Claytor Lake Trail, which circles the southwest tract of the park, is generally easy, except for a few rugged climbs and descents. It offers good views of the winding lake.

Although hiking is limited at the park, the Sandy Ridge Trail, a half-mile interpretive loop, offers eight learning stations and a booklet that explains trailside marked areas. You will see the land much as it was when the state acquired it in 1948. Tall pine, cedars and sunny fields that sprout saplings are scattered throughout the tract. Some fine examples of Carolina hemlock show how much things have changed in the last 200 years. These majestic trees are a sample of a mighty forest the once thrived here. Hikers should look among these aged trees for dead wood that now harbors a variety of insects, a delight for chiseling woodpeckers. These dead trees are important habitat for raccoon, owls and squirrels, too.

Nature's decomposing crew—insect, bacteria, fungi, mosses, worms and small animals—are important workers. They help turn old logs into soil so that healthy and new plants can thrive. Look beneath the Japanese honeysuckle at station No. 8 for decomposers. Also enjoy the fragrant honeysuckle that was introduced into America in the 1700s. Now Japanese honeysuckle has taken over many areas, growing up to 30 feet in height.

Claytor Lake has 12 waterside cabins.

Day-use areas: The hilly day-use areas are mostly around the marina and visitor center, consisting of mowed areas, shady spaces of conifers and hardwoods, bulky-appearing picnic shelters, large rest room buildings with soft drink machine, play apparatus and tables.

Beach: In the summer, especially on hot days, the sandy beach is the focal point of the park. It has a newer concession stand and angular bathhouse. Claytor Lake's guarded beach is one of the few swimming areas on the entire lake. Several wooden and wire mesh benches and tables sit along the perimeter of the beach, overlooking the action. The conditioned beach is about 450 feet long and has an offshore diving platform. The view from the beach is of tree-covered hills, occasional boat traffic and waterfowl and gulls that ride the tiny waves and sometimes fly just above the water.

A pay phone, soft drink machines and potted plants along the walkway make this a tidy beach perfect for family outings on hot summer days.

Nature: Seasonal interpretive programs are offered that include guided

Skulling boats get a work out on the lake.

walks, astronomy, bats, insects, storytelling and campfire programs. Small acoustic bands also occasionally play at the park. Many of the interpretive programs begin at the gazebo behind the Howe House visitor center.

In November, the park organizes a large lakeshore cleanup.

Hunting: A controlled deer hunt is conducted using blackpower and bows. The hunts are highly regulated. Call the park manager for details. Cabins are available during these special hunts.

Insiders tips: Lodging, private marinas, mini-golf and restaurants are scattered around the lake. Each Labor Day weekend, the park hosts an arts and crafts festival on the front lawn of the Howe House.

7 Clinch Mountain Wildlife Management Area

Land: 25,000 acres Water: 330-acre lake

The humble facilities include 22 wilderness campsites, a hand pump well, pit toilets and small bait and supply store, all in the middle of the largest and most scenic wildlife management area in the state. The Clinch Mountain Wildlife Management Area is more than 25,000 acres in the southern mountains of Virginia with an elevation of 2,200 to 4,600 feet.

The mountain range features significant and diverse habitats ranging from the boulder-strewn Big Tumbling Creek and haystack-like beaver dams at the foot of the mountains to towering red spruce and a large lake at the top of Beartown Mountain. The rugged wilderness area is a popular place for quality hunting and fishing.

The drive through, and into, the wildlife management area is exciting. Try rolling down your windows as you slowly drive the gravel road and listen to the cascading streams with step-like rapids, or calling songbirds, waterfalls and other sounds of nature. Wildlife viewing by auto-touring on Route 747 and hiking the roads are good ways to view wildlife.

The zig-zagging switch-back roads, which are carved into the side of the mountain, were once railroad beds. In places along the road you can still see where the salt-laden trains needed extra space to back up so they could maneuver the twisting turn up the steep incline. Today the road is very narrow. In places, if you should meet an oncoming car, one of you will have to carefully back down the road to the nearest wide spot so the other can safely pass.

The land for the wildlife management area was purchased in 1961 from the Stuart Land and Cattle Company. Since then smaller tracts have been added, equaling one solid block of mountains where northern and southern forests overlap. The diverse forest includes basswood, beech, birch, hickory, locust, maple, oak and poplar. A significant stand of black cherry has been designated by the Society of Foresters. The huge trees are near the lake and some measure three feet in diameter and are more than 85 feet tall.

The cold streams and lake offer some of the best trout fishing in the state.

Information and Activities

Clinch Mountain Wildlife Management Area
Virginia Department of Game and Inland Fisheries
(703) 944-3434 or
Hungry Mother State Park
(703) 783-3422

Directions: From Saltsville take Route 613 north to Route 747 and follow the signs. The park is north of Saltsville. The state park facilities are in the wildlife management area owned by the Department of Game and Inland Fisheries. The park touches four counties: Russell, Smyth, Tazewell and Washington.

Emergency number: Rescue, 628-7117.

Campground: The 22 campsites on the mountain are well spaced and primitive. Sites are not well numbered—often just a mark on a tree—but are easy to find along the narrow gravel road. Most of the sites are level, dry and face an open area adjacent to the road. Sites have a trash barrel and a small fire ring.

The campground is open from the third Saturday in March to Labor Day. Rental is first come, first served. One vehicle is allowed per camping site.

Concession: Open seasonally, the woodframe building with a patio, sells soft drinks, live bait and tackle, ice, light snacks and sandwiches. Live bait available include waxworms, mealworms, redworms and crawlers. The board-and-batten-sided building is outlined by a stained split-rail fence and a gravel parking area.

Boating: Non-gasoline powered boats only are permitted on the lake. The mountaintop lake, depending on the season and dam settings, can have wide mudflat-like shores. Cartop boats and occasionally windsurfers share the 300-acre lake that is 3,600 feet above sea level.

A single-lane, hard-surfaced launching ramp is on the lake. There are no courtesy docks.

Fishing: Daily fishing permit fees are required for Laurel Bed Lake, Big Tumbling Creek and tributaries. There is a creel limit of six trout per day. Fishing hours are posted. The use of minnows is prohibited in the lake and tributaries. Shoreline anglers should try the rocky shores on either side of the dam.

A trout stocking schedule is posted at the concession stand. The schedule details times and locations of fish stocking.

Fly fishermen will work hard climbing car-sized boulders to reach pools at the base of stair-step rapids. Use a short rod and bring some light Cahills, minnow imitators, light-colored dry flies and some terrestrials. Stick with light colors in the dimly lit streams. Much of the overhanging bowers are hemlock and oak.

Hiking: Many park roads make for exciting hiking through deep gorges, along steep mountainsides and on top of ridges. The best known of the

The mountaintop lake and surrounding lands are rich with wildlife.

---

designated hiking trails is the 2.5-mile Clinch Mountain Trail. The strenuous trail features rugged scenery of forested valleys and wildlife. The trailhead is near the parking lot at the dam.

Red Branch Trail (8 miles) is also a rugged hike through red spruce that are normally found much farther north, along ridge lines and into some secluded areas.

Nature: The wildlife management area has several trails where hikers can explore the bio-diverse habitats; from Southern Appalachian hardwoods typical of north Georgia to northern hardwoods and spruce typical of New England, and from desert-like cliffs and grassland to northern bogs, rivers, streams and a lake with beaver ponds. The valleys are narrow and the mountains steep throughout the entire wildlife management area.

The park has 30 types of amphibians, 24 species of reptiles, 140 birds and 51 mammals (including three types of bats).

Some of the most interesting species sighted at the park include black duck, bufflehead, pied-billed grebes, sandpipers in the mudflats, bald eagles, black bear and herons. Owls, wild turkey, deer and raccoon are also commonly seen from the roads and trails. Serious songbird watchers should concentrate in the shrublands and mowed sections.

Hunting: Hunting is excellent in the area. Mountain hunting can be tough, but the abundance of squirrels, deer, wild turkeys and rabbits make the effort worthwhile. Bird hunters can try for dove, ruffed grouse and woodcock. Some night hunters still pursue raccoons, opossums and bobcats. Call the park manager for details.

Insiders tips: Nearby privately operated Rainbow Campgrounds offers hook-ups and camping services. The Wild Turkey Brood Range Area, operated by the local chapter of the Wild Turkey Federation, plants many birds in the area. Visit during berry picking time (June). The cable and pulleys that cross the stream are used to lower containers of fish into pools for stocking.

Some of the rushing mountain streams have car-sized boulders and are stocked with trout.

8 Douthat State Park
Land: 4,493 acres Water: 50-acre lake/streams

Douthat, one of Virginia's six original state parks, opened in 1936. It's a huge tract nestled in the Allegheny Mountains not far from the West Virginia border. The remote park has a rustic flavor, with much of the development built by the men of the Civilian Conservation Corps. Many of the bulky wood and stone CCC amenities are still in use. You will see wonderful examples of their craftsmanship in stone walls, log and timber pavilions, carved doorknobs, and wrought-iron hinges, shutter latches, doors and light fixtures.

The terrific park lies between two massive ridges that reach up to 2,600 and 3,100 feet. The lake is at an elevation of 1,146 feet and shimmers in the valley, a focal point of the many activities and facilities.

For thousands of years people have been attracted to the Allegheny highlands. Prehistoric and historic Indian camps and burial sites attest to the presence of humans long before the highlands were populated by pioneers. The fertile Jackson and Cowpasture river valleys invited settlers and supported extensive agricultural development during the 19th century. The area's numerous hot springs were also popular in attracting people from up and down the east coast well into the 20th century. Mining was an important economic factor in the region during the 19th century. Local companies shipped pig iron to Lynchburg and Richmond via the James River and the Kanawah Canal until railroads reached the region in the 1860s.

Douthat lies in the Appalachian mountain system, which extends north to Newfoundland and southwest to Georgia and Alabama. The geological features in this region were created by a process of folding. Folded mountains are formed when internal stresses in the earth's crust push sideways against rock layers, causing them to rise upward in the form of gigantic folds or wrinkles. Upheavals of this sort usually require millions of years to complete.

Most of the mountain chains of the eastern United States and Canada were elevated during the geological era known as the Paleozoic, about 300 million years ago, long before the more advanced forms of life such as birds and mammals had appeared on earth. However, sections of Virginia's Appalachian region are even older. Rocks found in Douthat have been estimated to be about 1.1 billion years old. Time has mellowed Virginia's mountains. Because of their great age they generally lack the sharp peaks, abrupt cliffs and angular lines that characterize most ranges; their contours have been softened and their valleys broadened by the erosive powers of streams and rain.

In the 1930s, the Douthat Land Company donated almost 2,000 acres to the state which paved the way for the state park's development. Today thousands of park visitors have the opportunity to enjoy many of the same sights and sounds experienced by the first inhabitants.

Information and Activities

Douthat State Park
Route 1, Box 212
Milboro, VA 24460
(540) 862-8100

Directions: Near Clifton Forge. Take exit 27 off I-64 to State Route 629, then seven miles north.

Emergency numbers: Police (800) 542-5959, fire 862-4121.

Visitor center: The park office is adjacent to the visitor center and open 8 a.m. - 8 p.m. Monday - Thursday and 8 a.m. - 10 p.m. Friday and Saturday during the summer. Take a look at the three-ring binder filled with information about nearby attractions, covered bridges, scenic vistas, shopping, waterfalls and much more. Also in this book are interior photographs of the park's cabins.

The yellow walls are a bright background for many educational displays in the visitor center. Park users should start their visit here, learning about the unit's rich natural and cultural history.

Douthat State Park received its name from Robert Douthat, who in 1795 was granted a large tract of land which now includes the park and adjoining national forest. However, Douthat State Park's place in history is rooted not in the name, but in its origin as a park. Douthat was one of the many places around the country where the Civilian Conservation Corps employed many young men during the Depression of the 1920s and 1930s. Here over a course of nine years, some 600 men labored for one dollar per day plus room and board to create one of Virginia's first state parks.

Douthat is special since most of its buildings, trails and other structures built by the CCC have been well preserved. Few changes have been made to the park since opening in 1936. In its 50th anniversary, the park was placed on the Virginia Landmark Register and the National Register of Historic Places.

The visitor center has wood samples and information about how important a variety of woods were to settlers and craftsmen many years ago.

Sassafras trees grow to more than 120 feet tall and have dull-orange wood. The tree has always been known for the tea extracted from its bark and is still used in the manufacture of root beer. Colonists relied upon the hot tea to help them sweat out fevers. The bark was also used to die wool.

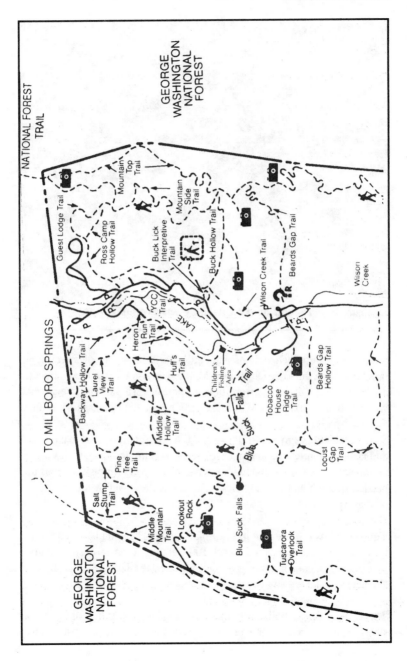

Log cabins were built by the Civilian Conservation Corps.

Sugar maple provided Indians and settlers with a supply of sweet syrup produced from the sap each spring. Maple was also used in the production of soap because its ashes were high in potash. The strong fine-grained wood was used extensively to make strong tools and beautiful furniture.

Shagbark hickory grows to 120 feet and is a fine-grained wood that is tough and lasting. While it makes an excellent slow-burning wood, it was highly regarded by Indians for making bows and by pioneers for making tools that needed strength and spring. Hickory nuts were enjoyed by the Indians, as well as by wildlife.

Tulip poplar was named for its tulip-like flower. The Indians prized the tree for its straight trunk that could reach 100 feet tall. It has a soft straight grain that made it ideal for carving canoes. In fact, the Indians called the tree "keeler," which means "canoe wood."

The white oak symbolizes strength and staying power because it grows slowly to a great size. Some of the trees have achieved a live span of more than 600 years. Wood of the oak is strong and heavy, ideal for ship building. Its acorn was an important food source for man and beast.

Visitors can also view and learn about some of the actual tools used by the men of the CCC. Rounded-off shovels, picks, worn-out leather boots and grainy photographs tell the tale of their back-breaking work.

The CCC legacy includes an uncommon use of natural materials and sensitivity to the environment. The CCC were advocates of using native materials in their project whenever possible. Douthat cabins were built with chestnut and poplar, which are hard and durable species. Cypress was used for shingles and pine for interior paneling. Oak was used for heavy beams and for strength, while chestnut was the choice for split-rail fences. Leaving little waste, the CCC crews used chipped bark as a dressing for hiking trails and planting beds.

Stone excavated during construction was used for fireplaces in the cabins, retaining walls found along the park roads and foundations. Types of stones found in the park and used in construction include sandstone, limestone, brown hematite, sandstone with quartz, malachite, chemung, quartz-pebble conglomerate and slag.

As the name implies, part of the Civilian Conservation Corps' mission was to do major work that would lead to the protection of the nation's natural and cultural resources. At Douthat, this was accomplished by protecting the 4,000 acres of mountain woodlands, and building durable facilities to accommodate people in the natural setting. While the managed and protected lands benefited the park's wildlife population, many visitors to the park developed a keener awareness of their environment which often led to support for conservation efforts far beyond park boundaries.

When the CCC began work in the park, many animals like deer, beaver and turkey were uncommon. Today they are abundant.

At the back of the visitor center is a wet lab complete with many aquariums and information about aquatic life. Large jars preserve common snakes including timber rattlesnake, black racer and northern copperhead. Also found in this smaller room are some archaeological artifacts, projectile points and arrowheads.

Yet another room is dedicated to blacksmithing. This room is actually a blacksmith's workshop complete with a coal forge and hand-operated blower, rusty anvil, and many tools of the blacksmith including tongs and pritchels that were used to make hinges, blades and tools. The shop was constructed by the CCC in 1933 and was a three-sided building (now it's connected to the visitor center). One side was open for ventilation and access for horses, wagons and large objects to be worked on.

Our vision of a blacksmith often is a husky man garbed in a soiled leather apron, bending over red hot coals that heated iron soft. Known for horseshoeing, most blacksmiths' work was actually comprised of making and repairing things made of metal. The blacksmith hammered iron into the shapes of tools, housewares, farm implements, latches, grinders, wheels, axles and fasteners. All of the hinges and latches in most of the park's buildings were made in this tiny blacksmith's shop. Samples of the hinges and latches are displayed in the historic shop.

Behind the visitor center are a small amphitheater and porch, where park benches and a small stage are next to the building. A mount of a black bear is under the porch roof at the small elevated stage. A fire ring and additional seating are next to the amphitheater.

Creasey Lodge: Across the narrow road from the park office and visitor center is the modern lodge that sleeps 18 people. It is used for meetings, small conferences and family reunions. The attractive building has rough-sawn siding, wood shake shingles and is pleasantly notched into the surrounding forest. Inside the lodge are hardwood floors, a stone fireplace, comfortable furniture, telephones, brass lamps and modern bathrooms.

A second CCC-built lodge near the campground can accommodate 17 people in six bedrooms. This log-style lodge is on the top of the mountain, up a narrow, switchback road. The steep shoulderless road is not for the faint-of-heart. From the rustic lodge with a small parking area is a beautiful view of the hazy rolling mountains. This is a perfect getaway lodge for an intimate family reunion.

Campground: The park has 116 camping sites in three areas. The campgrounds are as terrific as the rest of the park.

Lakeview Restaurant and Country Store.

Camping loop A is one big loop with 19 sites. It's the most popular section because it's on the lake. Many sites are just steps from the gently lapping water. Campers in the A loop should bring their fishing boats. There's plenty of mooring spaces for them. A creek also enters the lake near this loop and many fly fishermen enjoy wading the shallows, pitching feathery flies into quiet pools or at places where trout are seen rising. This loop offers a perfect view of the lake and tree-covered mountains that surround the park. The loop has plenty of shoreline fishing places and the water is shallow, making it a popular choice for families with children.

The C camping loop is southwest of the beach and accessed by a single-lane bridge over a stone-strewn creek. The Beard's Hollow trailhead is off the roadway that takes you back to the hilly campground. Many of the sites are outlined by landscape timbers and equipped with green-colored gas lantern hanging posts. Sites are neat and tidy and pads are coated with attractive blue chipped stone gravel. Some of the sites are L-shaped and have newer tables. Sites in the C section are dry, level and well-spaced.

Sites 16 and 17 can handle large motor homes or big trailers. Some of the favorite sites are at the end of the loop (sites in the 20s), where there's plenty of shade and privacy. Site 28 is at the end of the loop and has a view of a wooded valley. Electrical hook-ups are available in the loop. A soft drink machine is at the showerhouse. Site 3 is a pull-through and only 30 yards from the showerhouse.

Store/restaurant: The Lake View Restaurant and Country Store share space in a wood shingled building with a view of the lake. The restaurant has a lunch menu from 11 a.m. - 4 p.m. and dinner is served from 4 p.m. to 8 p.m. A buffet is served on Friday and Saturday nights and on Sunday. Wood tables and chairs and brass lights furnish the attractive eatery known for serving solid and hearty foods. A fireplace, hanging plants, vaulted ceiling and flagstone patio further contribute to a scenic and tasty eating experience.

The tan country store is open 6 a.m. -10 p.m. daily during the summer. The store sells ice cream, jellies, T-shirts, country crafts, mugs, hats, stationery, walking sticks, blankets, a few fishing supplies, newspapers, matches, marshmallows, candy, firewood, playing cards and pencil drawings of the park. From the high bank where the store and restaurant stand, you can see the lake where many fishermen drive small boats looking for their daily catch.

Fishing: Wilson Creek is a popular stocked trout stream. The rocky and scenic creek is stocked twice weekly during the trout season. These waters are highly regulated, including daily hours and catch limits. Anglers may take six trout per day as long as they are at least seven inches in size. Trout fishing is permitted the first day of the season (late March) until Sept. 30.

Local anglers recommend trolling tiny Meeps-style spinners behind your electric powered boat. Troll slowly, keeping the spinners out of your small wake.

Cabins: Of the 30 cabins at Douthat, 25 were constructed of logs by the busy CCC. The other five are cinderblock. The cabins have air conditioning, rustic furniture and fireplaces. All the log cabins are one-room and one-bedroom. Some cabins have two bedrooms. The cabins rent by the week or by the night with a minimum of two nights and are open nine months out of the year. Cabins are equipped with a picnic table and parking. Cots can be rented.

Cabins 1-9 are in a loop and have wonderful bulky log porch railings and solid walls under thick tree cover. The quaint cabins have stone foundations and tiny gravel walkways to each unit outlined by landscape timbers. All of these cabins are against a hill. Some of the cabins have a partial view of the lake through the thin trees. Cabins in this loop are within walking distance of the beach, concession, restaurant and country store. Cabin 7, which is on a low ridge above the rest, is a favorite.

Cabins 10 and 11 share a long gravel driveway and are by far the most private of the cabins at Douthat. Rocking chairs are on the porches of most cabins and almost all of the 30 cabins in the park are shaded.

Cabins 12-30 are grouped together on varying elevations along a narrow hard-surfaced road. Cabins 13-16 are on their own gravel spur along a tree-covered ridge line. A few modern cabins (26-30) are mixed into this group of units.

Split firewood is provided to cabin guests.

Boating: Electric-powered boats are permitted on the lake. Paddleboats and johnboats can be rented. The boat concession is near the beach along a gravel path that skirts the water's edge. The tiny boat ramp is across from the dam. Many small fishing boats are moored seasonally at the park.

Unique in the park system is the self-guided pedal boat tour of Douthat Lake. Seven interpretive stops around the lake include places to learn about the fish funnel (fish stocking point), cattails and their usefulness in a wetland, beavers and beaver lodges, flood control, fish, insects and lake history.

Fishing: Angling is fair in the lake, which is drained every two years. The lake is low in oxygen levels, resulting in sometimes less than average fishing.

The Wilson Creek Children's Fishing Area is a rocky stream where live bait (red worms) can produce lots of small trout. The area is for children 12 years and under. Kids should try the small pool using live bait or small spinners early in the season.

The popular beach is on a quiet cove and near a beautiful concession building.

Anglers also fish near the breast of the stone dam. The rocks used to build the dam are now worn smooth from years of water cascading over it. The shoreline near the dam is hilly and most of the lakeshore is tree-lined and firm.

Nearby Cowpasture River gathers its waters from Bath and Highland counties and flows south. Access is limited, but the fishing can be good to very good for smallmouth bass, muskie, pickerel, catfish and sunfish.

Hiking: The unit has 40 miles of hiking trails (24 different trails). Most are short, often a mile or less. The self-guided nature trail is 1.5 miles long. The trails connect to each other and to trails in the neighboring national forest. Many are moderate in difficulty and most offer panoramic views and scenic overlooks. Trailhead markers have brief trail descriptions and maps.

Douthat trails explore the valley floors, and others require some rugged uphill climbing. The trails that traverse mountain slopes are rated strenuous and should be attempted by experienced hikers only.

Douthat trails were built in the 1930s by the CCC. They are often up to six feet wide, and in addition to providing access to the entire park they serve as a fire break in the event of a forest fire. There are a number of fossil sites along Beards Mountain. These fossils are exciting evidence that this area was under water millions of years ago.

Beards Mountain Trail is a scenic trail offering panoramic views of Middle Mountain and Douthat Lake to the west and the Cowpasture River valley to the east. The interconnecting trails can be enjoyed by both advanced and beginning hikers.

Some hikers enjoy the trails in the summer, while others report that spring is the best time, especially before the leaves are out and when the waterfalls and creeks run strong. Hikers on their way to the Tuscarora Overlook should consider a hike at this time of the year. There are at least two waterfalls that you encounter, high-sulfur-content springs, woods of pines and dramatic views along the trail. The rock faces, rock cribbing constructed by the CCC and sparkling waters of the lake and stream make the trek to Tuscarora a wonderful experience.

The Buck Lick interpretive trailhead is near the restaurant and features a booklet (small fee) that details 17 learning stations along the trail.

Blue Lick Trail was built in the 1930s and has been well-maintained since. Hikers will learn about dogwood (which has a big bark) and that its showy flowers are actually leaves.

There is a legend that at the time of the Crucifixion, the dogwood was the size of the oak and other forest trees. So firm and strong was the tree that it was chosen at the time for Jesus' cross. To be used for such a cruel purpose greatly distressed the tree, and in His gentle pity for all sorrow and suffering said to it: "Because of your regret and pity for My suffering, never again shall the dogwood grow large enough to be used as a cross. Henceforth it shall be slender and bent and twisted, and its blossoms shall be in the form of a cross—two long and two short petals. And at the center of the outer edge of each petal, brown with rust stained with red, and in the center of the flower will be a crown of thorns, and all who see it will remember."

Black oak, white pine, skunks and mountains are along the trail. The interpretive trail takes hikers through the understory of the forest while explaining the significance of the overstory, tree canopy and fertile forest floor.

Along the banks and on the bottom of bubbling mountain streams live many specialized types of animal life, and to these banks come larger animals in search of food or a cool drink of water. You may see crayfish—a fine food for raccoons, birds, turtles and snakes. Salamanders may also be found under rocks and logs in the streams along Blue Lick Trail. Salamanders are small lizard-like animals which are not lizards at all, but are amphibians akin to frogs. They must keep their skin moist at all times. Therefore, they too are common in and around Douthat streams.

The trail is lined with mountain laurel, Virginia's most beautiful shrub that can grow 20 feet, forming a dense thicket. Hikers will also discover the native American chestnut tree, the evergreen hemlock (its bark was used to heal wounds and burns), and places where bobwhite, bear or deer may reside.

Biking trails: Cycling is allowed on all but six of the park's 24 trails. Cyclists must yield to hikers and follow these simple rules: Biking is allowed only in one direction on certain trails (indicated by an arrow on maps available from the visitor center); tread lightly; speak up; don't startle walkers; biking is permitted seasonally; stay on designated trails only; and maintain a slow speed. Finally, know your physical limitations and be nice.

Day-use areas: Two reservable picnic shelters are operated by the park. The shelters (one large, one small) can be rented by the half or full day. Horseshoe pits and open spaces surround the shelters. The park's amphitheater is at the beach.

Beach: Sandy and clean, the small guarded beach is on a cove and very busy on summer weekends and holidays. Offshore 35 yards is a diving platform that has green carpeting and a stiff single diving board where youngsters line up all day long. Swimmers can swim to the platform and use the diving board under the watchful eye of a lifeguard.

The 150-yard-long beach is divided into zones by buoys. There are safe, shallow areas for younger children to play. There is a small user fee for the beach that is open 10 a.m. - 7 p.m. daily. The white sand is highly conditioned and clean. Benches and picnic tables are scattered around the beach and near the stone retaining wall that outlines the popular sandy area.

The two-story beach concession is terrific, almost elegant. Constructed of large stone and recycled timber, its appearance is in keeping with the CCC style. The newer building houses changing rooms, rest rooms with showers and a food concession. The broad porch and bulky railings are perfect architectural elements that allow the building to fit into the park and natural surroundings. From the concession is one of the best views of mountain folds, quiet lake and white sandy beach.

The attractive concession sells flying discs, T-shirts, footballs, beach toys, popcorn, nachos, cold sandwiches, soft drinks, kick boards, sunscreen, candy, chips, inflatable toys, ice cream and slushes. One dining table is inside the concession that has a wall of windows facing the beach.

A conference room is on the second floor of the building.

Nature: The park has a number of small springs containing sulfur water, called *"suck licks."* The natural saltiness and pungent odor entice animals to the water and inhale the fumes. Large rhododendron thickets line the cascading streams and rocky creeks. If hikers are lucky, they might catch a glimpse of ruffed grouse, fox, turkey, deer and bobcat and the surrounding George Washington National Forest.

The park's nature center is near the group camping area. It was once a horse stable, then a bathhouse. The newly renovated nature center is the starting point for many outdoor learning activities. The center houses a naturalist's office and interpretive displays.

Black bear, deer and a variety of small mammals may be spotted. Wild turkey, various songbirds and reptiles can bee seen in the oak, poplar and hickory forests. Look for warblers and other small birds in the laurel, rhododendron and huckleberry thickets along the mountain slopes. The park is also known for large populations of opossum, the United States' only marsupial (meaning that the mother carries the young in her warm pouch). When the babies are born, they are smaller than a honeybee and spend a long time in the pouch, growing to a size were they can live outside.

Programming: The park offers a broad menu of recreational and educational outdoor programming, including self-guided paddleboat tours, line dancing, kids' fishing programs, Sunday morning worship, guided nature hikes, youth programs and more.

Insiders tips: Private camping (Whispering Pines) and a miniature golf course are nearby. Douthat is a very clean, safe-feeling park, great for family camping.

9 Fairy Stone State Park
Land: 4,868 acres Water: 168-acre lake

Home of the mysterious "fairy stones," Fairy Stone State Park offers beautiful scenery, rich history and ample outdoor recreation.

It is said that long, long ago fairies inhabited these quiet and remote regions in the lush foothills of the Blue Ridge Mountains. The tiny fairies roamed freely and enjoyed the beauty and serenity of the enchanted mountains and valleys.

One day they were playing in a sunny glade when an elfin messenger arrived from a city far, far away bearing sad news of the death of Christ. When the fairies heard the terrible details of the crucifixion, they wept. As their tears fell to the earth, they crystallized into little stone crosses. Though the fairies are no longer to be found, the "fairy stones" remain in that enchanted spot as mementos of the sad day.

Fairy Stone State Park derives its name from the amazing little crystals which are known as fairy stones. For many years, people held these little crosses in superstitious awe, firm in the belief that they protected the wearer against witchcraft, sickness, accidents and disaster. Formed and found within park boundaries, these stone crosses are composed of iron aluminum silicate. The mineral name of this composition is brown staurolite. Like other minerals, such as quartz and diamond, brown staurolite occurs as regular crystals.

Single crystals are hexagonal, or six-sided, and often intersect at right angles to form a Roman or Maltese cross or at other angles to form St. Andrew's crosses. The formation of the tiny (about three-quarter-inch) staurolite crystals involves an exact combination of heat and pressure, such as that provided by the folding and crumpling of the earth's crust during the formation of the Appalachian Mountains. Certain types of rock which have been folded and crumpled in this manner are known as schist. The staurolite crystals are usually harder than the surrounding schist and less easily weathered. As the staurolite-bearing schist is weathered away, the more resistant crystals are uncovered and come to lie on the earth's surface.

Staurolite stones are found occasionally in some sections of the mountains in North Carolina and in Switzerland, but nowhere else in the world are they found in such abundance and shaped so nearly like crosses as those in Fairy Stone State Park.

Opened in June 1936, Fairy Stone is one of Virginia's original six state parks built by the Civilian Conservation Corps.

Information and Activities

Fairy Stone State Park
Route 2, Box 723
Stuart, VA 24171-9588
(540) 930-2424

Directions: Fairy Stone is in the foothills of the Blue Ridge Mountains in Patrick and Henry counties. Access to the park is via Route 57 from Bassett or Routes 58, 8 and 57 from the famous Blue Ridge Parkway.

The tiny park office, surrounded by colorful planting beds, sells fairy stones and offers park information.

Emergency numbers: Sheriff, 694-3161; rescue squad, 930-2222.

Visitor center: A thick three-ring notebook with wood covers is on a counter inside the center and filled with historic photographs about whiskey and iron making, state park features, and bits and pieces of the area's railroading and CCC history. One of the most interesting photographs is of the restaurant soon after it was completed many years ago. Visitors can compare the old pictures with what the building looks like today. There is even a yellowing picture of the old wooden contact station when admission to the park was 40 cents. The center is open noon - 4 p.m. Saturday and Sunday.

A recipe for whiskey is also displayed in the visitor center. Here it is: "Boil two tubs of water, throw in one bushel of corn meal and a handful of barley malt. Let cook one hour, then break up and drop the temperature to 150 degrees. Put in one gallon rye or wheat and one quart barley malt. Let sit for two hours, break up and cool to 120 degrees, add cold water to fill barrel to bring the temperature down to 90 degrees, add yeast and let it 'work off'' for about two days. Put into the still, raise temperature 190 degrees, cap off and let it run." The last arrest in the area for an illegal still was in 1888.

Other displays in the small visitor center are an active honey bee hive, information about iron making, apple cider press, aquarium, animal mounts and hundreds of fairy stones.

The primary hunting area for the tiny stones is in an old creek bed. After a strong rain, when a layer of soil has been washed away, is the best time to look for the legendary stones.

The huge pulleys in front of the visitor center operated from 1780-1911, manipulating heavy cables that pulled ore cars up and down the hill, servicing the nearby mine. Bat gates are now installed over the old mine's entrance.

Finding fairy stones: From the park entrance, go left on Route 57 for 2.5 miles to the first white store (an auto repair garage-like building) you will see

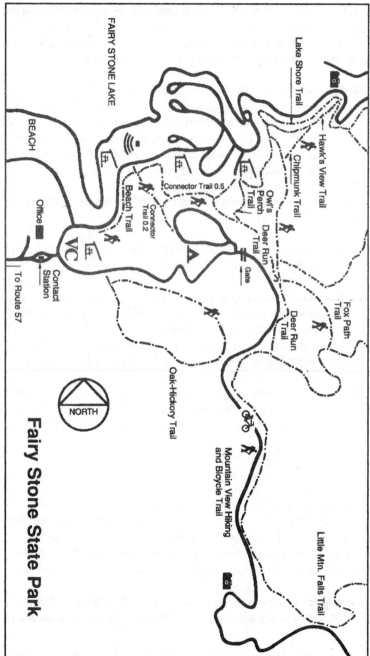

Fairy Stone State Park

on the left. A small gravel parking area and sign are at the trailhead of the park-owned property, where visitors may try their luck finding fairy stones along the dirt trail and dry streambed. No commercial digging is permitted; however, individuals may gather a few of the irresistible stones.

Campground: Fairy Stone is a rolling park with tall hills and tree-covered knobs in each direction. The 51-site campground has a wide entrance and is tucked into a valley and along hillsides. Sites have gravel pads, ground-mounted fire rings and picnic tables. Many are backed up against dense wooded tracts. The campground has one centrally located bathhouse, and all sites have water and electrical hook-ups.

The showerhouse has showers that are accessible by persons with disabilities and are clean. Sites 36 and 37 are near the showerhouse.

Sites B2, 3, 19, 25, 29, 33, 36, 39, 42, 43 and 48 (very large) are pull through sites. Many sites are outlined by timbers.

Cabins: Fairy Stone has eight log and 16 concrete block cabins available for rent on a weekly basis. The attractive log cabins are part of the original facilities built by the Civilian Conservation Corps in the 1930s. Each unit has rustic wood furniture, fireplace, air conditioning, electric appliances, kitchenware and linens. Firewood is provided to guests of the tidy cabins.

The surrounding oak forest has been selectively thinned, offering a perfect mix of sun, breeze and shade to the cabin colony. The forest, criss-crossed by shallow valleys and brushy gaps, also allows parents to watch children at play in the distance.

Cabins 11 and 12 have a wonderful lake view from a porch. They are surrounded by lawn and open spaces. Cabin 9, a log cabin, has white chinking, broad porch with timber railings and lawn. Cabin 18 has a partial lake view. Cabin 17 has the best view of the water, with its inviting porch facing the quiet lake. Cabins 1 and 2, are log units on the lake, offering shoreline fishing from the backyard. Cabin 8 also has good lake access, if you don't mind scrambling down the dirt bank to the water's edge.

Cabins 21-25 are up a single-lane gravel road. The entrance to this group of cabins is near a large day-use area. The private, rugged road climbs the

The author searches for the tiny minerals. They can also be purchased at the park office.

---

mountainside, then back down halfway to the modern cabins. Perched on a ridge, these cabins are very private. Cabins are on different elevations, forcing guests to climb up or down a series of steps to access the units. Cabin 22, at the end of the spur, has a through-the-woods view of the lake. A 40-yard-wide cove is also at the foot of the hill, offering a gentle shoreline, perfect for children to play along or fish from. This group of cabins is within walking distance of some open and day-use areas, perfect for family play.

The modern cabins have screened porches that are outfitted with blue rocking chairs and fire extinguishers. Inside, they have tile floors, quality wood furniture and stone fireplaces. Guests with pets must pay an additional fee. Extra linen and cots are available for a small fee.

Fishing: A 24-pound channel catfish was caught on the day I visited the park (taken on chicken livers). A 50-pound catfish was taken many years ago, according to staff. Early season crappie fishing is excellent in the lake, with most serious anglers fishing at night with minnows. Children catch plenty of bluegills using redworms suspended under a bobber. A few walleye and blue catfish have been planted in the lake.

Many 10-pound largemouth bass are taken from the lake. The best time to fish is during the week.

Some of the best fishing is from the handicapped fishing pier. In front of the wooden pier are structures that are said to hold fish. Other good places to fish are near the boat launch and in front of the cabins along the low banks. Check with local experts to determine where sunken Christmas trees have been placed around the lake.

Bass anglers should explore weedy coves and backwater areas using rubber worm rigs and topwater lures during the early part of the season. Nearby Philpott Reservoir produces lunker trout and largemouth bass. Smallmouth fishing is good until mid-summer.

Boating: Paddleboat (four passengers, small fee) tours are often scheduled on Wednesday mornings during the summer. Guides often talk about waterfowl, watch for wildlife and interpret the lake ecology.

Non-gasoline powered boats only are allowed on the small lake. Adjacent to the beach is a small boat rental with 40-foot-long courtesy dock. The park rents rowboats and purple paddleboats, called "paddlewheelers."

Hiking: A number of pedestrian pathways, some outlined by stone retaining walls, connect sections of the park. In addition, 25 more miles of hiking and biking trails are in the park.

The park publishes an excellent trail map that includes information about two of the most strenuous trails, Chipmunk and Little Mountain Fall. Many moderate trail loops are under one mile in length. For serious hikers, try the Stuart's Knob Trails, which has four difficult trails. To find them, take Route 346 out of the park and turn right onto Route 623. Look for the trailhead and parking area on Route 623.

Day-use areas: Bulky timber-frame and stone picnic pavilions are well-kept and grand. Wooden boardwalks cross small valleys, gaps and hollows, connecting day-use areas and other amenities of the park.

Lit by knee-level lamps, the gravel path to the amphitheater is heavily used when the park staff conducts fun or educational programs. A small parking lot and a scattering of picnic tables are near the small outdoor theater that is close to camping area B.

Beach: The well-conditioned sand of the 150-yard-long beach is blazing white. A diving platform with two ladders, three lifeguard chairs, two small CCC picnic shelters with tree trunk-style benches, drinking fountain and a wooden dock surround the pleasant beach. The tan log-style concession stand offer snacks and cold drinks. Beach hours are typically 10 a.m. - 7 p.m. daily unless otherwise posted. The water is divided into three patrol sections and guarded. The cove beach is the summer focal point of the park and offers a wonderful view of the wooded shoreline across the lake.

Nature: The environs at Fairy Stone are a rich mix of upland soils, towering white pines, oaks, hickories, poplar, beech and valleys filled with rhododendron. Naturalists will find many spring and summer wildflowers and habitats ideally suited for wild turkey, white-tailed deer, spring warblers, woodpeckers and many small mammals. Birders will find the most species along brushy edge areas, and open fields, and many types of waterfowl along Philpott Reservoir and Smith River.

A variety of interpretive programs are offered by the park's staff including guided hikes, bluegrass music, a gospel festival, guided fairy stone hikes, slide presentations and youth programs.

Hunting: Lands along Route 623 are opened for deer hunting during the fall. Some monster bucks have been taken from the old orchard area. The second-growth hardwoods and farmed plots offer excellent squirrel, dove and turkey hunting.

Nearby attractions: The unit is only minutes from Mabry Mills, Stone Cross Mountain, Chateau Morrisette Winery in Meadows of Dan, Booker T. Washington National Monument in Hardy and the Virginia Museum of Natural History in Martinsville.

Insiders tips: About every other Saturday, at the Allied picnic shelter, bluegrass music is played. Reynold's Homestead (to register call 703-694-7181) occasionally puts on programs at the park.

10 False Cape State Park
Land: 4,321 acres Water: Atlantic Ocean/Back Bay

The combination of False Cape State Park and adjacent Back Bay National Wildlife Refuge (7,700 acres) offers the best beach hiking in the East. The pristine coast of wild rolling dunes is one of the last undisturbed coastal environs in this part of the country, and it is just 20 miles south of Virginia Beach. The state park has nearly six miles of ocean shoreline.

False Cape is the least-visited of Virginia's state parks, but it is one of the best for environmental education, primitive oceanside camping and beach walking along miles of unspoiled shoreline. The isolated paradise has a forest of loblolly pines, tall oaks and broad maples. The park is closed to vehicles. The only way to access the park is by walking, biking or boat. The unit is about five miles from the refuge parking lot down gravel paths that thread along sand dunes, barrier beaches, salt marshes and scattered woodlands. Bring your own water, at least a gallon per person per day in the summer, because there is no water at the primitive state park. The park is well worth the sometimes dusty hike or bike.

The park got its name from mariners who falsely identified the slight curve in the beach for Cape Henry at Chesapeake Bay. Some of the sailors who stayed enjoyed the relatively mild climate caused by the close proximity to the Atlantic Ocean, surrounding bays and sounds. The area is buffeted by winds and offers little protection in a storm. Strong fall winds blow through the winter months. Potentially stormy, they are known as "nor'easters."

Survivors of numerous shipwrecks built the area's first community, Wash Woods, using cypress wood that washed ashore from the wrecks. From the turn of the century until the 1960s, False Cape was a haven for a number of prestigious hunt clubs.

About 22,000 people per year visit False Cape.

Information and Activities

False Cape State Park
4001 Sandpiper Road
Virginia Beach, VA 23456
(804) 426-7128

Directions: Virginia's southernmost park, bordering North Carolina. From I-64, take Indian River Road east to Newbridge. Take Newbridge to Sandbridge, then go south on Sandpiper Road.

The park is open year-round and there is no motorized vehicular access. The contact station is staffed April to October, 8 a.m. - 3 p.m. Monday - Wednesday and 9 a.m. - 3 p.m. Friday-Sunday. A pay phone is at the shingled-sided contact station that has sand instead of a lawn surrounding it. Bike and brochure racks are next to the contact station.

Daytime parking (small fee) is available at the Back Bay National Wildlife Refuge. Overnight parking is at the Little Island Recreation Area (small fee). Stay on the trails and do not bike or hike on the dunes.

Campground: Primitive camping is by permit only and permits must be obtained in person at Seashore State Park, 2500 Shore Drive, Virginia Beach,

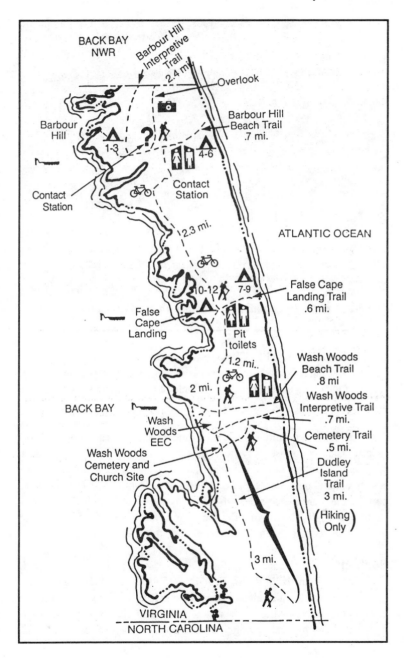

BACK BAY
NWR

Barbour Hill
Interpretive
Trail
2.4 m.

Overlook

Barbour Hill
Beach Trail
.7 mi.

Barbour
Hill

1-3

4-6

Contact
Station

Contact
Station

ATLANTIC OCEAN

2.3 mi.

10-12   7-9

False Cape
Landing Trail
.6 mi.

False
Cape
Landing

Pit
toilets

1.2 mi.

Wash Woods
Beach Trail
.8 mi

2 mi.

Wash Woods
Interpretive Trail
.7 mi.

BACK BAY

Wash
Woods
EEC

Cemetery Trail
.5 mi.

Wash Woods
Cemetery and
Church Site

Dudley
Island
Trail
3 mi.

(Hiking
Only)

3 mi.

VIRGINIA
NORTH CAROLINA

The beach is the finest and most isolated on the East Coast.

VA 23451, (804) 481-2131. Sites are available on a first-come, first-served basis. Camping is limited to six persons per site, seven nights in any 30-day period. Open fires are not permitted. Some of the camping sites are a mile apart; all are quite near the ocean.

The park has 12 primitive sites, including beachfront camping, with pit toilets. Campers must carry in all of their water (and, of course, other supplies). Campers (and day-users) should wear a wide hat, wear lots of sunscreen, and pack insect repellent and a shade tarp. Staff says the most popular sites are beach-side, 4-6 (about one-half mile from the contact station) and 7-9 (about two miles from the contact station). Sites 7-9 are south of the contact station, directly east of the small boat landing.

Boating: Boaters can access the park across Back Bay by using park docks at Barbour Hill, Walsh Woods or False Cape Landing. Many launching ramps are also along Princess Anne Road on the west side of the bay outside the boundaries of the refuge and state park. Expect about a 10-mile round trip by boat. Bring your own boat, or you can rent a canoe or kayak in Virginia Beach.

Fishing: Surf-fishermen have miles of ocean beach from which they can cast for black drum, channel bass, croakers, flounder, whiting, hogfish, speckled trout, spot, striped bass, bluefish, albacore and other saltwater types.

Freshwater anglers can try the state's second largest body of fresh water, the 25,000 acres of Back Bay. The bay has wind tides up to three feet and eventually empties into the Atlantic about 50 miles from the park. Bass anglers have long probed the shallows using spinners for largemouth bass, while pan fishermen toss jigs or small spoons with live bait (mostly minnows and small worms) for good-sized crappies and other panfish. Catfish (try prepared stinkbaits and ripe chicken livers), sunfish and perch are also taken. Back Bay is a 12-mile-long shallow body of water with a surface area of about 44 square miles.

Offshore anglers can take advantage of the Gulf Stream and underwater hills where tuna, marlins, dolphins and other big fish frequent. Check with area bait and tackle shops for charter captains and boat rentals for offshore fishing off Virginia Beach and southward.

Hiking: Avid naturalists will want to make the easy five-mile hike through the refuge to the park as early in the morning as possible. From the winding paths along the diverse coastal habitat, walkers may see river otter, white-tailed deer, feral ponies and pigs, mink, muskrat, opossums, raccoons, all kinds of waterfowl (the park is under the Atlantic Flyway) in the impoundments, and turtles slipping off logs plopping into still-dark marshes.

Once in the park, five trails totaling about 22 miles, are on soft sand. The park's location on a barrier spit allows hikers to observe beaches with sandpipers scurrying along the surf, bristly rows of dunes, maritime forests of live oak and pine, yaupon and wax myrtle, small bays that capture the wind, bogs and rich, wet woodlands. Trails also pass the ruins of an old Methodist church, heavily shaded cemetery and wooden observation platforms.

The 2.4-mile Barbour Hill Nature Trail has a 20-page booklet that describes 24 learning stations along its square-shaped loop. Numbered posts have white lettering on a teal blue field. Barbour Hill, once a distinct hill of sand known as a medano sand dune, was the home of John Barbour's family. Since that time the large dune has migrated and dispersed into many smaller sand dunes that are interesting and explored along the way.

Hikers on the self-guided interpretive trail will learn about the numerous loblolly pine, a pioneer tree of the forest that requires few nutrients but lots of direct sunlight. The decaying needles of the towering pines eventually enrich the soil for future plant growth.

Prevailing ocean winds have created a southwest movement among the dunes. In some places trees have been buried by the moving sand. In other places sand has blown away from the trees, exposing the lower branches and roots. These "migrating dunes" often form shallow valleys and washouts where fresh water collects and serves as a watering hole for wildlife that calls the sand spit home. Hikers along the educational trail will also see and learn about thicket habitat—areas of dense growth of small trees, shrubs and underbrush that contain abundant food and shelter for many species of wildlife.

One favorite activity is to look for footprints in the sand. If you look carefully, footprints in the sand are among the most obvious signs of animals. Hikers will also learn about the water cycle, Back Bay, wetlands, grasses, aquatic plants, waterfowl impoundments, reptiles and amphibians, and have a chance to visit the observation tower for a panoramic view of the area you are exploring.

Additional interpretive signs are on some of the trails. One, for example, does an wonderful job explaining the five stages of sand dunes. You'll learn that the winds and water combine forces to break off large deposits of sand, leaving them on shore. Soon small dunes begin to develop at the thicket's edge and are gradually covered by sparse grasses and other vegetation clinging to the sand, sucking every nutrient possible from the windblown sand hill. Finally, secondary dunes develop and become firm and established. The huge private dunes are fun to view on designated trails and learn about.

Biking: The gravel and dirt trails back to the park meander through the refuge, which is about 75 percent salt marsh. Biking back to the park along

There is no motor vehicle access to the oceanside park.

dikes and past wildlife management pools (they are drained in the summer and filled in the other seasons for waterfowl use) is the most popular way to visit the unspoiled coastal tract. The easy routes can accommodate street bicycles, but a fat-tired mountain bike makes the 10-mile round trip more pleasant. Bikes can be rented in nearby Sandbridge.

The biking paths begin on the east side of the refuge's visitor center. Riders can follow either the west or east dike south five miles to the humble state park entrance. Cyclists can also choose to ride the beach to the park, but select a low tide period which permits peddling on hard sand at the ocean's edge.

Many wooden bike racks, usually next to small timber benches, are scattered along the many trails.

Day-use areas: After a brisk five-mile hike or bike ride, visitors can relax along the beach, sitting on the sand or picnic tables that are scattered throughout the linear park. The park has two boardwalks, several observation towers, fishing, occasional programs, and the long beach. There are no concessions inside the state park.

Nature: Interpretive programs include guided hikes, loggerhead sea turtle programs (the only sea turtle that nests in Virginia), bike, pontoon and canoe trips and more at the Wash Woods Environmental Education Center south of the contact station and directly on the bay. The busy environmental education center, located in a renovated hunting camp, can accommodate 22 people overnight. Bed linens, blankets and towels are provided the kitchen is equipped with stove, microwave oven, sink, refrigerator, and cooking and eating utensils. Food, food preparation and drinking water must be provided by the group. There are day-use and overnight fees.

Demand for the center is high. Reservations must be made and confirmed well in advance by calling the park office. Groups arriving at the center will be provided with an orientation to False Cape that includes an overview of the area's history, flora and fauna. Groups can request a six-hour environmental education program by the staff for a fee that covers a range of study areas within the park, from bayside to seashore. Examples of staff-presented educational programs include wonderful wetlands, Back Bay exploration, profile of a barrier spit, ocean notions. aquatic food chain and undercover, a program in the event of foul weather.

All seasons are interesting at False Cape. In January the bay freezes and migrating waterfowl are present; in March the waterfowl migration is complete; April marks the return of osprey, egrets and many songbirds; May welcomes long-legged shorebirds that probe the moist sand and shoreline for meals; in June nests are active and eggs are hatching and crabbing begins; July and August are hot and quiet with nests vacant; September brings back flocks of migratory waterfowl, swallows and martins; October is filled with ducks, geese, coots and numerous migrating raptors; and finally, waterfowl observation is best in November and December. Access to the park through Back Bay National Wildlife Refuge may be restricted December through February. Contact the park first if planning a visit during these months.

Hunting: Call the state park manager for details about lottery-style deer and pig hunting.

Access to the state park is through the Back Bay National Wildlife Refuge.

Back Bay Wildlife Refuge: Like False Cape, Back Bay is a premiere natural area featuring a beach, sand dunes, shrub lands, wetland, maritime forest and bay habitats unique to barrier islands. The refuge manages water levels in water impoundments, conducts prescribed burning, disking, dike construction and controls access to the refuge. About 100,000 people annually visit the refuge. Call the refuge at (804) 721-2412; for hard of hearing and deaf visitors, (804) 721-0496 TDD. Back Bay is one of 500 refuges in the National Wildlife Refuge System administered by the U.S. Fish and Wildlife Service.

The refuge operates a visitor center near the parking lot at the trailheads that lead south to False Cape. Inside the center is a small classroom with a dozen chairs, a number of small interpretive displays and a fascinating and large decoy collection (including some Dudley, Ivie Stevens, etc.). Inside the glass decoy display cases are photos and descriptions of local decoy makers and other history. Other information and educational elements include a touch table, description of the sand dunes, display of endangered

Biking into the park is easy along firm dirt and gravel roads. Don't forget to bring lots of water. There is no water at the state park.

species that have been confiscated (tiger skin and skulls) and mounts.

Public programming is offered during the season. The visitor contact station is open 8 a.m. - 4 p.m. weekdays and 9 a.m. - 4 p.m. weekends and is closed Sundays December through March. Outdoor facilities are open dawn to dusk.

During peak migration time (December), more than 10,000 snow geese and a large variety of ducks visit the refuge. The mission of the narrow strip refuge is to provide habitat for an assortment of wildlife, including threatened and endangered species such as loggerhead sea turtles, piping plovers, peregrine falcons and bald eagles.

The protective marshland of the refuge and water impoundments offer valuable food plants such as three-square, smartweed and spikerushes. The shifting sands of the barrier beach are constantly exposed to ocean waves, currents and tides. Little vegetation can withstand these powerful forces, but ghost crabs, gulls and migrating shorebirds are common along the rolling mounds of sand. These dunes actually form a line of defense, protecting the refuge impoundments, marsh and woodlands from high tides and storms. The refuge is in many ways a safe haven for many species of flora and fauna.

Wax myrtle, highbush blueberry, bayberry, wild black cherry and persimmon flourish along side woodlands and wetlands. Edges between major habitats, such as between land and sea, are places where wildlife are most active. In fact, coastal barrier habitats are thought to harbor a greater variety of bird species than any other ecosystem in the continental United States. Nearly 300 species of birds have been recorded in the mile-wide refuge. Brightly colored warblers dot shrubs and woodlands each spring. Bird watchers should also look for shorebirds lining the inter-tidal zone each spring.

Avid wildlife watchers might also spot glossy and white ibis in the pools, terns and pelicans on the beach and glimpses of bottlenose dolphins in the ocean. Staff says birders see the greatest number of avians along the canals, pool edges and shrub lands. A birding checklist with 288 species, as well as 31 accidental species, is available from the visitor contact station.

Snakes, including the poisonous cottonmouth, are often seen.

The refuge provides fishing, hunting, boating, limited biking, trapping, educational programs for school groups and a volunteer program for those who would like to keep the refuge improving and protected.

Insiders tips: Bring sunscreen, hat and lots of water, or this remote ocean-side paradise might not be much fun on a hot summer day. The south inlet overlook, depending on the season, can be a very good place to observe wildlife. Walk the beach; it is truly one of the finest in the country.

11 First Landing/ Seashore State Park

Land: 2,770 acres Water: 1.25 miles on the Chesapeake Bay

The Spanish moss dripping from branches, thick-kneed cypress trees and temperate conditions could fool anyone into thinking their much farther south—maybe Florida or southern Georgia. Remarkably preserved, considering its close proximity to the Virginia Beach strip, reddish-brown pine needles cover the forest floor and pathways in the sprawling park. First Landing/Seashore is a wonderful and interesting natural area. More than 600 types of plants grow here due to the unusual meeting and overlapping of habitats (subtropical and temperate) and climates.

First Landing/Seashore has wonderful cabins, maybe the best and most scenic campground in the system, interesting hiking trails, more than a mile of beach on the ocean, a well-stocked store, picnic areas and much more. According to a Department of Conservation and Recreation publication, "Early settlers called this area the great desert because they found its dense woods, swamps and huge sand dunes to be uninhabitable. Thousands of years ago the ocean lapped upon the shoreline about 50 miles west of here.

As ocean and bay waters gradually receded, the wind and waves built a succession of sand dunes. As one row of dunes was being created, plant life was growing up on the one behind. Vegetation stabilized the shifting sand and the dunes became a permanent part of the landscape." Some of the dunes are 75 feet high.

The idea for a state park on the coast was advanced in 1929, sparking enough interest by 1931 to form a Virginia Seashore State Park Association. The group proposed studies and concluded that the Cape Henry area (Cape Henry is where the English landed in 1607, before settling in Jamestown) possessed significant natural features and beauty that would make it an excellent site for a state park. Just two years later 1,064 acres were donated to the state and an additional 2,373 acres were added only months later. The timing was wonderful. This was the era of the Civilian Conservation Corps (CCC) who came to Seashore to build trails, cabins, offices, maintenance buildings, roads and day-use amenities.

This Herculean effort and skills of the corps allowed the park to open in 1936, with development continuing until 1940. As park development ended at the beginning of the war, German U-boats slipped into the offshore waters and were sinking one ship a day for a period. In an effort to protect the Chesapeake Bay, the U.S. Government occupied more than 700 acres of the park, mostly along the beach. At the end of the war, more land was added to the park, more cabins built, beach lengthened and other improvements made until the park was closed in 1954 due to court litigation about integration. Happily, the park reopened in 1961 and everyone has enjoyed the facilities since.

In 1965, the state park and natural area were deemed a National Landmark. The park was also honored in 1977 as a part of the Department of Interior's National Recreation Trails system. The visitor center opened in 1981. In 1995, the Virginia Board of Conservation and Recreation voted to rename the park to First Landing/Seashore State Park, recognizing the Cape Henry area as the site of the first landing site of the English explorers who settled in Jamestown.

More than one million visitors annually come to Seaside.

Information and Activities

First Landing/Seashore State Park
2500 Shore Drive
Virginia Beach, VA 23451
(804) 481-2131

Directions: North of the public beach in Virginia Beach, about 110 miles from Richmond. Take I-64 east to Exit 282 (U.S. 13) and then turn right onto U.S. 60 to Cape Henry. Registered overnight guests are allowed on the bay front during the summer. A small parking fee is charged at the park.

Visitor center: Open 9 a.m. - 6 p.m. daily, the shady center is tastefully painted medium-green and is surrounded by landscaping timbers that hold back soils and colorful plantings beds.

Inside the visitor center are professional-quality displays that line the walls and include how the earth was formed, dune and tidal marsh interpretive panels, beach zones, dune zones, middle beach zone information, artifacts, an Atlantic leatherback turtle (they can weigh up to 2,000 pounds) model and an audio/visual room. The modern center also has a touch table, books for sale, labeled natural history features, facts about the cypress tree (did you know its roots are called "knees?"), mounts and brochures.

Environmental education center: The two-tone green education center is next door to the visitor center and is the starting point for a broad menu of outdoor education programs. In back of both of these buildings is a wooden boardwalk that disappears into the forest.

Campground: First Landing/Seashore's sandy campground (say that three times, fast) has nine loops and 235 sites stretching almost the entire length of the park's bay beachfront. Four elevated boardwalks arch across the delicate dunes for beach access. The beach is high-quality, wind swept and popular. The tract is comprised of rolling dunes, wooded sections, shallow ravines and plenty of sandy sites. Seven showers and six rest rooms, with exterior sinks, serve the sand dune campground.

The park has a full-color map of the campground that depicts which are tent sites, tent/trailer/pop-up or motor home/trailer sites. Most of Loop E is for groups, meaning you must reserve three or more sites to be considered for this area and to guarantee that your sites are adjacent. The park campground is one of the best in the system, with intimate sites scattered among and on top of sand dunes that are sparsely covered with vegetation. Campers can also choose more open and larger sites on the back of most loops. This is one of the few places you can camp on the sand, just a short walk from a long beach, near a complete camp store and only minutes from all the Virginia Beach high-energy attractions and amusements.

Loop G, which is both close to the beach and mostly shady, is the most popular section. Many sites in Loop G are between sandy dunes and often are well-separated by a wall of vegetation. Some pull-through sites are in this area. Site 18 in the loop is a terrific, sandy and private site for a small rig or tent. From some of the sites in this area you can hear the waves breaking against the hard packed sand shoreline.

In the summer, when it's very hot, loops A and B, with their shady cover, become popular with campers.

Some of the tent camping sites, which are outlined by landscape timbers and appear as yellow circles on the campground map, are close to the road. Rail fences also outline some sites.

Loops A, B and C are attractive and shaded by many conifers, offering a thick bed of soft needles to camp and walk on. During slow times, these loops might be closed. Loop H is an open grassy area next to the camp store and most often used by larger RV rigs because of extra room to maneuver. Site 19 in this loop is well located, near the boardwalk, showers and store. For shady sites, try 27, 28, 31 or 32.

Camp store: In a long two-tone tan brick building, the campground store, rest rooms, park office and laundry are open daily. The laundry is open when the camp store is open. Bikes (beach cruiser-type) can also be rented from the back of the store, where an amphitheater with bleachers is also situated.

First Landing/Seashore's camp store is well equipped. You will find considerable fishing equipment (live bait including blood worms, shrimp and crawlers), books, sunglasses, chips, ice, ice cream, propane, lighter

Cabins are modern, quiet and cozy at First Landing/Seashore.

fluid, charcoal, soft drinks, milk, inflatable water toys, T-shirts and beach clothing, batteries, limited oil and marine supplies, towels, souvenirs, folding beach chairs, low-cost surf boards, bread and other basic grocery items. Fishing licenses can be purchased at the store. Some picnic tables and mowed spaces surround the camp store.

Cabins: Six wood-frame and 14 block cabins are rented on a weekly basis. Each cabin is climate-controlled and has furniture, electrical appliances, a fireplace, kitchenware and linens. Cabins are located on a private loop on the west end of the park. Cabins are usually rented by the week, though they can also be rented for as little as two nights. They can be reserved in advance.

Cabins are on varying elevations in each rolling spur. Cabin 1 has parking for two cars and has a view of a wooded hollow and a screened porch. Cabin 2, with a large stone chimney, is more open and sunny than the others. Overflow and extra car or trailer parking are near cabin 4. Cabin 6 is along its own private land and very secluded. Cabin 7 has a screened-in porch

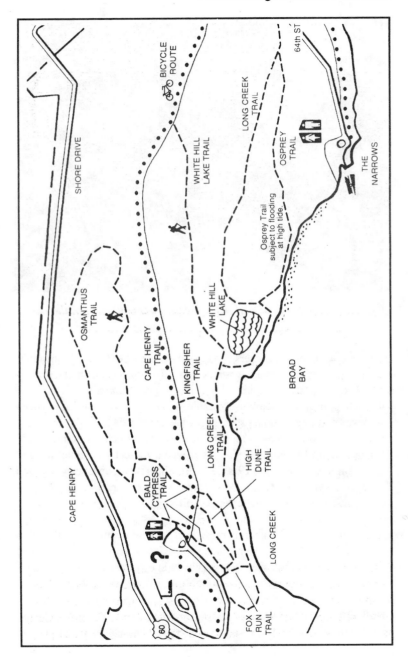

Cypress wetlands are part of the wonderful natural areas in the park.

with two antique blue rockers. Many cabins have field stone foundations and two-tone trim. Cabin 8 is perched on a rise protected from the road by a wall of vegetation. Cabin 11 receives a good mix of sun and shade throughout the day. Many of the cabins have some landscaping, a gravel walkway and tiny yard-like spaces for play and relaxing. Cabin 15 is on a rise with a lawn covered with pine needles and two chairs on the porch. Cabin 19 is up 15 steps to the low ridge where guests have a quiet wooded view. Directly across from 19 is Cabin 20, which is on a lower elevation and shady. Each cabin has outdoor chairs on a screened porch and fire extinguisher, but no picnic tables or grills.

The cabins are a long walk from most other day-use amenities. At the cabin entrance is a small shady picnic area with pedestal grills and hard-surfaced parking lots that often staging areas for in-line skaters and day-users. A picnic pavilion (reservable) and portable rest rooms are in the area.

Boating: Jet Skiing from the Narrow's Marina area is increasingly popular. This ramp is also a great access for anglers and pleasure boaters. Parking and rest rooms are at the marina.

Nearby, the Virginia Beach Scenic Waterway System is the first locally-developed comprehensive water trail system in the state. The first segment of this system, West Neck Creek, was formally opened in September 1986. This quiet water recreation system is the product of a citizen initiative and cooperation among local, regional and state agencies. The system allows small boats to traverse a varied aquatic environment.

Beginning on the north with the beach and tidal marshes at Lynnhaven Inlet, the main trail, the Lynnhaven River-West Neck Creek-North Landing River Trail, follows the Lynnhaven River through tree-lined suburban areas to a canal. The route also follows West Neck Creek through dense wooded areas and widens near the North Landing River, the main route of the Intra-Coastal Waterway. The unique water trail has services along the way, access points, rest rooms and camping in several parks. For more information contact the Public Information Office, City of Virginia Beach, Municipal Center, Virginia Beach, Va. 23456-9080.

Fishing: Anglers (and crabbers) can fish anywhere along the bay. Local anglers report blue croaker lures with a blood worm attached is a good basic bait. Offshore fishing is popular and charters can be a great way to take part in the action. Check with the local tourist association for information about half-day, day and night deep-sea fishing trips. Most large charter boats furnish equipment and even a license. One of the best known operators is the Virginia Beach Fishing Center, (804) 422-5700.

Full day offshore charters chase blue and white marlin, wahoo, tuna, dolphin and other species from May through October. Half-day charters stay closer to shore where bluefish, mackerel, amberjack, cobia, spot, croaker and sea bass abound. Excursions to the world's largest artificial fishing reefs, the Chesapeake Bay Bridge-Tunnel, can also be arranged. This entire region offers more species and more fishing that just about anywhere in the country.

On shore, anglers can fish from piers or the shoreline throughout the region. A well-executed cast into the waves of the bay or Atlantic can yield a variety of species including spot, croaker, sea trout, bluefish, kingfish (roundheads), flounder and many others.

One of the best beaches in the state.

Hiking: Nine easy walking trails totaling 19 miles loop around the unit. All of the trails are interconnected, making for many possibilities for circuit hikes. A free trail system brochure or the small book, "Seashore State Park: A Walking Guide ($3.95)," is available at the visitor center. The handy book features a naturalist primer and a complete (but slightly outdated) guide to the park and trails.

First Landing/Seashore's trails are well marked, defined and thought out. Each passes scenic and significant areas of the park.

Cape Henrys Bike Trail (6 miles hard-surfaced), marked in dark green, passes bald cypress swamps and crosses 64th Street and along old dunes. Users (hikers and bikers) will pass over a wooden bridge spanning a salt marsh where osprey are sometimes seen. The trail ends at the Narrows, where there is a small beach (no swimming), boat ramp, vending machines and rest rooms.

Bald Cypress Trail (1.5 miles) is the featured and most popular trail in the park. It offers handsome elevated boardwalks that cross caramel-colored waters of swamps filled with stately cypress, black gum and folds of Spanish moss. The rich habitat is filled with life. Listen for rapping woodpeckers, water-plopping turtles, snakes skimming the shallow waters and songbirds perched or picking at the thick understory. The trail also passes a forested series of dunes. Part of the trail is a self-guided area with a booklet available from the office or visitor station.

Osmanthus Trail (3.1 miles, marked in blue) gets it name from devilwood, or the American olive tree. The trees (and many ferns) are abundant along the path, which reaches into the northernmost limits of the natural area. The trail is low and can be wet. The easy trail is good for all ages and well-shaded under a canopy of trees.

High Dune Trail (.25 mile) ascends a steep ridgeline dune for a view of lowlands and dark beer-colored cypress pools. The trail can be reached from Cape Henry Trail or the second leg of Bald Cypress Trail.

Fox Run Trail (.3 mile) is a gentle walk and connector to Long Creek Trail, Bald Cypress and the main park road. Named for the rarely seen gray fox, the trail is an excellent birding trail. Loblolly and towering American beeches are favorite perching and nesting trees for warblers and other forest-loving songbirds.

Kingfisher Trail (.6 mile) parallels a series of dunes connecting the Cape Henry and Long Creek trails. The dry trail is shady with many blueberry bushes and beech trees lining the way.

Long Creek Trail (5 miles one way) starts at the main park road and continues to Broad Bay. The popular trail passes through salt marshes, terrific places to look for wading and shorebirds in the marsh grasses. Spring nesting birds are easy to observe along Long Creek Trail.

Osprey Trail (1.2 miles) floods at high tide, but is worth the effort to time your hike for a view of the bay and easily-harmed cypress swamps.

White Hill Lake Trail (1.4 miles) is for all ages and abilities. The easiest access is from Long Creek Trail. Hikers will discover many small cypress ponds, thick sweet gum trees and beech trees with smooth gray bark. Oysters and fiddler crabs can be seen along the sides of the bridge.

Biking: See Cape Henry Bike Trail above.

Day-use areas: Picnic shelters in the park can be reserved by the half day or full day by calling (804) 481-2131 or stopping by the main park office.

Nature: The low and shady environmental education center offers public outdoor education programs for a variety of school groups. Many programs originate at the center (near the visitor center), others at the amphitheater. Programs may include beach walks, history of the CCC, themed and guided nature hikes, a crabbing program, swamp secrets, kritter kids, dune programs, osprey hikes, evening programs, junior rangers, birding hikes and lots more.

First Landing/Seashore has some of the best printed material about the natural world of any state park in the East. Nature loving visitors should pick up a tastefully designed packet of checklists that includes lists and natural history of birds, ferns and fern allies, mammals, reptiles, amphibians and fish, trees and wildflowers. Each list offers a brief overview, rules and tidbits of information.

The park has strong diversity, which accounts for the many species of flora and fauna found there. More than 150 birds, 23 mammals and 46 species of reptiles and amphibians, 71 trees and 11 types of ferns have been recorded.

You may see the endangered chicken turtle (whose neck is as long as its body) or yellow bellied slider, tree frogs, egrets and herons, common mammals like raccoon, rabbits (two types), fox, opossum and flying squirrels, snakes, crabs, or trilling warblers, as well as bats in the evening and moles that live just below ground.

Flora lovers can find blueberries, flowering dogwood, wild grapes, many oaks, hickory, sassafras, cane, wild oats, holly, prickly pear cactus, threadsoftly (a plant to avoid!) and poison ivy (another plant to avoid).

Insiders tips: Enjoy the nearby tourist attractions and Virginia Beach boardwalk. The strip is crammed with surf shops, pizza joints, neon signs, hotel after hotel, amusement parks, specialty restaurants and more.

12 George Washington's Grist Mill Historic State Park

Land: 3 acres Water: Stream

George Washington was a busy guy. Aside from his military, statesman and presidential duties, he also was a farmer, miller and businessman. The grist mill was one of several agricultural enterprises he was involved in, and it represented the transition from tobacco to wheat farming in Northern Virginia.

The present mill is a reconstruction of the mill Washington built and operated for almost three decades. That mill was the second one he owned at Mount Vernon. Washington got into the mill business after leasing one from his half-brother's widow in 1754. This was a period between military service in the French and Indian War. Washington married four years later and inherited the title to Mount Vernon in 1761. On this property was a water (grist) mill that was probably located across the Dogue Run stream from the present reconstruction.

When Washington acquired the mill, he found it in poor condition. He learned that the old mill took 55 minutes to grind just one bushel of corn. He was uncertain if the slowness was due to the lack of water or to worn machinery, so he decided to build a new mill and began constructing it in 1770. A year later the new mill was in operation.

The new mill operated two pairs of stones, one to grind wheat for the merchant trade, the other to grind either wheat or corn for the "country trade," as Washington called it. Over the years Washington renovated the mill by adding water-powered hoisting machinery, which lifted the grain from ground level to the upper floors of the mill.

Washington operated the mill most of his adult life, including the eight years he served as the first President of the United States. In 1799, however, he rented it to a nephew, Lawrence Lewis. That year Washington died, leaving the mill to Lewis in his will. About 50 years later, after sporadic operation and little maintenance, the walls of the mill fell. Later, the stones were used for other buildings.

After considerable research, the current mill was constructed in 1932 (by the Civilian Conservation Corps) and completed in 1940 to help celebrate the Washington Bicentennial Celebration.

Information and Activities

George Washington's Grist Mill
Historic State Park
5514 Mount Vernon Memorial Highway
Alexandria, VA 22309
(703) 780-3383 or (703) 550-0960

Directions: Mount Vernon Highway, Route 635, one-quarter mile south from U.S. 1 or three miles west of the Mount Vernon estate. Parking is immediately in front of the mill on Route 635. The mill is open 10 a.m. - 6 p.m. Saturdays, Sundays and holidays.

How a grist mill works: Long before electrical or engine power, the process of grinding flour from wheat was long and hard. Water, men and crude machines did the work. Inside the mill visitors will readily see how the creaking gears, flapping conveyer belts and water wheels must have been difficult to build, maintain and operate.

Farmers brought their grain to the mill through the back door on the first floor, and the miller made an agreement to either buy the grain outright or to make a deal, such as "I will grind your wheat for one-eighth toll." Grinding for a share of the flour was a popular bartering agreement at mills throughout the East. After the agreement was reached, the grain was poured into the wheat hopper over the stones.

Water entered the mill through the flume box, hitting the water wheel slightly above the mid-point, turning the wheel. The wheel is connected to the master gear by a long shaft. Power for the two sets of millstones was derived from the master gear. On both sides of the large master gear were smaller lantern gears, which rotated on a shaft perpendicular to the main shaft. The lantern gear transferred the power to another set of gears that were connected to the drive shaft which connected to and turned the huge millstones.

The drive shaft entered the millstones from the bottom of the stone and was fastened securely in the top of the stone by a rynd. The bottom stone was stationary and the top stone turned.

The miller poured the grain into the hopper, which controlled the speed which grain met the milling stones. As it was ground, the grain worked its way into a metal container on the ground floor.

Making flour was the final step. Up from the metal bin by way of conveyors to the second floor went the rough ground wheat (or corn) for the final process of flogging. Flogging was a type of sifting using a cylinder-shaped device covered with a fine woven cloth. Ground meal entered the floggers, which went around and around separating the middlings and bran and allowing the sifted flour to fall to the bottom of the flogger into the worm gear. The worm gear worked the sifted flour out to a conveyer that allowed it to fall to the first floor for packaging.

Washington's mill has four floors. On the fourth floor, or attic (which is closed to the public), are a storage area and a point where all gear shafts, pulleys and conveyor systems terminate.

The third floor is the primary storage area for the mill. Barrels, grain and rough materials for making barrels were also housed neatly.

The second floor saw the most activity. Sifting (flogging) was the main work being done on the thick plank floors. Next to the gear structure in the center of the floor is the strange-looking flogger covered with cloth. It was originally housed in a hopper, in which ground meal was placed for sifting flour. The finished flour was conveyed back to the first floor for packing. Along the wall of this floor is a collection of cooper's tools (barrel makers) and other items important to operating the mill.

The first floor is where the grain entered the mill. Farmers often brought in their grain in heavy wooden barrels strapped to a mule. To the left of the stairs is a trap door directly over the hopper and conveyor on the ground floor. If the grain were to be stored, it was dumped into this hopper which conveyed it up to the third floor.

At one time Dogue Creek had ship traffic that took the flour and grain products to market.

Other history: There was a still operated on this site between 1797 and 1832. It was owned and operated by George Washington who made whiskey, bourbon and brandy, all byproducts of the grain milling process. The liquor was stored in barrels at the cooper's barn across the street.

Day-use areas: The tiny historical park features a handful of picnic tables and mowed areas surrounding the building and along the trickling stream. The rest room is in a white clapboard building and open when the mill is open on weekends and holidays.

Children can fish in the narrow mill pond and stream.

Insiders tip: Be glad you can buy flour at the supermarket!

13 Grayson Highlands State Park

Land: 4,935 Water: Mountain creeks

Towering northern hardwoods, cool sphagnum bogs, spruce-fir forests, rocky outcroppings and the occasional scream of a soaring hawk are set against a backdrop of rugged mountains and broad valleys at Grayson Highlands. Grayson Highlands State Park has the most inspiring alpine mountain scenery in the Commonwealth. Ribbon-like roads are carved through the mountain passes offering wonderful views in every direction. Views of grassy balds and clear streams are two of the main attractions of the park. Grayson Highland is adjacent to Mount Rogers National Recreation Area, a part of Jefferson National Forest.

From the park's trails you can see the two highest peaks in Virginia, Mount Rogers (5,729 feet) and Whitetop Mountain (5,520 feet). Much of this scenic mountain range is believed to have been an active volcanic field millions of years ago. These now rounded mountains are composed of rhyolite, a volcanic rock similar to granite. Since rhyolite is more resistant to weathering than most other kinds of rock, Virginia's highest mountains are clustered in this scenic region.

The park projects an country atmosphere—a back home feeling—both in the general surroundings and the visitor center, of a bygone era of mountain traditions, folklore and crafts. With a little imagination visitors can see how rugged it was for the hardy pioneers that settled this corner of mountainous Virginia.

Grayson Highlands, originally named Mount Rogers State Park, was established in 1965, the first of eight parks acquired through Virginia's State Park Expansion Program. The local community has been a strong support of the park, beginning with a fundraising effort for land acquisition and continuing with the donation of items for exhibit in the visitor center. Many areas in the park are named for early settlers. Massie Gap takes its name from Lee Massey, who lived in the gap with his wife and five children in the late 1800s and early 1900s. At that time, the present park was a lightly settled area with people living mostly off the land. Wilburn Ridge is named after the famed hunter Wilburn Waters. His reputation as a bear hunter and wolf trappers make him famous throughout the region.

Over 145,000 people annually visit the mountain park.

Information and Activities

Grayson Highlands State Park
Route 2, Box 141
Mouth of Wilson, VA 24363
(540) 579-7092

Directions: The park is on U.S. 58 midway between Independence and Damascus and is reached from I-81 at Exit 45 in Marion, then south on Route 16 to Volney, then west on U.S. 58. Inside the park office are rest rooms, comfortable seating, wood stove, brochure rack and park information.

The elevation at the gray contact station is 3,698 feet; visitor center, 4,958 feet; and Little Pinnacle, 5,089 feet above sea level. Park roads can be gated and closed in the winter.

Emergency numbers: 911 system; state police (800) 542-8716.

Visitor center: Inside the angular visitor center of stone and wood and beam ceilings, is a cozy seating area with a checker board, audio-visual viewing room (an 18 minute orientation video is shown), gift shop and rows of quality interpretive displays and dioramas. Toe-tapping bluegrass music plays in the background of the visitor center.

Items displayed include a kitchen scene, hand tools, moonshining apparatus and photos of a working mountain still, grinding wheels, leather ware, bullet molds, two-stoke hit-and-miss engine, long gun, farm tools, bedroom setting and late 1880s houseware and utensils. Each of the dioramas and displays have excellent narrative descriptions and accompanying photographs. Of special note, a mandolin and six-string guitar are on display near main entrance of the visitor center. Timbering in Grayson County dates back to the Civil War.

A terrific geology display, across the from reception desk, features samples of minerals and rocks found in the park. A cross-sectional displays shows that area strata and rock layers that compose the mountains. Many of the rocks and minerals are one billion year old. Examples include granite, gneiss, rhyolite, basalt, conglomerate, quartzite and many other common samples.

One of the most sophisticated displays at the center is about whiskey making. Before 1862, when it became a federal offense, whiskey making was the right of every American family. The art of whiskey making was an important part of the lives of the Scotch-Irish ancestors of the settlers of this region. Passed down from generation to generation, its was a means of easily transporting the product of the bountiful corn crop. It also produced the basis for countless home remedies.

It was difficult to get ground corn meal and flour out of the mountains to the market on the coast, especially when the average farmer produced 40-60 bushels per acre. But when the grain was turned into distilled spirits a pack horse could carry the equivalent 24 bushels. A horse could only carry about four bushels of solid grain. In this manner, whiskey paid the farmer's taxes and bought him whatever necessities he didn't make for himself.

Many mountain families lived in the cabin which they built themselves

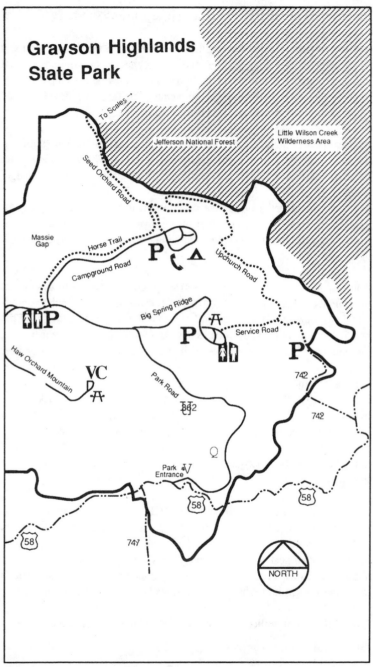

The large visitor center is filled with a variety of displays.

using timber from the trees felled from where the house would stand. Much of the furniture and many utensil were also handmade. These items were often handed down through many generations. Settlers to this area of the state raised most everything they ate and traded for such staples as sugar, salt and other things not provided by the land. On display is a fireplace that not only provided heat during the winter but most of the cooking was done there too. Kettles and pots were hung from crane or bar. Pickles, tomatoes and beets were canned for later use. These hardy settlers cured their own meat, ground sausage and took grain to nearby mills to be ground into flour.

Settlers also made their own butter in wooden churns, they made their own clothes, rugs, quilts and curtain and any thing that could be made of cloth. They did their washing using wooden washboards; after the clothes were hung up and dried they were ironed with heavy irons heated in the coals of the fireplace.

Men made crude brooms by whittling from a single branch, peeling back stiff slivers that were good for sweeping the rough floorboards of a small cabin.

They kept a supply of sour dough in a dough box and worked up a batch of biscuits in a dough tray. Many foods were dried including apples, beans, peaches, pears, sweet potatoes and herbs. Properly dried, foods contain about 5-10 percent of their moisture, but retain all of their nutrients.

Herbs provided most of their medicine. Settlers made many of their own home remedies.

When all of the hard chores were done and the coal lamps lit, its was a time for prayer and scripture reading. Prayer was said for ill relatives, thanks given for the gift of good health in the family and petitions sent for the sinful and lost of a round-about settlement.

One of the most interesting displays is a hanging ham and a story about pork curing. Pork is preserved today by families much as it has been for many generations. In the dry-curing method, the meat is rubbed with a mixture of about eight pounds of salt and two pounds of sugar for every 100 pounds of meat. For an eye-appealing red color, two ounces of saltpeter was added to the blend. Some also added about four ounces of ground black powder. The meat was kept at a cold temperature in a covered barrel. Ham needs about 2-3 days pound to cure.

A small wildflower garden at just outside the main entrance to the visitor center contains beebalm, flag fireweed, wild strawberries, daisies and other common wildflowers.

Craft shop: Local vendors and craftspeople from a 50 mile radius sell a variety of items in the Rooftop of Virginia Cap Crafts Shop that is located in the back of the visitor center. The shop has everything form a "cake of lye soap to the finest of handmade quilts." In a cathedral type setting native crafters offer authentic items that include books, quilts, decorative country-style items, birdhouses, textile products, placemats, T-shirts, hot pads, wooden children's toys, jewelry, dolls, wall hanging, musical instruments, wooden calendars, all chestnut miniature log cabins and more. The craft shop is open daily in the summer from 10 a.m. - 6 p.m.

Campground: Grayson Highlands has 73 camping with gravel pads, steel firerings and metal-legged picnic tables. Two bathhouses are centrally located. In addition, there are 24 campsites with a centrally located bathhouse adjacent to the overnight stables for visitors with horses. Bathhouses have laundry sinks and drinking fountains. The main campground (not the stable-side sites) are heavily wooded. Campers are asked to not hang lantern on trees. The heat from the gasoline-fueled lanterns can kill the trees and may start a fire. The most interesting thing about Grayson Lake camping sites is that some sites seem to cling to the mountain, often peering into deep valleys and forested ravines.

In loop 1-30, sites 1, 3, 5, 7, 9, 11, 13 and a handful of others are small, best suited for popup campers. Sites 2, 4, 6, 8, 10, 12, 14 (pull through) are large and can accommodate most RV rigs. Many of these sites are on varying elevations. Sites 23, 24 and 27 are on a ridgeline facing a valley that plunges down to the forest floors several hundred feet below.

Near sites 31 and 32 are nearly an acre of mowed fields. Inspect the sites, many are pull-throughs, other are easy access whiling being near rugged ridge and drop-offs. Site 45 is a wonderful pull-through sites ideal for a medium-sized RV rig.

Site 60-73 are dotted by rocky areas and along the steep mountainside. Sites 71 and 73 are pull throughs and are sunny. In fact, site 73 is in full sun all day long. The view of bald mountaintop from sites is the 60s is terrific.

Sites 47-73 are on the mountain. Some of the sites skirt a steep ridge and have a lofty view of the densely wooded valleys and hollows. Site 52, 54 and 55 are some of the most pleasant sites, surrounded by a scattering of rock outcropping and boulders. In places, the rock outcroppings look like huge stone pillows that have been tossed around the land.

Fishing: Native trout are found in the rocky creeks that criss-cross the mountain park. Wilson Creek is stocked with trout and lined with rhododendrons and trailer-sized rocks. The bottom is of stone and pebbles with many stair-step falls and small pools are frequent. Fly fishermen should bring a variety of stoneflies in the spring. Black stonefly nymph patterns are also great along the freestone headwaters. With all of the overhanging trees and vegetation, bring lots of terrestrials, especially beetles, says the park staff expert.

Other creeks in the Mount Rogers National Recreation Area worth trying

Grayson Highlands has horse camping.

---

include Fox Creek, Holoston River south fork), Hurricane Creek, Laurel Creek, Lick Creek, and Whitetop Laurel Creek. Its a challenge to match the hatch on the creeks that run on varying elevations. All of these creeks are good places to try floating midges, black ants, nymphs, Hendricksons, light Cahills, drakes and stoneflies.

Hiking: Grayson Highland has six dramatic trails, each are about two miles in length. Parking at the Massie Gap area (head-in parking) can be used as an overnight parking area for Appalachian Trail backpackers. The AT trailhead is three miles from the entrance gate. A few scattered picnic tables are in this area and often used by tired hikers. From the Massie Gap parking area a number of adjacent backpacking trails that can be accessed including Pine Mountain, Mount Rogers Loop, and Elk Garden Loop.

Twin Pinnacles Self-Guided Interpretive Trail (1.6 miles) leads to the two highest points in the park. Hiking along the "sky country" trails is easy. You'll reach Little Pinnacle in a half-mile and Big Pinnacle one third mile farther. On your way to the top of Haw Orchard Mountain, hikers will see the forest change from northern hardwoods to a forest of spruce. The trailhead is behind the visitor center and a small booklet accompanies ten learning stations along the loop.

Haw Orchard Mountain's remoteness, high elevation and harsh climate protected its red spruce and Fraser fir from destruction until the early 1900s. At that time, logging and fires eliminated much of the virgin forest. While walking the trail notice how different kinds of plants grow at different elevations. The cooler temperatures found at the top of the mountain support plants not found at lower elevations. Between the elevation extremes is a transition zone which supports a mixture of plant types. Trees with peeling, papery yellowish-gray bark are yellow birches.

The base of the mountain was once covered so thickly with hawthorn trees that early settlers called it Haw Orchard Mountain. The shrubs and small trees among the boulders and spruce trees are mostly hawthorn and witch hazel. In the spring, hawthorns bear fragrant clusters of white flowers that are visited by honeybees for their pollen. Among the tree's thorny, leafy branches, songbirds find protection for spring and summer nest building.

This mountaintop once looked like the summit of Mount Rogers (the nearby highest point in Virginia at 5,729 feet above sea level)—dark with a thick covering of old-growth evergreens. In the early 1900s, a spur of the railroad came up through Massie Gap. Trains carried cut trees to the boom town of Fairwood on the north slope of Mount Rogers. It took the logging company only 12 years to clear the magnificent virgin spruce, hemlock and fir forest from Haw Orchard Mountain. Some of the trees were three to four feet in diameter and over 100 feet tall. The harsh climate and strong winds will make regrowth a long. slow process.

Cabin Creek Nature Trail (1.9 miles) has some waterfalls and pools that contain native rainbow and brown trout. The trail begins at the Massie Gap parking lot and starts with a .6 mile downhill walk to Cabin Creek and the falls. The stream gets its name from a small hunting cabins that was once creekside. The trails passes scattered mountain laurel, Rosebay rhododendron and thickets of huckleberries. The rush of the creek is deadened somewhat by the canopy of yellow birch, quaking aspen, Fraser fir and red spruce trees. The understory of this interesting trails is of rhododendron thickets and is as lush as a rain forest.

Rock House Ridge Trail (1.2 miles) starts near the picnic area and cross a meadow and tracts near the Jones's homestead. The trail derives its name from a huge boulder on the left across the road from the second parking lot in the picnic area. Many Indian artifacts have been found the boulder that slants inward forming a simple shelters.

Stampers Branch Trail (1.7 miles) connects the visitor center to the campground using the east slope of Haw Orchard Mountain. The visitor center is 600 feet higher in elevation than the campground. Along this trail you can notice the distinctively different vegetation between the two elevations. Near the center the trees are northern types (spruce, beech, birch and maple), at the campground the trees are making a transition into oaks and hickories. A rhododendron tunnel and clubmoss are along the firm trail. Also found here is the black locust, one of the most durable trees, often used for sturdy and long-lasting fence posts.

Listening Rock Trail (2 miles), also referred to as Wildcat Rock, where farmers once came to listen for the ringing of bells hung around the necks of their livestock to find out where they were grazing on the mountain slopes. When the farmers spotted the cattle, he often called them in for salting. Sounds can be picked up and carried for a long distance from the rock because it juts out from the ridge. The trail is rugged winding around and under boulders, often near sheer drops offs. The mixed deciduous forest consists of a dozen species. Watch out for stinking nettles, which has course stinging hairs on its stem.

Wilson Creek Trail (1.8 miles) is a steep .7 mile walk to Wilson Creek during which hikers will pass through beach and sugar maple forest. In the summer the forest floor is heavily covered with ferns. After the trail levels out you can see the large whorled leaves of the Fraser magnolia. This tree produces large fragrant blooms. Striped maple seedlings can also make up part of the understory here. Wilson Creek waters originate from Pine Mountain. The brown or tea-colored waters is due to tannin, which is leached out of the decomposing materials in the bog and the creek headwater. Tannic acid produced by boiling certain types of barks has been used by leather tanners in the caring and staining of leather hides. Mild tannic acid is present in teas that we drink. Wilson Creek also features a 25 foot tall waterfall. The trail returns on a gentle grade through a thicket of rhododendron. Fishing on the stream is allowed by permit during the open season.

Rhododendron Trail (1 mile) is famous for its mid-June blooms of catawa rhododendron. These scented flowers are sometimes called purple laurel. The trail begins at the Massie Gap parking area.

Cross-country skiing: Grayson Highlands is one of the finest places in the state for winter camping and cross-country skiing. The snow-covered scenery and snow conditions are excellent.

Bridle trails and horse camping: Park trails also lead to bridle paths in the adjacent Jefferson National Forest. Bridle trails are a combination of open fields, hilly tracts and wooded corridors.

Horse trails are blazed in orange. A trail starts from the stable area leading to two trails; one leading to the Virginia Highlands Horse Trail and the other leading past the campground to the Little Wilson Creek Wilderness Area. The Appalachian Trail and other trails are for foot traffic only.

Grayson Highlands is the only Virginia State Park that offers a special area for people that bring their horses. The camping area has 23 sites and is near the long covered, walk-in and box stall barn. Each stall has a hay manger, grain box and water bucket hook. Near the well-lit 57 stall barn are hitching posts, soft drink and candy machines, and an extra wide parking lot where turning trailers around is easy.

The mostly shady camping sites can accommodate, trailers, tents and there is often room for horse trailer parking on site. Each of the horseman's camping sites have pedestal grills, firm gravel pads and picnic tables. A modern bathhouse with hot showers, laundry and dish washing sinks is centrally located. Sites 5 and 7 are oversized and can accommodate large gooseneck horse trails and camping equipment. Sites 22 and 23, at the end of the spur, are shady, private and up against a natural area.

The park is required by law to examine a valid equine infectious anemia test form for each horse brought into the park. Please have your Coggins papers with you when you arrive. Call the park office for additional details.

Day-use areas: The main picnic area has drinking water, grills and modern rest rooms. Picnic shelters are available by reservation or on a first-come basis. The scenic overlooks along the park roads are spectacular. The

Wild Cat Overlook is one of the more convenient, complete with nearby picnic tables, grills and a pathway to the vantage point. From the towering overlook you can see a cemetery with gravemarkers that appear as tiny dots, farmfields that are carved into the valley and a view of the rolling wooded mountains that seem to go forever. There is plenty of parking and mountain views near the visitor center.

Interpreter's cabins: Near the park office, a small log cabin surrounded by a rail fence was originally built by the Pender family on Shippies Creek branch. It was moved to the park 1993 and authentically restored. The oak logs and natural stone chimney have been chinked with clay and the roof is hand-rived oak shingles. The rustic cabin is presently providing housing for the interpreter.

Nature: Evening deer viewing in the park is excellent. Lucky hikers might also spot a black bear ambling about the slopes, or wild turkey and ruffed grouse pecking around in the understory. During the summer hawk watching is popular. Broad-winged, red-shouldered and red-tailed hawks can often be seen soaring along ridgelines and near the bald mountaintops. Other fauna include cedar waxwing, summer tanagers, raven, eastern and New England cottontail rabbit, red start, groundhog, bobcat, opossum, red fox, grosbeak, black-capped chickadee, northern junco and beaver.

Wildflowers include Turk's cap lily, mountain laurel, Dutchman's breeches, pink lady's slippers, fireweed, asters, trillium, catawba rhododendron, flame azalea, bloodroot, sorel and many other species that thrive on the shaded hardwood slopes. The visitor center has terrific displays and information about the mountain-building process that took place in the region millions of years ago. Various seasonal naturalist programs are offered including guided hikes, cultural demonstrations and evening amphitheater programs.

Hunting: Significant public hunting lands surround the park. The area is known for excellent deer hunting. Call the park manager for details.

Insiders tip: The peak for fall colors in late September, maybe the first few days in October. From the visitor center you can see the Blue Ridge Parkway more than 70 miles away.

14 Holliday Lake State Park

Land: 250 acres   Water: 150-acre lake

Holliday Lake State Park is minutes from the famous Appomattox National Historical Park. The state park features a variety of marvelous outdoor recreation opportunities and is located deep within the sprawling Appomattox-Buckingham State Forest. The clear park lake is the focal point of activity, offering very good fishing, swimming, boating, a unique aquatic trail and nearby camping, hiking and shoreline day-use areas.

There are five known archaeological sites around the park, including Morris Field along the Appomattox River that served as a base camp as long as 8,000 years ago. South of the park in Prince Edward County is a prehistoric soapstone quarry that eventually produced some of the highest grade soapstone and steatite in the region. East of the park, there is more evidence of habitation at Willis Mountain, where several rock shelters provided temporary shelter for hunters and foraging parties of the past.

Also nearby is the Jordan site, commonly called "old stone fort" that possibly served as a prehistoric ceremonial grounds. From the woodland cultures to the first European explorers, Bolling and Bell in the early 1700s, the park has been used for hunting, agricultural and natural resources. Tobacco farming has been an important export commodity since the earliest days of settlement.

The fertile region was quiet and peaceful for most of the millennia, but the Civil War swept locals into the fight. The war had its biggest impact on the area when the Confederate Army of North Virginia passed within 1.5 miles of the park, retreating under General Robert E. Lee's command to Appomattox.

More than 70 years after the Civil War, construction of the lake began by the Depression-era Works Projects Administration. The lake was completed in 1938. It was cleared by hand using cross-cut saws, axes, mule teams and dynamite. The average worker made $1.05 a day; he was paid an extra $1.00 a day for each mule he had. Foremen were paid $2.05 a day. There were 10 foremen who had 10 men under them working 10 hours daily, five days a week. The workers either walked, rode their mules, or hitched a ride to and from the hard work every day. Today, the scenic park is one of the more quiet family units in the system.

Information and Activities

Holliday Lake State Park
Route 2, Box 622
Appomattox, VA 24522
(804) 248-6308

Directions: In Appomattox County, reached via Route 24 (between Appomattox and U.S. 60) and routes 626 and 692.

Emergency numbers: Sheriff 352-8241; rescue squad 352-5433.

Visitor center: Near the beach and main day-use complex, the small visitor center is in a wood clapboard building on a ridge. Inside the small visitor center are wall-mounted displays depicting the history of state parks, Depression-era photos of park development, general photographs of the park, aquarium, description of Holliday park development and examples of some old tools including a sled auger, buttress, sheep shears, wedges,

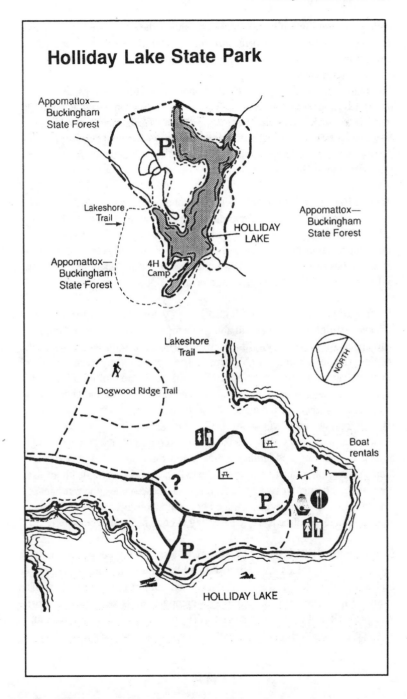

Holliday Lake State Park

Appomattox—
Buckingham
State Forest

P

Lakeshore
Trail

Appomattox—
Buckingham
State Forest

HOLLIDAY
LAKE

Appomattox—
Buckingham
State Forest

4H
Camp

Lakeshore
Trail

NORTH

Dogwood Ridge Trail

Boat
rentals

?

P

P

HOLLIDAY LAKE

coffee mill, sausage mill and a map that shows the march to Appomattox. Two small brochure racks offer information about nearby parks and other attractions.

The map that depicts the march to Appomattox shows the route of Lee during his final retreat. It shows the section of the Lynchburg to Richmond stage road, which was the route followed by Lee's Army of Northern Virginia on April 8, 1865. The Confederate army was being closely pursued by Humphrey's 2nd Corps and Wright's 6th Corps of the Union Army under the command of General U.S. Grant.

General E. P. Alexander, Lee's Georgia gunner, records the march: "It was the third consecutive night of marching and I was at least scared...able only to keep from falling off of my horse for sleep. With my staff I left the column and went a quarter-mile more off to our right to old broom grass and second-growth pines by cloudy moonlight until we found a secluded nook near an old worn fence. There we all laid down and slept for three or four hours."

Trooper Boykin of the 7th South Carolina Cavalry recalled April 8 as "the most weary night march that will always be remembered." Colonel Magnus Thompson of the 35th Virginia Cavalry, who rode with the rear guard, summed up the situation of Lee's army: "The few men who still carried their muskets had hardly the appearance of a soldier. There clothes all tattered and covered with mud, their eyes sunken and lusterless and their faces peaked and pinched from their ceaseless march through storm and sunshine without food or sleep. Many of the men from exhaustion were lying prone upon the ground, only waiting for the enemy to come and pick them up, while at intervals horses and mules lying in the mud struggled to extricate themselves until exhaustion forced them to be still and wait for death to ease their wildly staring eyes. And yet through all these scenes, the remnant of that once invincible army still trudged on. With their faces still strong, only waiting for General Lee to say where they were to face, and about to fight."

Campground: The park has 30 newer sites and a centrally located bathhouse. Most pads are comprised of blue gravel and are outlined by timbers. Each site has a picnic table, wood lantern post and steel grills mounted on a cement pad. Holliday's campground is sunnier than most state parks; it is about 65 percent open. The campground is within walking distance of the tree-lined lake, beach, boat rental and snack concession.

Sites 8, 10 and 12 are cozy against a natural area, perfect for tents or pop-up campers. Site 13, at the end of the loop, is L-shaped and large enough for big RV rigs. Site 14 is also oversized. Sites 16-21 are pull-throughs; all are good for just about any type of rig. These sites can accommodate fifth-wheel or large motor homes. About half of the pull-through sites are open and sunny much of the day.

The brick bathhouse has showers, soft drink machine and drinking fountain.

Fishing: Bass have a 12-inch minimum size limit. The boathouse sells bait and other angling supplies. Fishing in the lake is considered good to very good. The small lake has a good variety of fish species, including some striped bass. Four creeks feed the lake and are good places to fish.

You will find northern pike, one of the fiercest predators, lurking in weedbeds waiting to ambush suckers, although any smaller fish will do as a meal. Medium- and shallow-running lures and large live bait are used with success at Holliday Lake. Crappies are an excellent catch and abundant in the lake. They have sweet flaky meat. You'll find both black and white crappies hiding under fallen logs, under pad beds and in other underwater vegetation. When the lake level drops in early summer and when marginal weedbeds can no longer hide minnows, crappies move out to deeper water. Spinner baits, minnow rigs, wet and dry flies and popping bugs are effective bait.

Sunfish, commonly called bream, include bluegill, pumpkinseed and redear sunfish. Bluegills, recognized by their deep yellow to coppery-red complexion and green or brown vertical bars, prefer quiet weedy areas where they can hide and feed. Live bait, flies, bright-colored jigs and grubs are often used at the lake. Bluegills provide excellent sport on a fly rod.

Channel catfish have deeply forked tails and 24 - 29 anal rays. Their body is gray to greenish and they can reach large sizes, often 10-20 pounds. They will take shrimp, squid and chicken innards, the preferred bait for bottom fishing. Largemouth bass are in good numbers and can be recognized by a conspicuous line down its side that reaches past the eye. Eight to 10-pounders are taken here. Largemouth bass are usually found in shallow weedy habitats from which they will strike with a smashing blow at nearly any live bait. These fish are good fighters, often leaping high into the air, running in each direction and diving as deep as they can.

The lake has at least two underwater fish attractors and an underwater island in the upper arm of the lake. A lake map with depth and fishing information is hung at the boat rental concession. Buoys mark where Christmas trees have been sunk. The lake can reach 30 feet in depth. There are many shoreline fishing opportunities along a well-worn path that skirts the lake's edge through the main day-use areas.

A small live bait well at the boat rental sells worms and minnows.

Boating: Paddleboats, rowboats and canoes can be rented by the hour or day to explore the cozy lake. Gasoline motors are prohibited. A tiny gravel boat launch is for small cartop boats. It is next to the clean beach and gray and blue boat rental concession. The boat rental is surrounded by a narrow wooden dock. You can purchase limited fishing gear, paper plates, post cards, inflatable toys, ear plugs, T-shirts, inflatable toys, propane, candy, soft drinks, goggles, sunscreen and other items.

Behind the boathouse is the hull of a boat sunk in knee-deep water. The boat, called the Batteau Appomattox, was built in 1986 at a length of 50 feet and width of eight feet. The long boat is a replica of a 1790 James River cargo boat. This style of craft was built to haul heavy cargoes over shallow whitewater sections of Virginia rivers. These boats continued in use until the early 1900s, when they were replaced by larger canal boats and a developing rail system.

The Batteau is still used during an annual weeklong event in the James River. When not in use, it is stored at Holliday Lake. It is sunken in shallow water to keep the timbers of the hull swollen.

Also behind the boathouse and near the old sunken boat is a tiny cemetery with six worn headstones. One of the gravestones is dated 1862. These shoreline gravesites prohibited the CCC from making the lake any bigger.

Next to the cemetery are a grove of trees and a shady picnic area.

Aquatic trail: Holliday Lake is one of the cleanest in the state, and is one

The lake is the focal point of the park.

---

of the few with a self-guided aquatic trail that canoeists and paddleboaters can tour.

You may rent a boat or bring your own. The journey will take about 45 minutes and there are 10 learning stations. Along the way you will learn about mountain laurel that grows on the slopes and offers a glorious blossom in late May. If you are sharp-eyed, you might see some dragonflies, aggressive predators with ancestors millions of years old, patrolling the shoreline. Dragonflies can fly up to 25 miles per hour.

Aquatic trail travelers will also learn about "edge" habitats, alders, freshwater invertebrates, beaver dams, erosion, life in the shallows and the northern water snake. A six-question quiz at the end of the booklet will test your aquatic nature knowledge. The booklet is available from the park office and boat rental concession.

Hiking: From the Lakeshore Trail, hikers can see some of the aquatic self-guided trail signs. Along the easy Lakeshore Trail is a stream crossing where you can take your shoes off and wade across. The park has a variety of easy hiking trails.

Day-use areas: The best picnic sites are scattered around the lake. Near the shoreline, picnicking areas are furnished with pedestal grills and refuse cans. Picnic pavilion No. 2, near the beach, is constructed of huge timbers and is one of the most popular day-use amenities.

Near the campground exit is a two-panel display that has a sample of the Pulaski tool, an ax-like hoe. This tool was used to fight forest fires on trees that seem to have been extinguished, but can often be rekindled by smoldering stumps. The Pulaski tool is used to uncover and break up these hazards, as well as scrap a fire line. A fire rake, used for controlling small fires, is especially designed with sharp blades that can cut through brush and rake a fire line. Also on display are a helmet, 55-pound backpack water pump, brush hook and shovel.

Beach: A split-rail fence outlines the sandy beach, which is outfitted with an offshore two-board diving platform. A volleyball net is on the 125-yard-long beach, just below a changing room and snack concession. Yellow floating buoys divide the water into sections that are patrolled by lifeguards during the summer. A small fee is charged for using the beach; a tag may be acquired at the ticket window behind the concession.

The snack bar and angular bathhouse have four showers with skylights, blue awnings and three umbrella picnic tables on a small deck that overlooks the lake and beach. The concession sells ice cream, sandwiches, soft drinks, foot-long hot dogs and mint chip strawberry cheesecake that is incredible.

Nature: The diversity of habitat at Holliday Lake State Park and the surrounding 19,710-acre Appomattox-Buckingham State Forest allow for a wonderful variety of flora and fauna. The region is comprised of 80 percent pine species (50 percent are loblolly pine) and upland hardwoods of red oak, hickory, beech, yellow poplar and sweetgum. The bottomland is 80 percent hardwoods. Open grassland and seeds are composed of orchards and meadows. Biologists have recorded 40 species of fish (most are minnow-sized types), 23 species of amphibians, 21 reptiles, 129 species of birds and 40 types of mammals.

Seasonal programs at the park include nature hikes, canoe trips, beaver programs, campfire programs, night hikes, fishing tournament, discovery hike, bluegill basics and a variety of youth programs.

Insiders tips: Rent a paddleboat and take the self-guided water trail. The park is a pleasant, quiet getaway park perfect for family camping vacations.

15 Hungry Mother State Park
Land: 2,215 acres   Water: 108-acre lake

The Virginia state parks system was the brainchild of William Carson, chairman of the Virginia Commission of Conservation Development. He envisioned easy-to-find and inexpensive recreation for all people of the Commonwealth. Even through the commission, which was created in 1926, lacked funds to purchase land, it sought funding. In 1933, after a discussion with President Franklin Roosevelt, Carson received federal funds and the help of the Civilian Conservation Corps to help construct a system of state parks.

Carson also requested land donations from the people of the Commonwealth. Within a year, large tracts of land were donated by corporations and citizens around the state. Marion businessmen John D. Lincoln and Charles C. Lincoln along with other citizens donated more than 2,100 acres at Lake Forest. Lake Forest Inc. ceased to exist in December 1933 when its corporate charter was revoked, making possible the development of Hungry Mother State Park.

Carson and state park boosters realized their dream when Hungry Mother, along with five other state parks, opened in 1936.

The legend of Hungry Mother takes many forms, but the one that is generally accepted is also tragic. The legend has it that when Indians destroyed several settlements on the New River south of the park, Molly Marley and her small child were among the survivors taken to the raider's base north of the park. Molly and her child eventually escaped, wandering through the wilderness eating berries. Molly finally collapsed and her daughter wandered down a creek until she found help. The only words the child could utter were "Hungry Mother."

When the search party arrived at the foot of the mountain where Molly had collapsed, they found her dead. Today, the mountain is Molly's Knob and the stream Hungry Mother Creek. When the park was developed in the 1930s, the creek was dammed to form Hungry Mother Lake.

The park was built by the Civilian Conservation Corps and opened to the public June 15, 1936. Hungry Mother is one of the best equipped units in this region of the state and has the second highest visitorship annually. The park's various amenities are nicely spaced out, offering plenty of parking and are easily accessed.

Information and Activities

Hungry Mother State Park
Route 5, Box 109
Marion, VA 24354
(540) 783-3422

Directions: In Smyth County, take Exit 47 from I-81. Travel one mile on Route 11 toward Marion, and turn right on Route 16 four miles to the park office. The small office has an exterior plaque with the legend of Hungry Mother printed on it. A collection of Indian projectile points is inside the small office.

Emergency numbers: Sheriff, 783-7204; fire, 783-8144; rescue, 783-

8144.

Cabins: Five log, eight frame and seven wood-sided cabins are rented on a weekly basis or a minimum of two nights from March to early December. A gentle creek winds though the loop of 20 scenic cabins. The log cabins are part of the original facilities built by the CCC. Each unit has rustic furniture, a brick fireplace, electric appliances, kitchenware and linens. Cabins have wood floors, thick wood paneling, cushioned seating, four-burner stoves and colorful posters on the wall. Pets are allowed in the state park cabins for a fee. No outside fires are permitted. Cabins 1, 4-8 and 10-20 are two-bedroom units; the others are one-bedroom.

Each cabin is tucked into a hillside under a tree canopy of maples. They are well separated from each other. Thickets of rhododendron screen off the roads and dot the entire tract. Cabin 3, an old log cabin with white chinking, is up a small ridge and has a porch and woodland view. Chopped, stacked wood is offered near most of the cabins. Cabins 16 and 18 are the most private and appealing units. No. 17 is above cabin 18 and looks up over the rolling forest and dense hollows. Nos. 4 and 7 are old log cabins, and have a restful wide porch and thick timber railings that have been skillfully mortised together. Each cabin has rocking chairs on the porch and picnic tables in the side yards. Cabin No. 2 is near the lakefront and is the most expensive one-bedroom unit.

Some of the cabins have newer poured cement porch, walkways and parking areas outlined by landscape timbers. Log cabins 2 and 3 are surrounded by huge rhododendrons and have a gentle view of the mixed deciduous forest and songbirds that inhabit the rich area.

The former log visitor center is now a lodge for park guests.

Shoreline fishing, quiet park roads and trailheads are near the scenic cabin colony.

Campgrounds: Hungry Mother has three small campgrounds with a total of 43 sites. The bathhouses are centrally located and 32 sites have electrical and water hook-ups. Campground hosts are on duty much of the season. Campground B, which is shady, manicured and updated, is the preferred loop.

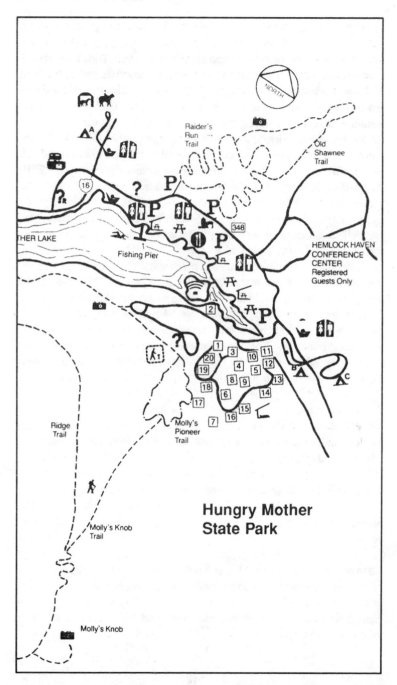

Hungry Mother
State Park

Campground A is a small loop near the stable. Depending on prevailing winds, you can sometimes smell the horses and hear the giggling riders take their turns. Sites are small, with gravel pads and hook-ups. Smaller sized travel trailers, tents and popup campers are best suited for this loop. Site No. 1 could accommodate a larger RV rig. This loop is near the road and a small white church.

Campground B offers many pull-through hard-surfaced sites. Site 2 is an intimate pull-though site that can accommodate medium-sized campers and trailers. A small creek bisects the loop and most sites are under a heavy canopy of shade. Sites 12, 14 and 16 are terrific sites next to the creek and near thickets of tall rhododendron. The small creek is popular with small children. All of the sites in this fine loop have hook-ups. Site 20 is adjacent to a small sunny opening. The showerhouse is up about a dozen steps that are illuminated by lampposts.

Campground C is the only loop in the entire state park system that features elevated wooden camping platforms. The platforms, complete with picnic tables, provide a flat tent camping space among the hilly terrain. The cantilevered platforms will remind you of the wooden deck you may have behind your house. Site 2 has a woodland view and is near the cement block showerhouse. The showerhouse has exterior sinks useful for doing dishes and hand laundry. Site 7 is on a knoll and pleasant. Each site has a metal fire ring and metal-legged picnic tables.

Conference center: Once an Episcopal Church camp, the 35-acre complex was purchased by the state in 1986, refurbished and opened in 1989 as the Hemlock Haven Conference Center. Facilities include meeting rooms, cabins, swimming pool, sports complex and picnic area. Construction of the original facilities was completed in 1942 by Charles Collins, a Marion, Va., native. A lodge with 10 guest rooms and a dining/kitchen complex were the main features. Eight guest cabins, lacking plumbing, were added in 1947. The Virginia Episcopal Diocese purchased the site from Collins in 1957 and added the swimming pool, two lighted tennis courts, three new cabins and a large meeting facility, Ferrell Hall. Hemlock Haven was a popular site for training meetings, conferences and a summer camp for many years.

The conference center offers six lodges and five housekeeping cabins for adult conferences, youth retreats and family reunions. Ferrell Hall is a red

The park has a large conference facility.

brick multi-purpose building with various sized meeting rooms, including the Rhododendron Room that can accommodate up to 250 people for banquet services and 375 people for stand-up receptions. The Dogwood Room can seat 50, Redbud Room up to 40 people and the Laurel Room provides a lounge atmosphere for about 20 people. A break-out area with drink machines, room for food preparation, a refrigerator and storage is on the first floor. Ferrell Hall is accessible to those with disabilities.

Comfortable lodging is provided at the rolling Hemlock Haven complex for up to 78 conference guests. Six shady lodges which accommodate up to eight people are available for overnight functions. These lodges offer single and bunk beds with group bathrooms and showers, and some have sitting rooms. Chestnut Lodge is handicapped accessible and all lodges have decks, several have small refrigerators. One lodge has a wet bar.

Five tidy housekeeping cabins are on a shallow ridge and offer fully equipped kitchens for up to six people. Additional cabins may be available for groups which need more accommodations. Overnight users may use the swimming pool (up to 75 swimmers, open 10 a.m. - 8 p.m. in the summer) and sports areas (volleyball courts, softball field, two lighted tennis courts with bleachers, and basketball and horseshoe courts). The flat ball field area is often used for large outdoor banquets.

The conference center is open from April through November for overnight rentals and until Dec. 22 for day use. No alcohol is allowed in the park.

Restaurant: About 200 yards from the beach, the clapboard-sided building is also near the gray boat rental that offers paddleboats. The full service restaurant has a screened-in eating area with a view of the lawn and wooded shoreline. Some park benches are in front of the eatery around a planting bed filled with annuals.

Inside the restaurant are vaulted beam ceilings, polished wooden floors and country-style tables and high back chairs. Lantern-style lights and ceiling fans further provide a casual atmosphere.

The dinner menu includes baked Virginia ham, Southern fried chicken, grilled chicken breast fillets, open pit barbecued steaks, salad bar and family-style dinners.

Gift shop: Connected to the popular restaurant is a small upscale gift shop that features souvenirs for children (rubbers snakes and such), books, walking sticks, T-shirts, sweatshirts, country crafts, wrought metal artworks, small framed nature drawings, candies, dolls, note papers, wreaths, figurines, pottery and post cards. One of the most interesting items is a cookbook entitled *"Favorite Recipes of the CCC."*

Fishing: The narrow lake is tree-lined and the shoreline is hilly. Many shady coves and productive shallows are around its perimeter. An accessible fishing pier near the beach offers good panfishing and is convenient to cabin guests, campers and day-users. Twice the state record northern pike came from Hungry Mother Lake. Today, anglers catch a variety of species, mostly from the coves. Upwards of 30-pound channel catfish are sometimes caught using cutbait and old liver. The park has about 5.2 miles of streams inside its boundaries.

Most local anglers use crawlers and Powerbait, hooking up with good-sized largemouth bass and other species. Some anglers also make corn and peanut butter mixtures that seem to work.

Two artificial reefs made from Christmas trees have been placed near the dam. Buoys make the small reefs. The reef is especially useful to protect fry and small fish; it acts as a nursery. The lake, which has spots that are 30 feet deep, is not stocked.

Mobile anglers might also want to try the nearby Holston River for large- and smallmouth bass, trout, panfish and white bass.

Boating: The boat rental, complete with a wide hard-surfaced staging area, is one of the larger paddleboat concessions in the state. Both paddleboats and rowboats are offered for rent by the hour, day and week. The blue and gray paddleboats are mini-pontoon-style and riders often cruise close to the nearby pedestrian bridge and along the shoreline of the shallow, intimate lake. The lake is 2,220 feet above sea level and has about six miles of shoreline to explore.

Tree-covered banks jet up the mountainside and the quiet waters offer excellent views and a peaceful time on the water. The restaurant is only 100 yards away from the waterside boat concession. A drinking fountain and a few picnic tables are in the immediate area.

The boat launching ramp is about 1.5 scenic miles from the park office (2.9 miles by foot trail) and is at the end of a winding gravel road past the water treatment lagoon. The narrow road passes one small wildlife viewing station. The gravel single-lane launch is for small gasoline-powered boats. It does have a hard-surfaced apron that angles into the shallow water. Two benches and two picnic tables are at the quiet ramp. The views from the cove-side ramp are of mountains, flat water, tree-lined shores and the occasional fish surfacing to nibble at floating insects or maybe just take a look at the air-breathing side of the world. There is a portable toilet at the ramp.

The trailhead for the Little Brushy Mountain Trail system is at the boat launching ramp.

Hiking: The park has eight popular trails. Most are easy, but several offer a challenge for energetic hikers.

Raider's Run (1.5 miles) is blazed in blue and accessible near the restaurant. The trail has some rugged climbs and narrows in place, but offers some excellent views of forested hollows.

Lake Trail (3.1 miles) is perfect for the entire family, but also has side trails and a connection to Molly's Knob for hikers who are looking for a more challenging trek. The trail is often 10-feet wide and tracks above the lake offering scenic views.

Molly's Knob (1.6 miles) is steep and difficult, but the outstanding views are worth the effort.

CCC Trail (1 mile) crosses woods and wetlands, climbs along a stream and has some steep switchbacks.

Nearby Little Brushy Mountain Trail offers panoramic views of Hungry Mother Lake and Walker Mountain on the west and Mount Rogers and the Balsams to the east. With 8.3 miles of trails, both the beginning and advanced hiker can enjoy the moderately difficult trails. Six trails comprise the Little Brushy Mountain Trail system.

Day-use areas: The small amphitheater with wood benches is on an island near the boat rental that is connected to the shore by a wooded footbridge. A vertical log picnic pavilion is near the foot of the bridge, behind the restaurant. The park has several elegant CCC timber-style pavilions and other structures scattered around the park. At picnic area No. 3 there is a wonderful stone building with bulging walls that are wider at the base than at the top of the wall. The last CCC company, which constructed so much of the park, left in 1941.

Horse stable: Horses are stabled and pastured on the property. The gentle equines give half-hour guided trail rides. Pony rides are also offered. The easy trail loops behind the stable. Rides are offered during the summer from 10 a.m. - 5 p.m. daily. After Labor Day the stable is open noon to 5 p.m. on weekends, weather permitting. Hungry Mother State Park is the only unit in the state that rents riding horses. A drinking fountain and picnic tables are at the stable area near a tiny creek that runs past the building. Some of the horses there go by the names of Dusty, Mac, Doc, Duke, Beau and Red.

Beach: Across the road from the tan park office is the sandy guarded beach on a cove and protected by a rail fence. The beach is within walking distance of the campground. A bathhouse, concession stand and diving platform are open seasonally. The beachfront is 580 feet in length.

Nature: The steep slopes and dense woodlands that surround the lake is a good place to observe deer, beaver along the lakeshore, a variety of warblers, groundhogs, chipmunks, great blue and green heron, raccoons and occasionally common loons crying mournfully in the distance. The park has a heavy covering of hemlocks and thickets of rhododendrons and laurel.

Guided weekend canoe tours are one of the best ways to see the park and wildlife from the placid lake. The park has one of the better interpretive programs. The senior park ranger/interpreter offers guided hikes, campfire and amphitheater programs, youth programs and other natural history programming. During the summer, programs are offered daily and on weekends through the end of October. Music programs are sometimes scheduled.

Hungry Mother manages the Lick Creek Natural Area, a 836-acres tract that is 20 miles away on the southern slope of Carter Mountain and the northern slope of Brushy Mountain. The highest elevation in the natural area is 3,200 feet above sea level. It was donated to the state by the Old Dominion Foundation acting through the Nature Conservancy in 1961. Lick Creek was the fifth addition to the natural area system established in the early 1960's with the mission to protect the state's most important natural area. Jefferson National Forest bounds the pristine property on two sides. There are about five miles of mountain streams in the designated natural area. The creeks are freestone and become modest in the fall. Ants and minnow replicas are suggested by local fly fishermen. The area is also open to hunting.

Hungry Mother also manages Clinch Mountain about 37 miles away, and Pinnacle Natural Area Preserve which is 63 miles away.

Pinnacle Natural Area Preserve, which was donated to the state in 1993, has 100 threatened or endangered species of fauna and flora. Some of the creeks in the lush preserve are stocked twice annually. There is no camping there, but there is one small picnic shelter.

The Clinch River and Big Cedar River flow through an extraordinary landscape known as karst topography. The rugged Pinnacle terrain has been shaped by the weathering of calcium carbonate rocks which were formed more than 400 million years ago. The dissolving action of water on limestone and dolomite has created a landscape of sinkholes, caves, sinking streams and unusual rock formations. The pinnacle, a towering dolomite rock formation that rises 600 feet above the Cedar Creek, serves as the namesake for the preserve. Freshwater mussel is found in the Clinch River at the preserve. Some excellent trails skirt the banks of the Big Cedar and the Clinch rivers.

Seasonal outdoor programming is offered at Hungry Mother, including guided canoe trips on the lake, critter calling, fly fishing school, wild turkey hunting school, ruffed grouse workshop, nature photography, and black bear hunting school.

Hunting: Deer and small game hunting are offered. Call the park manager for details.

Insiders tips: Hungry Mother has some terrific CCC-built log buildings. For a directory of attractions, accommodations, shopping and recreation, call the Smyth County Chamber of Commerce at (703) 783-3161. The third weekend in July is the annual arts and crafts festival featuring more than 130 exhibitors. Molly's Knob (3,270 feet) offers a spectacular view. In a shopping plaza about three miles from the park, try the Great Wall Chinese food; it's pretty darn good.

16 Kiptopeke State Park
Land: 375 acres Water: Chesapeake Bay

Kiptopeke (pronounced *Kip-toe-peak,* which means *"big water"*) State Park is well-known among bird watching enthusiasts as one of the best places in the state to watch raptors and songbirds during the fall migration. The park is also known for a quiet, open campground, sandy beach, hiking, picnicking, crabbing and fishing.

The park was once the northern terminus of the Virginia Beach to Eastern Shore Ferry. A huge terminal still stands at the park, where thousands of people over the years boarded a ferry for the back and forth ride across the Chesapeake Bay. In 1949, when the terminus was moved to Cape Charles, the site was renamed Kiptopeke Beach in honor of the younger brother of a kind of the Accawmack Indians who had befriended early settlers to the area. In 1950 the terminus opened after completion of a $2 million pier, promoted as the world's largest and most modern ferry.

The old terminal building once had a busy upstairs restaurant and passenger business. The old 13,000-square-foot building is under consideration for renovations including development as an educational center, store, classroom and wet lab.

In 1933, the Virginia Ferry Corp. began operation between Norfolk and Cape Charles, Virginia. Eighteen years later the corporation decided to relocate the northern terminus to Kiptopeke Beach. The newly completed pier operated 24 hours a day, and up to 90 daily bay crossings occurred. Thanks to the breakwall of concrete ships, ferries were able to operate in all types of weather. By the mid-1950s, however, even this busy schedule could not handle the demand for transportation. In 1960 work began on the Chesapeake tunnel. It opened in April 1964, making ferry service to and from East Shore obsolete.

The nine ships (sometimes called the "Kiptopeke Navy") lying end to end offshore are actually made of concrete. They were originally built by the U.S. War Shipping Administration at a reported cost of $30 million. In 1948 the ships were purchased by the ferry corporation for $270,000 to form a protected harbor for ferry operation.

Kiptopeke State Park opened in 1992.

Information and Activities

Kiptopeke State Park
3540 Kiptopeke Drive
Cape Charles, VA 23310
(804) 331-2267

Directions: The park is three miles from the northern terminus of the Chesapeake Bay Bridge-Tunnel on Route 13. Turn west on Route 704; the park entrance is within a half mile. A marked bike lane is along the main park road. The park office is in an attractive colonial-style building with a red tin roof and well-cared for landscaping. Rest rooms and a brochure rack are inside the park office.

Emergency number: 911 system.

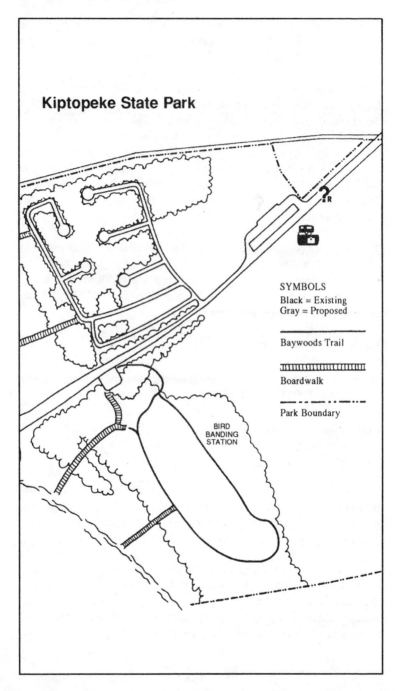

Kiptopeke State Park

SYMBOLS
Black = Existing
Gray = Proposed

Baywoods Trail

Boardwalk

Park Boundary

BIRD
BANDING
STATION

The park has a long oceanside beach and wonderful views.

Campground: The mostly open, flat and dry campground has 27 tent sites and 94 water/electric or water/electric/sewer sites. A quality shower building has outside and indoor showers. Each camping site offers a picnic table and a fire ring. Firewood is sold in the campground. The campground is about one-third shady. The campground host is near the slate-gray colored bathhouse, near site 60. Attractive modern lampposts provide subtle illumination for late evening walks.

Loop 1-42 includes a picnic area and utility hookups. Many of the sites are open and sunny, with a gravel road that wanders through them. Larger RV rigs like this open-style campground due to the ease of getting in and out. Many pads are neatly clipped grassy, not gravel or muddy, spaces.

Sites 72-94 are open and grassy. Sites 95-110 are shady under pencil-straight conifers, with pine needles littering the ground. A timber-style play structure, gazebo and rest room are at the end of the loop. Sites 111-121 are also shady and are slightly more private. Each site's gravel and cracked shell parking space is neatly outlined by ground-mounted timbers.

The concrete ships off the park's waterfront offer some excellent fishing from a boat. The sunken ships act as an artificial reef holding and attracting a variety of saltwater species. The ships were sunk in 1950, filled with sand and water, and helped to protect the harbor for ferry boat traffic (the ferry stopped operating in April 1964). The old ships once served in the south Atlantic during World War II. In part because of these sunken ships, the beach is actually growing and fishing in the area can be very good.

The quarter-mile-long non-swimming beach is open for surf fishing, crabbing and beach combing.

Boating: A single lane hard-surfaced ramp can accommodate small boats, except at low tide. The launch is tidal dependent. Use it only when the tide is in. A tide chart is posted at the narrow ramp. A new expanded boat ramp is in the works.

Steady offshore winds and a mix of protected and open waters draw many windsurfers to the area. Some of the board sailors stage and launch from the park; others just sail by. Park staff warns the windsurfers to watch out for the many pound nets that are placed along the coast. Otherwise, the colorful sailing boards are welcome and add to the ocean vista.

Hiking: The 1.5-mile Baywood Trail leads visitors through the part of the park most used by migratory birds. Along the trail you will see a bird banding station and various boardwalks that protect the dunes.

Day-use areas: About 150 acres of the park are in agricultural fields, leaving plenty of room for a picnic area, campground, swimming beaches, shoreline, pier and parking. The tidy and shady picnic area has portable rest rooms, nearby soft drink machine, water hydrants and defined parking areas near the mowed day-use spaces. Picnic tables have rugged metal frames and wood tops. Bald Eagle Bluff walkway, a short trail, starts in the day-use area.

Swimming beach: Stay on the walkways (to protect the dunes) to the sandy beach. The beach is one-half mile long and fronts the Chesapeake Bay. The two clean changing rooms at the beach have skylights and a deck that surrounds them.

Nature: The coastal land and bay funnel huge numbers of migratory songbirds and raptors (birds of prey) through the park. Since 1963 Kiptopeke has been the site of bird population studies and banding programs. Sponsored by the Virginia Society of Ornithology and Hawk Migration Society of North America and licensed by the U.S. Fish and Wildlife Service, volunteers capture, examine, weigh, band and release resident and migratory birds in September and October annually. In the Raptor Research Area, hawks, kestrels, osprey and other birds of prey are observed and banded from September to early November. Raptor banding and counting has been conducted since 1977.

The hawk observatory is an elevated wooden structure where hawks, owls and eagles can be watched, counted and sometimes lured close. The deck is about eight feet above grade and has benches for comfortable wildlife watching. Many migrating raptors are attracted to the observation deck area to hunt in the grassy and open fields. This area is the site of one of the heaviest concentrations of migratory birds on the East Coast. For this reason, good numbers of birds are easily seen during migration times as they stop to rest and feed.

Banders work mist nets every day during this period. The general public may watch and learn on Wednesday and Saturday mornings. On a good day, banders will catch, record and carefully release up to 300 birds before 2 p.m., when the nets are usually taken down. About 15,000 raptors, mostly sharp-shinned hawks, migrate through the park each fall.

Kiptopeke is well-known for the annual Eastern Shore Birding Festival, held in early October. The event is an annual celebration during the fall migration of the neo-tropical songbirds and raptors. Virginia's eastern shore (northern Delmarva Peninsula and the tip near Cape Charles) creates a natural narrow funnel focusing the migration of birds to the southern tip of the peninsula. The area provides an extraordinary opportunity for novice and experienced birdwatchers to witness incredible numbers of birds congregate in preparation for their flight to the tropics.

The goal of the birding festival is to increase the awareness of the role that Virginia's eastern shore plays in bird migrations, highlight the importance of protecting habitat within this migration corridor and emphasize the mutual benefits to the local economy and habitat conservation through

Kiptopeke was once a busy ferry port.

responsible nature tourism. There is a small fee to attend the colorful event.

Activities include dozens of exhibits, art work, food and beverages, kids adventure tent, workshops, a butterfly walk, bird feeding exhibits, falconry, butterflies, marvels of avian flight, and trips to Fisherman Island, Saxis Wildlife Management Area and Chincoteague National Wildlife Refuge. Other tours include a canoe trip, a trek to Glebe Farm and Marsh Point Farm, habitat hikes and hawk observation.

Birders may also see a variety of water birds in the park including royal tern, common tern, great black-backed gull, laughing gull, herring gull, double-crested cormorants and a variety of ducks (oldsquaws, mergansers, gold-eneye, bufflehead, surf scoter, canvasback and other diving species) and shorebirds.

Blue crab, one of the most abundant inhabitants of the Chesapeake Bay, can also be found at the park. There are many fascinating things to know about the sea dweller. Did you know that "callinecdes sapidus" is their scientific name and that "callinecdes" means "beautiful swimmer, " and "sapidus" means "tasty?"

Crab live only 2.5 years, shedding their shells in order to grow, a process called molting. A blue crab will molt more than 20 times during its life. This crab gets its name from the bright blue pinches of the adult male. Crabs migrate up the bay toward fresh water each spring and back down the bay in the fall. Crabs are known by many names, sometimes called Jimmie, Buster or soft shells. They area also known by the name "Sook," referring to an adult crab, or "Peeler," a crab that is in molt.

Recreational crabbers are often called "chicken neckers" by anglers. Commercial crabbers harvest about 80 million pounds of crabs a year from the Chesapeake Bay. This is almost 500 million crabs. If you laid that many crabs side by side, the line would stretch more than 47,000 miles, or 1.5 times around the earth.

Females produce eggs only once during their lifetime. But then, they produce between 750,000 and 3 million eggs.

Wildlife watchers should also scan the ocean vista in search of bottlenose dolphins and bobbing pelicans.

The park also features seasonal naturalist programs for camping and day visitors. Typical programs include snake identification, junior rangers, campfire programs, crabbing and fishing clinics.

Insiders tips: Enjoy the trip through the Chesapeake Bay Bridge-Tunnel. Call ahead and visit in the early morning when bird banders are tending their mist nets and attaching numbered bands to birds' legs. The Fisherman's Island National Wildlife Refuge is only minutes away (look for big flocks of pelicans and shorebirds in the flats) and has a wonderful visitor center with lots of natural history about the area.

17 Lake Anna State Park
Land: 2,058 acres Water: 13,000-acre lake

Lake Anna is a sparkling lake with dozens of intimate coves nestled in the undulating hills of central Virginia. The 13,000-acre lake is wildly popular with boaters, skiers and fishermen. The park itself is resort quality, clean, well-groomed and a popular place for corporate outings, family reunions and daylong visits to the white sandy beach.

The region also has a fascinating history. A minor gold rush began in the area that is now Lake Anna State Park with the discovery of gold in 1829. Farmers began finding gold in the rich lowlands near the creeks and streams. After every rain, particles of gold became exposed on the surface of the ground, fueling the gold rush. Many farmers began panning for the gold which soon became a common practice during the 1830s.

The gold belt stretches from northern Virginia to the North Carolina border. This narrow strip is known now as the Gold-Pyrite Belt. What is believed to be the largest gold nuggets found in the United States came from

Spotsylvania County in which the park is located.

The Goodwin Gold Mine became established at the north end of the park. The shaft was 95 feet deep, and the tunnel extended for about 200 feet into the hillside. Today, the old foundation of the shaft mine can be found along Pigeon Run. The land in Lake Anna State Park was once known as "Gold Hill," but the gold was not easily or quickly extracted from the vein which the gold-bearing ore was found. The deposits also contained pyrite or fool's gold, so named because it was often mistaken for gold.

When gold was discovered in California in 1849, experienced miners from Virginia joined the gold rush in the West, and the production of gold in Virginia began to drop off. The last gold produced in the area was actually a byproduct of lead mining. What had once been known as "Gold Hill" became "The Big Woods" by the 1900s. Panning for gold demonstrations offered at the park is one of the most unique interpretive programs offered in the commonwealth's state park system.

Lake Anna began in 1967-68 when the park base was cleared in preparation for the dam on the North Anna River to supply cooling water for the Virginia Electric and Power Company nuclear power plant. In January 1972 the dam gates were closed. Six months later, with the help of excessive flooding created by hurricane Agnes, the lake basin was filled. In December 1972 the lake was dedicated and turned over to the people of the commonwealth of Virginia. Shortly thereafter 2,000 acres of land and 8.5 miles of Lake Anna shoreline were acquired by the state for development of the state park.

Information and Activities

Lake Anna State Park
6800 Lawyers Road
Spotsylvania, VA 22553
(540) 854-5503

Directions: The park lies adjacent to Route 601 off Route 208, 25 miles southwest of Fredericksburg and 55 miles northwest of Richmond. There is a small parking fee. You are within 10 miles of the North Anna Nuclear

Power Station. Private campgrounds are scattered around the lake.

Visitor center: The attractive, modern, gray visitor center is surrounded by landscaped planting beds and tightly mowed grass. The center overlooks the lake and beach. Inside the center, the history of the park and impact of gold are interpreted by words and displays.

The first recorded history of gold in Virginia was in the early 1800s. It was usually found in and along stream beds. The Whitehall Mine in west Spotsylvania County was the first recorded gold mine in operation in Virginia in 1806. Spotsylvania County during this time had no less than 23 active gold mines. Between 1830 and 1850 Virginia was the third largest gold producing state in the nation. In 1849, for example, 6,259 ounces of gold worth about $130,000 were found in the state.

But as mining costs increased and known gold reserves became depleted, production slowed and finally stopped. Gold was last commercially produced in Virginia in 1947. Gold mining was actively done within the park boundaries.

Panning for gold was the simplest and most primitive technique of gold gathering. The success of this method was limited in two ways. First, gold recovered with a pan was chiefly the coarser fractions of gold particles. Second, most of the fine and float gold was carried off with gravel and water.

Interestingly the first gold pans doubled as wash basins and skillets, out of necessity historians suspect. Panning for gold was best for prospecting, not mining and recovery. Other mechanical devices were used to help speed and increase the gold recovery process. One such device was the Long Tom, a wooden shaker device that screened gravel. One miner would feed the gold-bearing sand and gravel into the upper box, and another miner stirred the gravel, broke up clay and discarded particles collected at the grating. Even with this tool, much of the fine gold was lost. Two men working the Long Tom could find an average of $10 worth (half-ounce) daily. This might not seem like much money today, but in 1850 this would buy you a coffee pot (36 cents), bushel of coal, bottle of cough syrup, Valentine's Day card (six cents), Harper's Magazine, cemetery grave plot and still have change left over.

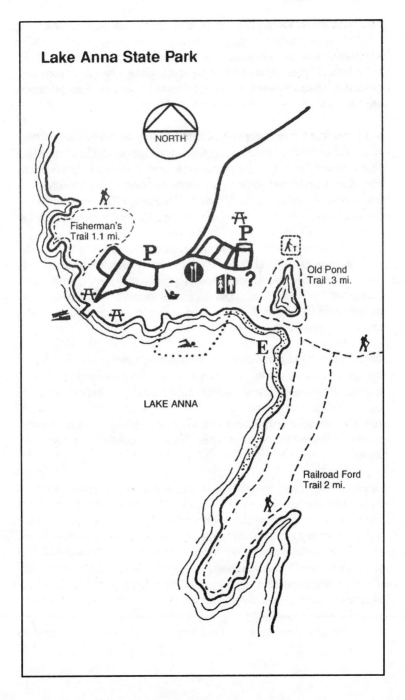

Lake Anna State Park

NORTH

Fisherman's
Trail 1.1 mi.

P

P

Old Pond
Trail .3 mi.

?

E

LAKE ANNA

Railroad Ford
Trail 2 mi.

Also in the visitor center are well-designed educational displays about iron mining, a video about gold, display about fuel for making iron, touch table with furs, skulls and antlers, information about the development of Lake Anna, natural history notes, weather station, telescope, two aquariums with native fish, insect display cases, colorful butterfly display, animals mounts and more.

Boating: Lake Anna State Park is 17 miles long and the park's launching ramp is one of only two public access points on the entire 13,000-acre lake (there are many privately-operated marinas around the lake). The two-lane launching ramp is hard-surfaced and shaded smooth-bark sycamore trees. Courtesy docks are at the end of the launching ramp. The small ramp area is well-organized with a tie-down area, staging lane and gravel parking lot.

Fishing: 5.5 million fish were planted in Lake Anna in fall 1972. The lake has more than 200 miles of shoreline and can reach a depth of 50 feet. Many more fish have since been added, including largemouth bass, bluegill, black crappie, channel catfish, redear, stripers, walleye and other panfish. Stocking programs continue today. The most commonly taken species include largemouth bass, shad, catfish and yellow perch.

Striped bass, the largest member of the sea bass family, can grow to 100 pounds in the open ocean and freshwater bass can easily weigh 15 to 20 pounds. In lakes like Anna, anglers attract these fish by trolling deep-running baits like plugs, spoons, lead heads or spinners with a plastic worm rig. Still fishing or drift fishing with live bait such as gizzard shad is also effective. Striped bass have also been introduced to Virginia's saltwater lakes.

Largemouth bass are recognized by the conspicuous line down the side of the jaw that reaches past the eye. Largemouth bass are a favorite in Lake Anna, with 8-10 pounders taken with regularity. The biggest fish are found in shallow weedy areas and will strike with slashing power at nearly every live bait. Some anglers tease the ornery fish into biting with buzz baits and flashy spinners retrieved near the surface. Once hooked, the bucketmouths offer an exhilarating fight, often leaping high into the air and making runs away from the boat and under structures.

Sunfish (bream) are numerous in Lake Anna. Bluegill is recognized by deep yellow coppery-red complexion and green and brown vertical bars. The gills prefer quiet weedy areas where they can hide and feed. Live bait, flies, jigs and grubs are often used. Fly anglers should try a tiny bit of live bait on a small lure.

Channel catfish have deeply forked tails and 24-29 anal rays. The body is gray to greenish-gray above and silver gray on both sides, with a white underbelly. Cane poles with a bobber, split-shot and small hooks baited with stink bait, worms, minnows and cutbait work well. Locals prefer shrimp, squid, chicken livers and prepared catfish baits fished at night.

Crappies are a favorite fish at the lake. Their sweet flaky meat make them a good meal. Look for structures; they love to hide under fallen logs, vegetation and other objects. After June, when the water warms, crappies head for deeper water. Spinners, minnows, live bait, wet and dry flies and popping bugs are effective baits.

A fishing pier on the pond near the visitor center is accessible by people with disabilities. A small bait and tackle shop at the visitor center features tackle for the pond or lake angler. Near the boat launch is access to Fisherman's Trail, a shoreline fishing area.

Anglers should also pick up a map that details 20 underwater fish structures in Lake Anna. The structures, placed by Virginia Power Company, U.S. Army Corps of Engineers and the Virginia Department of Game and Inland Fisheries, consist of cinderblocks, small trees and brush. Each structure is marked by a buoy with "Fish Structure" painted on the side. The blocks and brush provide cover and protection for young fish and serve as spawning and feeding areas for larger fish.

By providing a more suitable environment than was previously available, the structures should be of particular benefit to largemouth bass, bluegill and black crappie anglers.

Hiking: Some of the trailheads are off the main park road and defined by landscape timbers forming a parking lot.

Turkey Run Trail (1.5 miles) is blazed in yellow and leads over gently rolling terrain. While hiking through a mature forest of maple and oak, you will pass

The modern visitor center has excellent interpretive displays.

a filled-in well. This well once provided water for a steam-powered sawmill. Near the trail's end is a chimney marking the old Taylor homestead. Just before reaching the homestead look carefully for an old graveyard.

Glenora Trail (1.7 miles) winds gently down rolling terrain to the edge of the lake. On your way you will walk through an oak and maple forest past overgrown fields and down an old country lane. Overlooking the lake is a large plantation house built in the 1800s (that may soon be restored). Remnants of Glenora outbuildings include a smokehouse.

Mill Pond Trail is blazed in blue and leads .6 mile from the Turkey Run Trail to a cove of Lake Ann, where Hailey's Grist Mill ground local farmers' grain from 1857 to 1889. Around the shallow cove look for heron and evidence of beavers.

Cedar Run Trail (.7 mile) is a connector loop of the Turkey Run Trail offering views of Lake Anna. It follows a cedar-lined abandoned country lane and passes an overgrown homesite where dandelions still bloom in the springtime.

Big Woods Trail (1 mile) is blazed in silver and connects Turkey Run and Glenora trails. The trail passes through a forest of oak and maple down a former logging road and along the lakeshore. Look for signs of beaver near the water.

Old Pond Trail is self-guided (booklet is available at visitor center) loop along the edge of the pond behind the visitor center. Nine learning stations explain a variety of ecological themes.

The pond was built by a former owner and is now thick with hazel and common alder, members of the birch family. While walking the trail you will travel through several stages of forest succession from once cleared fields to areas where pioneer species such as red cedar and Virginia pines begin to take over. Look carefully and you will also see many sweetgum and hornbeam (ironwood) trees, both species representing members of the mature hardwood stage or "sere" in forest development.

The sweetgum is identified by corky wings on the twigs, its star-shaped leaves and round, prickly fruit. Pioneers used the sap found beneath the bark in medicine and in chewing gum. American hornbeam, or ironwood, gets its name from its muscular appearance (smooth, gray bark) and extremely hard wood. The wood is used in tool handles and the charred wood is used in gunpowder.

Also along the trail, in more mature areas, is the loblolly pine, one of the fastest growing southern pines which does well in this type of moist area. In its mature state, the loblolly pine cone provides food for birds and small mammals.

Spring is a wonderful time to hike the easy trail and view the yellow blossoms of the tulip poplar. The massive tree gets its name from its scented greenish-yellow flower, not from a relationship with tulips or poplars. It is actually a member of the magnolia family. One of the tallest eastern hardwoods, it is also one of the most important commercial trees, used in musical instrument and furniture making. Indians used the trunks to make long dugout canoes. Some wonderful sycamores, with whitish bark that peels off in flakes exposing patches of brown and green, are also evident along the trail.

Hikers should also look for signs of beaver. Other nocturnal residents that can be seen early or late in the day are raccoons and opossums. Look for footprints in the mud and sandy areas around the pond.

Along the pond's edge, visitors will see and learn about emergent aquatic plants, decomposing cycles and how the pond is gradually filling in and will one day become a grassy field, and eventually a mature forest.

Day-use areas: Lake Anna has some terrific day-use areas along the lake's edge. The neatly mowed park has plenty of picnicking areas, play equipment and places for family fun. The unit also has two 20-foot by 40-foot canopy tents that are set up for group outings and picnics. The most popular of the green and white tents is near the water. According to staff, family reunions and corporate rentals are equal users of the unique tents. The canopies can be rented by the half-day or full day. Each tent area has two or three grills and many picnic tables.

The park gets heavy day use, and picnic areas fill up on the weekends. Sometimes there are more picnickers than grills and tables to go around. Some of the finest picnic areas are along the shoreline near the beach.

Rest rooms and the bathhouse are modern and clean. All of the day-use areas are exceptionally well-maintained and tidy.

Beach: A large timber-formed play structure with five swings, five slides and climbing platforms is near the changing house. A pleasant grassy area is between the play structure and the beach. A small fee is required for using the beach, and it can be paid at the modern snack bar. The 125-yard-long sandy beach is outlined by a walkway and is open 1 p.m. - 6 p.m. Wednesday - Sunday. The beachside snack bar is open 10 a.m. to 7 p.m. Memorial Day to Labor Day (like the beach).

The snack bar is one of the best in the state. The gray-colored snack bar, which is surrounded on three sides by a wooden deck, sells adult and child inflatable rafts, flying discs, buckets, candy, hats, beach balls, sunscreen, T-shirts, hot dogs, beverages, nachos, onion rings, chips, subs and beach passes. On the deck are some umbrella tables that have a pleasant view of

The beach and facilities are super clean---and fun!

---

the beach and lakeshore.

Three lifeguards patrol the swimming area. The almost white sand is clean and conditioned at the cove-side beach. The bathhouse has an exposed beam ceiling, skylights, showers and clean rest rooms.

Nature: All that glitters isn't gold...or is it? Visitors can learn about geology, gold and panning for gold during programs offered throughout the summer. Environmental education programs are offered on a seasonal basis. Panning for gold demonstrations are popular weekend programs for the entire family. Other programs include birding by boat, meteor showers, evening cruise, bluegrass music and more. The park also features pond ecology programs throughout the season.

One of the most interesting residents of Lake Anna is the beaver. The largest rodent in North America, an architect, wood cutter, mason and hauler, the beaver has few equals in the animal world. For example, two adult beavers can cut down a tree in three minutes, build a two-foot high dam 12-feet across in two nights, construct a lodge of 1,000 cubic feet and store a pile of wood 30 feet long—all using only their teeth and forepaws. Beaver pelts traditionally used as currency still command an important place in the fur industry.

Lake Anna offers teacher in-service training, which is a teaching the teacher effort designed so students can have a quality outdoor education experience at the park. Some of the training is done at the pond-side environmental education pavilion, which is adjacent to the pontoon launch.

Education: The park's interpretive staff offers weekend programming aboard the 24-foot pontoon boat during the summer. Up to 12 visitors may take the tour at a time and learn about a variety of ecological principles. An entire lesson plan has been developed for school groups and teachers to help maximize the use of the pontoon boat and park visits. There is a small fee for the tour.

Park educators have also developed a comprehensive outdoor education lesson plan that is a terrific aid for teachers to base environmental study units on. Concepts and lessons included in the plan are fruits and seeds, limnology, hands-on outdoor activities, forest growth, shelling, wildlife notes, ecology and much more.

Hunting: Waterfowl hunting can be good on the lake. The lake, with warm water from the power plants, has a resident Canada geese flock. Call the park manager for details.

Insiders tips: Plan to see the panning for gold demonstration. You may find some real gold! Ask for the history booklet entitled, "Fortune's Wheel." The park's visitor center also publishes a list of area marinas, private campgrounds, motels and restaurants.

18 Leesylvania State Park
Land: 508 acres Water: Potomac River

Leesylvania State Park, about 20 miles south of Washington, D.C., features nearly three miles of heavily used frontage on the Potomac River between Neabsco and Powell's Creek. The park is best known for excellent boating facilities, day-use area and a rich history. Within the park is the house site of Henry Lee II, father of Light-Horse Harry Lee and grandfather to Robert E. Lee.

On a moss-covered knoll is the Lee family cemetery. On Freestone Point, a 110-foot bluff overlooking the Potomac, are the eroded earthworks of a Confederate battery of the Civil War. Henry Lee II was the first Lee to reside on the property, naming the plantation Leesylvania, a title meaning "Lee's woods." In 1753 Lee married Lucy Grimes ("the lowland beauty mentioned by George Washington"). Eight children were born to the couple, including a remarkable collection of gifted public servants.

Henry Lee II was swept up in the revolutionary ardor and fought to secure home and port. A militia leader, Lee later built roads to facilitate the transport of military goods and men. But Prince William County's greatest contribution to the Revolution was Henry Lee II's son, Henry Lee III, known as "Light-Horse Harry."

Light-Horse Harry was born in 1756 at Leesylvania and was a graduate of Princeton at age 17. Returning from college, he found that the issue of separation from England was the dominant topic of concern and that his superb horsemanship skills would be needed in the war that was breaking out.

Commissioned as a captain, Lee hand-picked the members of his 5th Troop of Continental Light Dragoons. After leading each potential recruit on a grueling steeplechase, he would wheel his horse about and charge them with a drawn sword. If the recruit did anything but meet the challenge steel on steel, he was politely refused into Harry's ranks. In this bold fashion, an aggressive, young group of 82 cavalrymen were chosen. They quickly showed their mettle.

Called to George Washington's Army, Lee's horsemen demonstrated the classic mounted and dismounted tactics of light dragoons. It was here that young Lee acquired the nickname, "Light-Horse Harry." The intrepid men had many exploits, including seizing convoys of British provisions, daring commando-style raids at British forts and more. Light-Horse Harry ended the war a hero, receiving a rare Gold Medal of Valor from Congress. He was also a member of the Continental Congress, Virginia governor and congressman. Harry was the father of another great American, General Robert E. Lee.

Information and Activities

Leesylvania State Park
16236 Neabsco Road
Woodbridge, VA 22191
(703) 670-0372

Directions: From the junction of U.S. Highway 1 and Neabsco Road (between Woodbridge and Dumfries), travel east on Neabsco Road for one

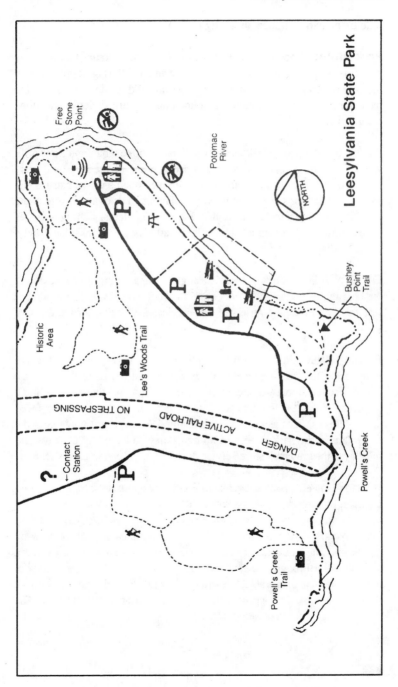

Leesylvania State Park

mile to the park entrance on the right.

Park store: Looking much like an old seaside colonial building, the nautical-like park store has a weather vane and a U.S. flag flapping above it. Lots of food and basic marina supplies are sold inside. In front of the park store are a bustling marine gasoline pump, courtesy docks and stone breakwalls.

From a broad wooden deck with picnic tables, coffee tables and a gas grill, visiting boaters or park users have a scenic view of the river and busy service docks. Inside the roomy store are seven booths where patrons can eat a light lunch or snack from the tiny restaurant. Handy items sold at the store include sunscreen, charcoal, basic grocery items, fishing supplies (lures, mostly), oil, charcoal starter fluid, batteries, soft drinks, ice, candy, T-shirts, diapers, sandwiches, coffee and Frosties.

Fishing: Join the ranks of shoreline anglers along the improved areas near the boat ramps and sailboat winches. The rocky breakwaters are popular structures for holding a variety of fish species. Live bait is sold at the park store.

Boating (launching fee): Boating is the primary activity at the distinctive state park. The park represents Virginia's largest access to the Potomac River. From sailboat winches to finger docks, marine store and two large launching ramps, boaters are catered to at Leesylvania. Huge hard-surfaced parking lots service the wide launching ramps. Showers are available in the rest rooms at the park store.   Motorboats may be rented by the half- and full-day at the gray park store/service dock. A private vendor rents Jet Skis.

Hiking: Howell's Nature Trail has a small parking lot at the trailhead along the main park road.

Lee's Woods Historical Interpretive Trail is outlined part of the way by ground-mounted timbers. The educational trail winds over small hills, along a tall bluff and through fields and forests. A 12-page self-guided trail booklet is available that interprets 11 learning stations along the twin-loop trail. Stations are marked by a post with a white number on a red field sign. The dirt trail is easy to moderately difficult.

Biking, boating, and hiking the interpretive trail is popular.

By using your imagination, the Lee's Woods walk can become a fascinating journey through time. You'll feel like you witnessed some of the events that brought national attention to this historic site.

At the top of the first hill are cannons surrounded by embankments, pointing toward the river. This artillery site on Freestone Point is one of several Confederate batteries along the Potomac. General Robert E. Lee once ordered a blockade of the river, hoping to cut off Washington, D.C.'s main avenue for military transportation and communication. From this site you can imagine the approach of the Union Navy sloops, exploding shells and barking cannons.

Other learning stations detail the busy port and tall schooners that sailed the Potomac and flat-bottomed barges that plied Neabsco Creek. The vessels transported firewood, lumber, livestock, fruit, hay and slate.

Maybe the most fun to imagine is the days when magnificent riding horses proudly trotted down narrow roads that bisected lush tobacco fields, woodlands and newly-cleared fields. These lands were once rich with game, waterfowl and settlers criss-crossing the river and lands. This was where Henry Lee II carved a plantation out of the forest and built a fine home that was richly furnished and filled with family.

In the cemetery on a mossy knoll lies Lucy Grimes Lee and beside her Henry Lee II. They were married 34 years, raised eight children and built a successful business.

The final leg of the trail talks about the 1870s when railroad tracks gleamed and area residents became accustomed to the distant huffing and shrill whistle of approach trains carrying products in all directions. You can almost smell the oily smoke and burning coal. Trains ran regularly from Washington, D.C. to Richmond, Virginia. This rail line is symbolic of the newly reunited nation that the Lee family was well-known in helping to create.

Over the past hundred years, this lush peninsula has been used by loggers and fishermen, bootleggers and squatters. It has been a hunting retreat and gambling resort. Thanks to Daniel K. Ludwig, a wealthy philanthropist, the land was deeded to the state in 1978 and the park has been growing and improving since.

Day-use areas: Most picnicking takes places between the historic site and the boat launching area. Tables, grills and bulky-looking shelters are scattered along mowed open spaces, shady tracts and near the river bank. In this day-use area is a modern rest room and the place where you can purchase a booklet that details the history of the park.

A nice touch in the rest rooms is the tall faucets that allow picnickers to easily fill water jugs or rinse coolers. A soft drink machine is also located at the rest room building.

The sandy beach (not open for swimming, but good for sunbathing) offers day-users a pleasant area to wander and great views of the tree-lined shore, wide river and boat traffic. Small bits and pieces of driftwood collect on the sandy beach and beg closer examination.

Along the river is Freestone Point, where the U.S.S. Freestone was docked.

Lee's Woods Historical Interpretive Trail.

It was a gambling ship that was part of a resort that was operated here in the 1950s.

Nature: Huge paw paw trees, bent with large fruit, are along some of the trails at Leesylvania.

Cormorants and gulls are commonly seen on the water and in the park. High numbers of resident and migratory waterfowl, including wood duck, canvasback, bufflehead, mallard and merganser are often seen in the winter and spring. Staff reports that at least two American bald eagle nests are in the region, and the birds are often seen patrolling along the river bluff and over the river. Eagles also roost along Bushey Point and Freestone Point during the winter. In the spring and summer, osprey can also be seen hunting above the river and soaring along the coastal bluffs. Look along the edge areas for deer during the early morning or evening.

Insiders tip: Hike the Lee's Woods Historical Interpretive Trail.

19 Mason Neck State Park

Land: 1,804 acres Water: Potomac River

Mason Neck (8,000 acres), famous as the location of both Gunston Hall and the first National Wildlife Refuge specifically established for the protection of the bald eagle, is a peninsula jutting into the Potomac River. The scenic peninsula is bounded by Pohick Bay, Gunston Cove, the Potomac River, and by Belmont and Occoquan bays.

The state park and surrounding outdoor amenities combine valuable natural, historical and recreational resources in a serene setting that belies its proximity to a large metropolitan area.

In addition to Gunston Hall (a National Historic Landmark and home of George Mason) and Mason Neck National Wildlife Refuge (site of an active bald eagle nest), the "Neck" is home to Pohick Bay Regional Park (703-352-5900), operated by Northern Virginia Regional Park Authority for recreational pursuits (swimming pool, boat rental, mini-golf, camping, picnic areas, boat launching ramp and so on). Mason Neck State Park, which has an environmental education center and trails, offers a public area for passive outdoor recreation. The park also has large tracts of land preserved in their natural state.

The various park and conservation units are part of the Mason Neck Cooperative Management Area, which strives to provide a spectrum of outdoor recreation and educational opportunities.

During the 1800s and early 1900s, logging was the area's primary industry. The removal of mature pine and hardwood, and use of the pesticide DDT, led to the decline of the bald eagle in the region. In 1965 the Conservation Committee for Mason Neck formed to preserve the area from increasing development. In July 1967, The Nature Conservancy made it its first purchase of land to protect areas of Mason Neck until funds were appropriated to federal, state and local agencies to further preserve the tract.

The Commonwealth purchased its first parcel of what is now the state park in 1967. The park opened in April 1985.

Information and Activities

Mason Neck State Park
7301 High Point Road
Lorton, VA 22079
(703) 550-0960

Directions: In the southwest corner of Fairfax County, 20 miles from Washington, D.C. Access the park via U.S. Route 1, then five miles east on Route 242 to the park entrance. The office is in a portable building across from the large visitor center. Inside the park office is a color-coded map that details the lay of the land including tidal ponds, open fields and wood lines.

The nearby George Washington Grist Mill is managed by the staff at Mason Neck State Park.

Visitor center: On the river bluff above the Potomac, the brown, rough-sawn, vertical sided educational center is the focal point of the park. Stretching in each direction from the center is a split rail fence, drawing your

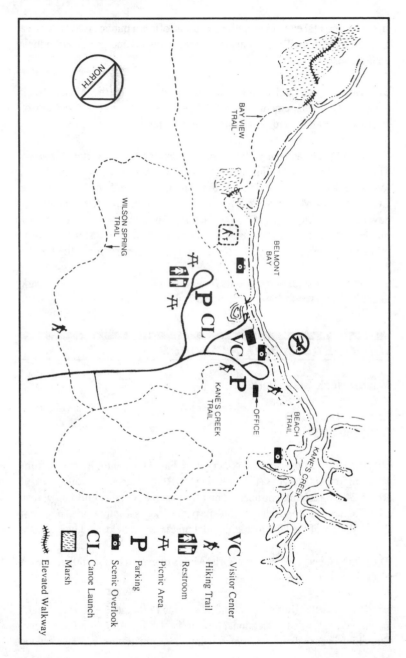

NORTH

BAY VIEW TRAIL

WILSON SPRING TRAIL

BELMONT BAY

KANE'S CREEK TRAIL

OFFICE

BEACH TRAIL

KANE'S CREEK

P

CL

VC

P

VC Visitor Center

👤 Hiking Trail

🚻 Restroom

🏕 Picnic Area

P Parking

📷 Scenic Overlook

CL Canoe Launch

▨ Marsh

〰 Elevated Walkway

eye to the wide views of ridges and water and boats full of anglers.

The center has a multi-purpose room, wet lab and two areas for natural and cultural history interpretive displays.

Operated mostly by volunteers, the center is open weekends (hours are posted) and contains a variety of natural history displays. The popular touch table includes plenty of nature items like furs, bones, feathers and stones. The visitor center has comfortable rocking chairs scattered around the building near colorful displays that detail the nearby wildlife refuge, area wildlife and flora.

During this century, millions of acres of forest and farmlands have become cities and suburbs. Many habitats were destroyed and wildlife populations declined. Thanks to society's changing awareness of nature's importance in the life of mankind, tracts of land are being set aside as refuges for man and animal. Here at Mason Neck, a refuge and state park have been established where humans can escape the rigors of contemporary life and animals can live free of many serious threats presented by a growing population.

Visitors to this 10,000-acre peninsula can explore nature in the state park and federal wildlife preserve, search for the past in some of Mason Neck's 13 historic sites and enjoy camping, swimming, boating and golf in a regional park. Here, visitors can explore the role of man and nature by visiting the center and many surrounding amenities.

Wildflower enthusiasts will enjoy the demonstration plantings that are carefully tended around the building. Species include depford pink, obedient plant, black-eyed Susan, ox-eye daisy, thin-leaf coneflower, New England aster, American holly, wild geranium, blue lobelia, wild ginger, golden Alexander, Christmas fern, purple coneflower and many others.

A single picnic table and rest rooms are under a small porch-like space behind the visitor center.

Hiking: Three miles of trails wind through the water-side park, providing routes to observe birds and wildlife. Elevated boardwalks allow visitors to explore some of the wetlands in the park.

The Bay View Interpretive Trail (1 mile) offers good views of the bay, boardwalks that cross a tidal marsh, a chance to follow a creek and easy hiking through a mature hardwood forest. Hikers will learn that a bay is only as healthy as the creeks that flow into it and the creek is only as healthy as the land from which it flows. Plants depend on clean water for survival and animals rely on plants for shelter and food. Along the educationally signed trail, walkers will learn how upland plants benefit aquatic plants and how the entire ecosystem contributes to the health of Belmont Bay. The trail traces the shoreline of the bay.

On the boardwalk above the tidal marsh you'll discover a sign entitled, "What's for Lunch?" This wet spot is one of nature's busy kitchens. Though not picturesque, many animals depend on the food produced in marshes. Ingredients like dead plants and leaves are broken down and consumed by bacteria, tiny worms and insect larvae. These tiny creatures are eaten by larger insects as part of the food chain and eventually devoured by fish, frogs, salamanders and songbirds.

Today, fishing in Belmont Bay is poor (but improving!) and the shoreline is eroding because the bay has lost its water plants. In a healthy bay thick tangles of underwater plants harbor small aquatic animals that are eaten by game fish. Plants also reduce the force of in-coming storm waves and boat wakes. Pollution in the Potomac River caused a dramatic die-off of aquatic vegetation in the 1970s. When the water plants died, fish populations declined sharply due to reduction in food and shelter. Without the plants, waves eat away at the forest foundation and one or two feet of shoreline erode each year. The effects of erosion are evident along the shoreline the trail follows.

The inlet you will cross via boardwalk along the Bay View trail is like a two-way street. Both the creek and Belmont Bay are affected by tides, which raise and lower the water twice a day. When the tides raise the bay, waters flow into the creek, and conversely, when the tides fall the creek waters flow to the bay. Thus algae and migrating fish ride the currents back and forth between the bay and the creek. If you look at something floating in the creek, you can see the tide rising or gradually falling.

This wetland forest is the home and food source for many creatures. Beavers topple trees, eat the inner bark and build dams and lodges;

Shoreline hiking is popular at the park.

woodpeckers chisel holes in trees in search of insects and to construct nesting cavities; songbirds scan the air, ground and treetops for seeds and insects; and deer, raccoon and opossum wander through the valley seeking food. From the trail, walkers should take the time to listen and look for animals that call the area home.

Trees in the wetlands are nature's best water filters. Raindrops strike tree leaves and branches, then break into small droplets and fall to the earth gently. Instead of washing away topsoil, they soak into the spongy ground. Sand, clay, decaying leaves and an intricate network of plant roots then filter bacteria and harmful chemicals from the rainwater. The purified waters eventually seep to the bay and the waters are used by man and animal.

Along with informational signs, some of the flora is identified by small placards. Learn to identify sweetgum, dogwoods, mountain laurel and others.

Kane's Creek Trail (1 mile) winds through the forest and ends up at an observation blind at Kane's Creek. The Wilson Spring Trail is a connector between the two hiking trails.

Fishing: Freshwater shoreline fishing is fair. Common species taken include panfish, rough- and gamefish. Largemouth bass, catfish and carp are the most popular catches. Belmont Bay is relatively shallow and affords little spawning and natural reproduction near the park's shore.

Boating: The wide bays beckon quiet boating, offering plenty of tree-lined shores to explore. A gravel cartop canoe launching ramp is next to the visitor station and is open daylight hours. There is no parking at the launch; you must move your car to the nearby parking lot.

Guided canoe trips are a popular way to see the Mason Neck park from a totally different perspective. The two-to three-hour trips are a great way to experience the waterway, explore Kane's Creek and possibly see muskrats, king fishers, beavers or bald eagles.

The park provides a trained volunteer guide, Personal Floatation Devices and paddles. Bring a hat, sunscreen, water, insect repellent, binoculars and a camera. Participants paddle their own canoe and the minimum age is three years old. There is a small fee for the trips, and the canoe tours are a fundraiser for the park. Up to 17 people can take a tour at one time.

Day-use areas: Picnic areas include drinking water, grills and modern rest rooms with soft drink machine. The Bay View Trailhead is the main picnic area.

Nature: The nearby Mason Neck National Wildlife Refuge was established to preserve and protect critical nesting, feeding and roosting habitat for bald eagles. Within the sprawling national wildlife refuge is the Great Marsh Trail that offers hikers a wonderful view of the 258-acre Great Marsh and surrounding diverse habitats. The wetland is the best place to look for eagles on the peninsula. In the winter, 50 or more bald eagles are known to visit, hunt and roost. A total of 15 immature and mature eagles reside in the area during the summer.

Look for eagles along the marsh edge, Bay View Trail and Kane's Creek Trail in the refuge, over the bay, and along the shoreline in the state park.

The neighboring refuge is also the site of a great blue heron rookery, where more than 1,000 pairs of the stilt-like birds fuss over twig nests, squawk at young birds and sit in trees staring down at the vibrant wetlands. More than 200 species of birds have been recorded on the peninsula . The area is also the home to a variety of small mammals, wading birds, marsh hawks, waterfowl, beavers, white-tailed deer and several types of reptiles and amphibians.

The hardwood forest consists of oaks, holly and hickory. Look for whistling swans, raptors and a wide variety of ducks that often raft in large numbers offshore in wide bays.

Inside the state park, birding is excellent. Spring is the time for waves of warblers passing through, and quacking waterfowls selecting mates and heading north to nesting grounds.

Seasonal naturalist programs are offered to school groups and to the general public. The park is raising funds to upgrade environmental education programming, and renovating and developing a recently ac-quired group of buildings for use as an environmental learning center.

Gunston Hall/history (small fee): When in the area, include a visit to the stately home of George Mason, father of the Bill of Rights (and the park's namesake). Gunston Hall was built in 1755 on land overlooking the Potomac River near Mt. Vernon.

The house, an outstanding example of colonial Virginia architecture, contains a fine collection of 18th century furnishings, a number of which belonged to the Mason family. Several outbuildings have been restored to illustrate daily life on the plantation. Visitors can walk through outstanding formal gardens, view a deer park, hike a rolling nature trail to the river, and enjoy interpretive exhibits in the visitor center.

In George Mason's time, Gunston Hall was a self-sufficient plantation of more than 5,000 acres, many of them devoted to growing wheat and tobacco. Groups of buildings on the grounds provided housing for servants and craftsmen, both free and slave, and their families.

Mason began construction of Gunston Hall before he brought William

Buckland from England in 1755 to complete the house and design the superb carvings. Gunston Hall was Buckland's masterpiece. Since this time the house has undergone extensive architectural study and research.

George Mason (1725-1792) was a noted political thinker and statesman whose writing and counsel played an important role in the founding of our country. He seldom left Gunston Hall and his family; his longest absence was the summer of 1787 when he stayed in Philadelphia to help write the Constitution. He exerted great influence on his friends, George Washington and Thomas Jefferson.

A prolific writer and scholar, Mason helped draft key documents fundamental to American government, the most important being the Virginia Declaration of Rights, which became the model for our federal Bill of Rights. Condorcet, a French philosopher, wrote of Mason: "The first Declaration of Rights that is entitled to be called such is that of Virginia. Its author is entitled to the eternal gratitude of mankind."

Mason's statement, "That all men are by nature equally free and independent and have certain inherent rights...namely, the enjoyment of life and liberty, with the means of acquiring and possessing property, and pursuing and obtaining happiness and safety," was written before Jefferson's Declaration of Independence.

The historic hall and museum are open 9:30 a.m. - 5 p.m. daily.

Hunting: In conjunction with the neighboring wildlife refuge, a managed shotgun-only deer hunt is offered annually. The entire park is closed for a few days to allow for the herd managing hunt. Call the park manager for details.

Insiders tip: Try a round of golf at the Pohick Golf Course, only minutes from the state park.

20 Natural Tunnel State Park
Land: 649 acres Water: Stream

Daniel Boone, in 1769, was probably the first white man to see the "eighth wonder of the world," as famed 19th century orator William Jennings Bryant called it. The 850-foot tunnel has been attracting sightseeers to the rolling mountains of southern Virginia for more than 100 years. Today, it's the focal point of the park offering, visitors not only a terrific view, but a modern swimming pool, camping picnicking, hiking, a visitor center, amphitheater and interpretive programs.

No one knows exactly how the tunnel was formed. The question of its age and origin continues to stir the imagination of naturalists, geologists and visitors alike. It's believed that the tunnel is more than one million years old. Scientific theories have been posed, but the actual means by which the tunnel formed remains a mystery. What is known is that Natural Tunnel is a wonder of nature. For centuries this rare passage has wound its way through a tall mountain of limestone and dolostone to emerge into a crater-like amphitheater that is more than one-half mile around its rim and more than

300 feet above the tunnel's entrance.

Nestled within the scenic beauty of the Appalachian Highland, Natural Tunnel is both amazing and mystifying. The spectacular rock wall of the amphitheater at the south portal or awe-inspiring overlooks enable the visitor to appreciate the grandeur of the tunnel and its dramatic surroundings.

Two geologists, Robert E. Milici and Herbert P. Woodward, have proposed theories as to how Natural Tunnel came to exist. Although their ideas differ in the final analysis, they are based on the same fundamental principle. Milici and Woodward agree that the shifting land mass prompted the rising of the ancient Appalachian mountains. This exerted tremendous pressure on rock layers in southwest Virginia and caused faults or cracks to form. Glenita Fault is exposed the length of the Natural Tunnel.

Both geologists believe that groundwater barring carbonic acid from decaying plant life percolated through crevices along Glenita Fault. This dissolved the surrounding limestone and dolomite bedrock and started the formation of the gaping tunnel. The action created caves, sinkholes, disappearing streams and underground drainage. Then, what is now greenish-blue Stock Creek was probably diverted underground to continue carving the tunnel slowly over many centuries. The sheer walls of the craggy tunnel show evidence of prehistoric life, and many fossils can be found in the creek bed and the tunnel walls.

Lt. Col. Stephen H. Long explored the site in 1831, 60 years after Boone first saw it as he was blazing the Wilderness Trail. He was the first to write about it in a geology journal in 1832. The surrounding areas and tunnel were mined for saltpeter (potassium nitrate) during the Civil War to make gunpowder. Evidence of the mining can still be seen from the Lover's Leap self-guided trail. In 1890 Southern Atlantic and Ohio Railroad arrived and, making use of the natural land form, laid tracks through the tunnel. In 1906 Southern Railway acquired the tracks and created a passenger line, the Natural Tunnel line, that went through the tunnel. Large coal deposits were discovered in the area shortly thereafter, and although they no longer carry passengers, trains continue to this day carrying coal through the huge, dark rock tunnel.

An area with this type of topography is referred to as "karstland." The park is an incredible example of the rock formation that was formed in the Pleistocene Epoch. The public is not allowed to enter the tunnel for safety reasons. The Commonwealth acquired the tunnel and 100 surrounding acres in 1967 from the Natural Tunnel Chasm and Cavern Corporation (they operated a lodge and restaurant here) to establish the state park. Since, about 500 acres were added. The park opened in 1971.

About 250,000 people annually visit Natural Tunnel, with 25,000 guests riding the chairlift.

Information and Activities

Natural Tunnel State Park
Route 3, Box 250
Duffield, VA 24244
(540) 940-2674

Directions: In Scott County, 13 miles north of Gate City and 20 miles north of Kingsport, Tenn. To get there, take U.S. Route 23 to Route 871. Travel one mile east on Route 871 to the park entrance. A soft drink machine is at the railroad depot-style park office. Inside the park office, some Natural Tunnel Ladies Auxiliary cookbooks are sold. Other small railroad-related souvenirs are also offered at the park office.

Climbing and repelling are not allowed at the park.

Emergency number: Fire/sheriff/rescue, 386-9111

Visitor center: The modern visitor center is at the trailhead of a fenced walkway that travels above the tunnel, offering a spectacular elevated view. Inside the visitor center that has a vaulted ceiling are many professionally designed displays including information about park activities, legends and lore of the area, a long gun, the making of Natural Tunnel, natural history displays, railroad history, large historic photographs of steam engines, railroad switch lights, signal lamps, inspector lights, large oil cans, locomotive jacks, hands-on geology display, diorama of the tunnel and a train, marine fossils formed in the tunnel (the entire area was once an ancient sea), gift shop with lots of railroad-related items and souvenirs, and other

193

Lover's Leap.

Natural Tunnel's huge opening.

interpretive displays. A video is also shown that details the history and formation of the tunnel.

One of the most interesting displays is about the brown recluse and black widow spiders. The two species are embedded in plastic and sit side-by-side so visitors can compare these two poisonous spiders.

Railroads helped make the tunnel a favorite destination. Samples of railroad track teach visitors that all trains aren't created equal. There are many rail gauges. The small gauge, or T-rail, came into use in America long before rail service reached western Virginia. The smallest rails were used for mining or industrial spurs. The medium gauge rail was used as equipment size increased. The common main line rail through Natural Tunnel during the Mallet-era was 100-pound rail, as measured per linear foot of rail. These 39-foot lengths of rail were joined by bolted angle bars. The large gauge rail used today are in the 132-136 pound range, and are welded together in a seamless strand running miles in length.

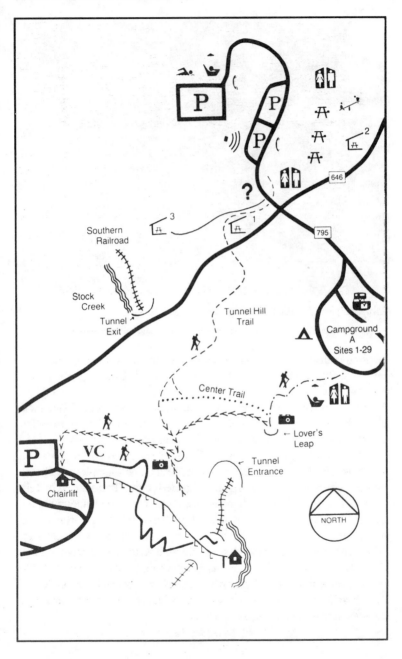

The chairlift takes riders to the floor of the tunnel.

Unseen are improvements in metallurgy that strengthen and prolong the life of the rail. There are example of these three types of rail in the visitor center.

Campground: Natural Tunnel has 22 camping sites; 18 have water and electric hooks-ups. Four of the sites are for tents. The newer, well-maintained campground is rolling, but open, offering little shade. Two swings and climber are at the end of the loop and near a trailhead. Firewood is available by the bundle. Each site has steel ground-mounted fire rings, gravel, hard-surfaced pads and picnic tables. Site 18 is a pull-through. Tent sites 19-22 are accessible down a set of stairs to level spots below the grade of the rest of the sites. The campground is open March to December.

Chairlift: The 536-foot chairlift ride descends 230 feet. Opened in May 1989, the twin-seat lift carries riders from the visitor center parking area to the breath-taking floor of the tunnel's natural amphitheater for a small fee. The chairlift is open Memorial Day to Labor Day seven days a week, and on weekends during the spring and fall.

Hiking: The park has seven walking trails, the longest 1.1 miles long. They lead to the tunnel floor, Lover's Leap, Tunnel Hill and Gorge Ridge. A 500-foot boardwalk and observation deck provide accessibility to guests with disabilities.

Gorge Ridge Trail (.3 mile), blazed in yellow, is moderately difficult and connects the campground with the main features of the park. From the campground, the trail follows Purchase Ridge to Lover's Leap, around the visitor center and the beginning of the trail to the Natural Tunnel. Along your hike, notice the difference between the open fields of the campground and the wooded trail. Wild grasses, young trees and spring wildflowers populate the open campground where the sunlight is strong and direct. In the moist shaded areas of the trail you will find ferns and thick ground cover.

Lover's Leap Lookout, which is at the crest of the tunnel opening, has a spectacular view of the deep gorge. A four-foot-tall wire fence and stone retaining wall are along the entire length of the moderately difficult ascending trail. The trail has many switchbacks and stairs.

The Tunnel Trail (.3 mile) is a 500-foot boardwalk and path that makes its way down the steep gorge through a series of switchbacks to the flat gorge floor. There are several resting places along the way that are outfitted with wood benches. The trail leads to an observation deck at the mouth of the dark tunnel. From here you can peer into the black hole and see the polished rails that are still used daily and the greenish-gray color of the rock that forms the roof of the tunnel. It's easy to imagine the steam trains that once huffed and puffed through the dark tunnel carrying people, coal and industrial products.

One of the things that strikes visitors to the mouth of the cave is how quiet it is at the base of the gorge. Except for the trickle of the stream, the sounds are muffled. The Spring Hollow Trailhead is off of Route 646.

Day-use areas: A broad and rolling mowed picnic area surrounds the pool and amphitheater. Many picnic tables and pedestal grills are scattered under trees and near a gray rest room building and angular picnic shelters. Also in the day-use area, along a ridge, is some quality play apparatus including climbers and swings. The park has four pavilions, about 100 picnic tables and two rest rooms.

The visitor center interprets the history of the region and railroads.

One of the nicest amphitheaters in the state park system is near the swimming pool. The stage and backstage building have vertical cedar siding, a wide performance area and five rows of benches and terraced seating formed by landscape timbers and earthwork. The theater can seat up to 2,000 people and is used for interpretive programs, performances and special events.

Swimming pool: Opened in 1983, the 5,400-square-foot, junior Olympic-size pool, a large shake-shingled bathhouse and concession building are open daily from Memorial Day to Labor Day 10 a.m. - 6 p.m., except Sunday when it closes at 7 p.m. The grill closes one hour before the L-shaped pool closes. The pool has comfortable lounge chairs scattered around its deck and grassy spaces inside the fenced area. The pool has two diving boards and a covered patio area that can accommodate up to 15 picnic tables. No coolers, food or drinks are allowed into the pool complex. A bike rack is near the entrance of the pool.

Insiders tip: The walk up to Lover's Leap and the story of the lovers who once plunged from the cliff are scenic and interesting and scenic.

21 New River Trail State Park
57-mile-long trail

The 57-mile stretch of old railroad bed is a ribbon-like multi-use trail that tracks along the shining waters of New River.

The twisting and turning trail travels through mountains and valleys, past Shot Tower Historical State Park, crosses 30 bridges and trestles, and winds through a 229-feet-long tunnel and a shorter one. The longest bridge, at Fries Junction, is more than 1,000 feet long and is at least 40 feet above the flowing river. Bikers, horseback riders and walkers also meander across a stone arch and near plenty of convenience stores, and skirt farmlands and picnic spots, past bike rentals, flowing springs, dams, campground, small towns and pulloffs. You'll also see remnants of mines that once flourished in this part of the state.

Much of the trail, about 30 miles of it, parallels the banks of the New River, which isn't so new. The placid river got its name in colonial times when Southwestern Virginia was called New Virginia. It is one of the few rivers in the world that flows north. Geologists believe the river is more than 350 million years old. Some experts says it is the second oldest river in the world.

The old railroad that once clattered along the way was called the Cripple Creek. It operated in the late 1880s and huffed and puffed through the hills and valleys carrying iron and lead from remote mines to industrial centers throughout the state. The area was once peppered with blast furnaces, huge stockpiles of minerals and ore. Rough and tumble "boom" towns sprouted up near the tracks and along the river. The boisterous history of the area is a topic for another time, but much of its flavor can still be detected along the route.

As the mines declined, the Norfolk and Southern Corporation abandoned the rail line and gave the right-of-way to the state for development of the rail trail in 1986.

Information and Activities

New River Trail State Park
Route 1, Box 81X
Austinville, VA 24312
(540) 699-6778

Directions: In Western Virginia, the 57-mile trail can be accessed in Carroll, Grayson, Pulaski and Wythe counties. It stretches from Fries to Pulaski. The trail is open 8 a.m. until dark every day.

New River Trail: Two public campgrounds, Buck and Byllesby Dam, and a private campground operate on the southern and middle sections of the trail. One trailside campground has overnight accommodations for horses.

Rest rooms and picnic areas are along the trail.

Outfitters along the linear trail offer bike, tube and canoe rentals.

Access: There are too many access points and parking lots to detail. From Draper Station to Galax Station, trail users will find lots of places to get on the trail. Call the park office for a brochure that details mileages.

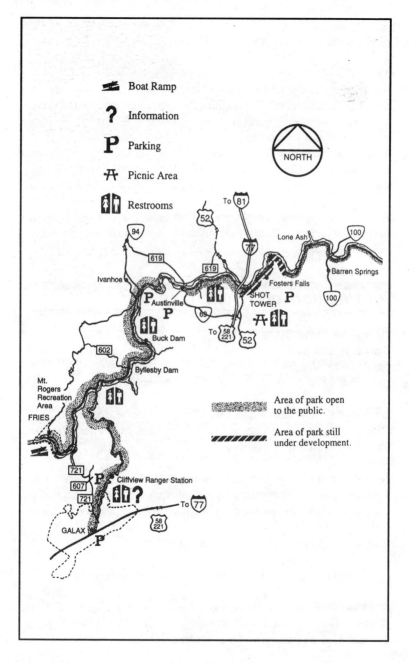

The 57-mile-long trail is popular with walkers, bikers and equestrians.

Horse trailers: May be parked at Shot Tower (where the New River Trail State Park office is), Cliffview and Draper.

Insiders tips: Galax is the "World's Capital of Old-Time Mountain Music." Tangent Outfitters is one of the larger outfitters who offer canoe trips of various lengths, shuttle service, paddle and mountain bike combined trips, and overnight trips. Call them at (703) 674-5202.

22 Occoneechee State Park

Land: 2,690 acres Water: Buggs Island Lake, 48,000 acres

The park is on Virginia's largest lake, Buggs Island Lake, also referred to as John H. Kerr Reservoir.

In 1839, William Townes settled along the Roanoke River and built a plantation known as Occonechee (original spelling). The sprawling 3,105-acre plantation included the Occoneechee Island, a huge two-story, 20-room house that was flanked by two annexes and many other buildings. The wealthy Townes owned a popular tavern in Boydton and imported fine thoroughbred race horses from England.

The Occonechee Plantation was a village in itself. The many buildings surrounding the main house included a kitchen, ice house, smokehouse, servants' quarters and a stable. Slave quarters and the overseer's house were a short distance from the main house. The plantation was best known for its spectacular terraced and formal gardens. The five terraces, with thick boxwoods on each corner and along the brick path, stretched the entire length of the garden.

Steps lead from one terrace to another. The upper two terraces were lined with white, pink, red and violet roses. The lower terraces were planted with crepe myrtle and Osage orange. Daffodil, spice and Japonica bushes, and periwinkle were also abundant throughout the highly-manicured garden.

When Townes died in 1876, the estate was divided among his children and workers. To his former slaves he gave four acres of land or its value in money. His maid also received a small amount of land or its value in money. The remainder of the lavish estate was divided among his children and grandchildren. William Townes Jr. inherited the house and grounds along with much of the fertile land. Sometime in the late 1870s or early 1880s, he sold the land to Dempsey Grave Crudup. Dempsey and his wife Novella and son Nathaniel Barter lived at the plantation until 1898, when the house caught fire on Christmas Eve and burned to the ground. Authorities attributed the fire to Christmas tree candles.

Today, visitors can walk around the plantation, view the terraces and see remains of the buildings along a self-guided trail.

Information and Activities

Occoneechee State Park
500 Occoneechee Park Road
Clarksville, VA 23927
(804) 374-2210

Directions: The park is 1.5 miles east of Clarksville on U.S. Route 58. Inside the park office are some small displays of arrowheads and other projectile points found on park property. The park office has a comprehensive list of area restaurants, lodging, marinas and attractions.

Emergency numbers: Sheriff, 374-2154; fire, 374-5411.

Campground: Two of the three campgrounds are open, offering about 100 sites, centrally located bathhouses with hot showers and flush toilets. A limited number of the sites have electrical hook-ups. Campground C has

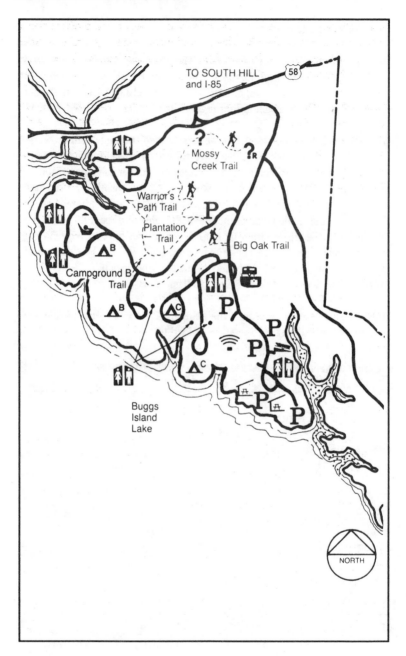

TO SOUTH HILL
and I-85

58

Mossy
Creek Trail

Warrior's
Path Trail

Plantation
Trail

P

Big Oak Trail

Campground B
Trail

B

Buggs
Island
Lake

NORTH

most of the tent sites and is closest to the lake. Campground B offers plenty of places for medium-sized RV rigs to park for a long relaxing weekend. Sites have gravel and grass pads, steel fire rings and picnic tables. Some of the picnic tables are made of concrete.

Sites 1-6 in the B section have a partial lake view and are near the showerhouse. A soft drink machine and drinking fountains are at the burgundy-trimmed showerhouse. The showerhouse also has two outdoor showers. At the end of the loop is site 7, which is private and above the lake on a high bank. Inspect sites carefully for levelness and size. Sites 19, 34 and others are walk-in sites off the road several yards into the woods. Some of the walk-in sites are near the water, shady and private. Tent sites 42, 44, 47, 48, 49, 51 and 52 are near the beach, along a cove and private. Walk-in sites 54 and 55 are private, down a wooded path and away from other sites and the road.

Campground C, according to staff, is the most popular. Sites 1-11 are small and along a narrow gravel road that is densely shaded. Sites have utility hookups. Sites 12-21 are also shaded and sought after by campers with medium-sized RV rigs. A modern showerhouse and level and large sites are in this section of the C loop. Sites 17 and 20 are the closest to the showerhouse in this loop. Sites 17 and 18 are along a cove with a view of sandy banks and the tree-lined lakeshore in the distance. Access to the water from these two sites is easy. Some of the sites in this loop are on a slight incline; inspect them carefully before pulling your rig in.

Sites 22-35 in the C loop are shady, but there are some sites where the sun filters through the tall canopy of leaves and branches. Site 23 is a a pull-through and terrific for large RVs. Many of the sites in this section have a partial view of the lake in the distance. Site 24 is more open than the others, offering some filtered sunlight and oversized pad. Sites in the 30s are near the showerhouse.

John H. Kerr Reservoir: Occoneechee and Staunton River state parks are on the huge reservoir that extends more than 39 miles up the Roanoke River along 800 miles of wooded, cove-studded shoreline. The Army Corps of Engineers opened the dam that generates hydroelectric power in 1953. To generate power, water from the reservoir flows through the gate-controlled pen stocks, rotates the turbines in the powerhouse and dis-

There's many shoreline campsites at the scenic park.

charges through the draft tubes of the river channel below. The turbines are connected to generators which produce electric power. The electric current is increased in voltage by large transformers for transmission away from the project.

Lake levels and current information are available by calling (804) 738-6371.

The Corps manages the lake in cooperation with private and other public agencies. Facilities around the huge lake include three major marinas, 24 launching ramps, 16 campgrounds, 22 wildlife management areas, lakeside day-use areas, boat repair, fueling stations, lodging, restaurants and much more. The entire lake and surrounding area are well-known for good roads, campsites, concessions and things to do for the whole family.

Fishing: South of campground C is one of the most productive shoreline fishing areas on the lake. Shoreline anglers also do well in the vicinity of both launching ramps in the park. Below the dam, the water can be muddy and the fishing slow. Many crappie anglers use live baits at night for the best results. Registered campers only are allowed to fish in the campground.

Serious bass anglers should probe deeper waters using plugs and larger plastic worms. The Corps has a lake map that depicts lake depth, channels markers, seaplane operation areas, public recreation areas and boat launches.

The immense reservoir is an excellent year-round fishery. It is very deep, especially in the channel and in front of the dam. Any shallow water is limited to the immediate shoreline. Deep fishing should focus on underwater structures that hold fish. They include old road- and creekbeds. Many local anglers say that feeder streams offer good action much of the year. Try points and feeder streams like the Dan, Roanoke and Hyco rivers, and Buffalo, Eastland, Grassy and Bluestone creeks.

The lake contains good populations of largemouth bass, striped bass, carp, catfish, sunfish and crappies. Increasing catches of walleye and white bass during the early spring are being taken on small jigs with twister-tails or minnows. Locals say white and yellow jigs are the best at this time of the year.

Boating: The unit has two launching ramps, one near Route 58 and a broad cove, the other a small launching ramp at the south end of the park. Any size boat and motor may be used on the lake.

The main launching ramp, near Route 58, is equipped with a small rest room building and floating wooden courtesy docks. These launching ramps are hard-surfaced and have a more gentle grade than the southern launching ramp.

The small, two-lane, hard-surfaced ramp at the south end of the park is on a narrow cove. This launch is steep, best suited for four-wheel-drive tow vehicles or launching of small aluminum fishing boats. The lake's shoreline and feeder creeks are terrific routes to paddle with a canoe.

Hiking: The plantation interpretive trail (1.2 miles, easy loop) has small signs along its course that winds through aged gardens. You will learn that plantation was a term used for any large self-sufficient farm establishment. A plantation usually included an icehouse, blacksmith shop, pottery shop and carpenter shop. A tutor was often retained to educate the children.

To prepare the untamed land for farming, colonists adopted the Indian method of clearing timber. A girdle of bark was cut from each tree and the tree was left to die. Dead wood would then be burned and seeds were sown along the hillsides between the stumps.

Hikers along the trail will also read about how in the late 1600s a sudden rise in tobacco prices made tobacco farming extremely profitable. Farmers wanting cheap labor to work the fields began buying slaves from English traders. By the late 1700s, during the struggle for independence from England, some Virginians began to understand that owning slaves while fighting for their own freedom was a bold contradiction. Opposition grew. By 1774 importing slaves became illegal in Virginia.

Thomas Jefferson, although a slave owner himself, summed up the rising sense of uneasiness in the book, *"Notes on Virginia,"* in 1782. "Can the liberties of the nation be thought secure when we have removed their only firm basis...that liberties are a gift of God?" Despite the rising concern of many, slavery continued until the signing of the Emancipation Proclamation in 1863.

A 35-feet-deep hand-dug well that is along the gently grassy trail. Using only shovels, grubbing picks 3-feet-wide, and a bucket, the well took days of back-breaking labor to dig, line with stone and set with mortar. Wells like this one were essential to plantation life. Since there was no indoor plumbing, wells were the only dependable source of water for cooking. bathing and washing clothes. On cold mornings, buckets of water were drawn from the well and warmed over a roaring fire in the kitchen. In the heat of the summer, cool water was drawn and splashed gratefully on sweat-soaked faces. A small drawing at the old well shows the wood crib structure, buckets and rope.

Near the well is a pit that was once an icehouse, and a sign that depicts the layout of the garden, fences, outbuildings and the huge house. At this sign you are standing at the first terrace of an extensive five-terrace garden built more than 100 years ago. From this point you can look at the profile of the land and see the wide stop-like terraces that were once thickly planted with ornaments and flowering plants. The trees with yellow-orange bark are Osage orange and native to the south-central United States. They are named for the Osage Indians, who often used the hard wood to make bows and war clubs. The bark was also used to produce a simple yellow dye. Farmers frequently use Osage orange trees for hedges and fences. When trimmed, they form a thorny barrier against livestock that was said to be "horse-high, bull-tough and pig thick." The milky sap from the round fruit may cause a rash in some people.

The park maintains three other short and easy trails at the north end of the tract. The trails are near the campground.

Day-use areas: Across the lake from the water tower is the grassy amphitheater, where various programs are offered during the summer. Picnic areas near the boat launching ramp have a shelter, pedestal grills, drinking water and nearby rest rooms. Many of the picnic areas have wonderful views of the shimmering lake, boats passing by and the wooded rolling hills of the Piedmont. One volleyball court is open during the summer. The day-use areas are pleasant and under-used—great, uncrowded park for your next family reunion. The park has a few pieces of playground equipment.

Nature: The tract is dotted with bluebird nesting boxes mounted on metal posts. The birds have made a dramatic comeback and pairs can often be seen during the nesting season gathering insects for fledglings. Seasonal naturalists offers night hikes, Indian heritage programs, tours of the plantation and junior ranger programs.

Topography of the area is characteristic of the northern Piedmont Plateau, with gently rolling hills occasionally dissected by deep drainages. Sections of the immediate area are managed for pulp and saw timber interspersed with small farms of tobacco, soybeans, wheat and corn. Some 50,000 acres surround the reservoir, with 40,000 acres open to hunting.

The region's habitats include oak and hickory; upland hardwoods and pine; loblolly, short-leaf and Virginia pine; and bottomland hardwoods, willow and pin oaks, green ash and sweetgum.

Bald eagles winter in the area, while osprey take up residence in the summer, fishing the lake and nesting along the secluded shoreline. A birding checklist is available from the Corps' office.

Hunting: Game species found on the 40,000 acres around the lake include deer, wild turkey, bobwhite quail, mourning doves, gray squirrel, cottontail rabbit, fox and raccoon. Resident waterfowl species include wood duck, black duck and mallard. Hunting is allowed in designated areas only.

History of Occoneechee Indians: Early records indicate that the Occoneechee Indians occupied the Roanoke River bluffs for more than 400 years. In the mid-1600s, they operated as middlemen in the thriving trade between the Virginia settlement and other Indian tribes. Rumor quickly spread that the Occoneechee, in an effort to preserve their trade monopoly, were intimidating and threatening many outside traders. They were even accused of murder.

In 1676, Nathaniel Bacon, in response to attacks on white settlers by Susquehanna Indians and other tribes, persuaded the aggressive Occoneechee to attack the Susquehanna. However, Bacon quarreled with the Occoneechee Chief Rosseechee, resulting in an armed conflict that nearly wiped out the Occoneechee. Shortly after this crushing defeat, the Occoneechee along with the Tutelo and Saponi tribes moved to North Carolina, where they remain to this day.

Insiders tips: Looking for arrowheads is a popular pastime at the park. Please look, but don't collect. The U.S. Army Corps of Engineers also operates campgrounds, swimming beaches and boat launches around the lake. Occonneechee Indians return to the park one weekend each May for their annual Native American Heritage Festival and Pow Wow.

23 Pocahontas State Park
Land: 7,604 acres   Water: Three lakes

Pocahontas is one of the most popular—and the largest—state parks in the system. Its broad entranceway is inviting and leads visitors directly to the park's offerings, which include a huge modern swimming pool, boating, hiking, bicycling, hiking and camping. The park is only 20 miles from the state capital, Richmond.

The park was the site of two Civilian Conservation Corps camps that housed a force of more than 300 men who constructed the recreation areas along Swift Creek. From the spring of 1935 to the summer of 1937, the workers built three group camps, barracks, maintenance buildings, water and sewer system, toilets, picnic shelters, campground, foot trails, day-use areas, blacksmith shop, amphitheater and three dams (one of which created Swift Creek Lake). All of these facilities except the barracks, group camp No. 7 and the blacksmith shop, remain in some form today. One of the most interesting remains of the CCC camp is an old bell that was used to warn men in case of emergencies. Today the bell is symbolically maintained as a warning to us to protect the sprawling park.

Pocahontas State Park was not named after the Walt Disney movie, staff was quick to point out. The name Pocahontas actually means "playful on." Nor does the park have any direct history dealing with the Indian woman. It was named by a third-grader in a "name the park contest" in the late 1930s. The lucky student won a $50 saving bond for suggesting the popular name. As it turns out, the park is the closest state park to the area where Pocahontas grew up.

According to legend Pocahontas, daughter of Chief Powhatan, leader of the federation of Algonquin tribes, both fell in love with Captain John Smith and saved his life. According to the story, Smith was captured by Powhatan's warriors and sentenced to death. Lovely Pocahontas, whose actual name was Matoaka, begged her powerful father to spare him. He did.

Pocahontas eventually married John Rolfe, a noted early settler and tobacco grower from Jamestown in 1614. They had one child named Thomas, then set sail for England. She was one of the first native Americans to visit London. Sadly, during her stay, she contracted smallpox and died in 1617.

The park's first year of operation was in 1941 and more than 250,000 visited. The park is just west of the Fall Line, the geographical point where the lush rolling hills of the Piedmont drop-off to the tidal influences of the coastal plain.

Information and Activities

Pocahontas State Park
10301 State Park Road
Chesterfield, VA 23838-4713
(804) 796-4255

Directions: In Chesterfield County, about 20 miles south of Richmond. To get there, take Exit 61 off I-95, then west on Route 10 to Route 655, Beach Road; or take Exit 67, north on Route 150 to Route 10; go east to Beach Road.

Visitor center: A new CCC museum is planned by renovating the old visitor center. It will be equipped with natural history displays, CCC artifacts and other educational materials. Some interesting photographs of the CCC camp, line drawings of their work, photo of the dam, tools used by Depression-era workers, clothing, water jugs and a variety of historical artifacts are in the center. A new environmental education center is also set to be constructed by the lake near the CCC museum and expanded day-use areas.

A path from the visitor center winds to an amphitheater and overlook of the lily pad-filled lake.

Campground: The current campground features 34 sites with grills and a centrally located rest room and showerhouse. Hilly and shady sites are on varying elevations and suitable for small RV rigs and tents.

When they are dry, sites 1-17 are shoreline camping sites ideal for tents. These sites are subject to flooding, however, they are equipped with steel ground-mounted fire rings and picnic tables. Site 17 is at the end of the waterside loop and offers extra space and privacy.

Site 18 is private, perched on a hillside and oversized with a view of a wooded valley. Site 34, on a knoll, is also private, set off by itself and airy. Some of the sites in the 18-34 loop are walk-ins and have timbers that outline the pads. Many also have steel lantern hangers.

A new campground planned for the park will be along a ridge above the lake.

Fishing: The 150-acre Swift Creek Lake is stocked with warmwater species including panfish, bass and channel catfish. This lake may have restrictions, such as catch and release periods. Crappie and bluegill are most often caught in the aging lake. Anglers typically use live bait and small, colorful jigs and twister tails in the spring and early summer before the water warms too much. A few trophy largemouth bass have been taken from the reservoir.

Serious local anglers recommend renting or bringing your own boat and fishing in deeper waters near the dam. A variety of underwater structures have been placed in the lake over the years. Local tackle and bait shops can offer tips on where to find the fish.

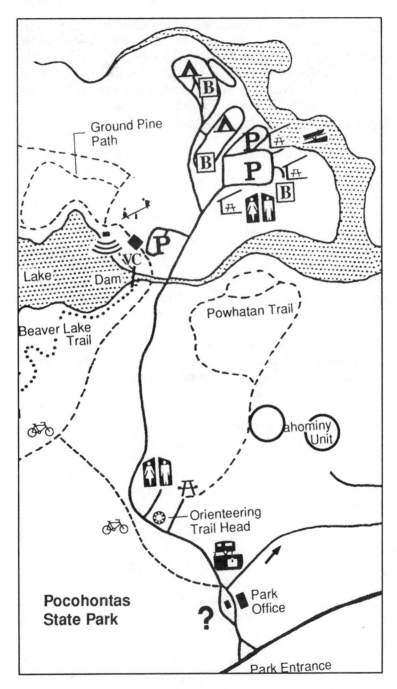

Ground Pine Path

VC

Lake

Dam

Beaver Lake Trail

Powhatan Trail

ahominy Unit

Orienteering Trail Head

Park Office

Pocohontas State Park

?

Park Entrance

"Waterskeeters" pedal boats can be rented to explore the shady coves.

You may fish from shore in most places in the park. Camping anglers may also want to travel to the Appomattox River.

Catch and release fishing is popular along the bank in the campground. Both Swift Creek Lake and Beaver Lake are silting in. In fact, swimming was stopped in the lakes in 1981 because of the enriching waters. That's when the jumbo swimming pool opened. Beaver Lake is becoming a freshwater marsh.

Boating: A tiny building with an oversized roof and porch rents rowboats, green canoes and pontoon-style pedal boats. The unique yellow pedal boats are called "waterskeeters" and are a favorite for cruising the shallows and carving a path through floating lily pads along the tree-lined cove. The boats have a clever hand-operated rudder that controls their direction. Canoes and rowboats can be rented by the day, pedal boats by the hour. Lifejackets are provided at the boat concession that is open 10 a.m. 7 p.m. daily during the summer. A small boat ramp offers access to Swift Creek Lake.

Hiking: Aside from an orienteering course used by staff to teach compass and map reading skills, the park features five miles of trails around Beaver Lake. The park has six trails totaling more than 10 miles in length.

Ground Pine Path (1 mile) is the park's 16-stop interpretive trail. The loop-style trail is gently rolling tracking along the lakeshore to hilltops. An interpretive booklet that accompanies the trail is available at the contact station. Numbered posts along the trail correspond with numbered sections in the illustrated booklet. Take your time, use your senses and you'll enjoy this easy and educational hike.

Along the trail you'll learn about wild grape that uses stringy tendrils to twine around twigs and into the cracks of trees, trying to get its leaves up into the full sunlight at the top of the forest canopy. These sometimes thick vines produce tart grapes in the early fall. The area is a favorite for staff, as well as for opossums, raccoons, songbirds and foxes.

Many loblolly trees are found in this section of the park. They thrive in moist conditions along streams and river banks. Indians collected the six-inch needles of the fast-growing tree and boiled them, making a pungent tea that was rich in vitamin C. Today, the tree is a valuable pulp and lumber commodity that is farmed in huge plantations such as those along the park's bicycle trail. When the plate-like bark sections are about the size of a man's hand, the tree is about 70 years old.

Along Beaver Lake hikers will see—and maybe smell—fragrant water lilies that float on the surface, but are rooted in the shallows. Look for fat bullfrogs that use the thick leaves as a gently rocking sunning deck. Near stations four and five are the wispy sensitive ferns and pawpaw trees that have banana-like fruit that are about four inches long. After the first hard frost, the fruits can be picked and eaten or cooked into custard-like desserts. Watch for bandit-like raccoons in the evening, feeding in the 40-foot-tall trees.

Other plants in the area include flowering dogwood, American holly, ground pine, huckleberry, Virginia creeper, blueberry, beech, black and white oak and many other hardwoods. Both the flowering dogwood and American holly live in the understory because they are shade tolerant, able to survive on the weak sunlight that filters through the dense canopy of the surrounding forest.

If you need to brush your teeth, stop at marker No. 9. Sassafras, known by its double-lobed or "mitten-shaped" leaf and tea-making potential, also produces twigs that can be used to scrub your teeth. The twigs have a distinctive flavor that hints of root beer and lemon.

Some huge towering beech trees stand like sentinels along the trail. Their gray, ghost-like bark and thick-reaching branches can quickly kill competing trees. Beeches have evolved the ability to grow well in dry, thick soil.

Ground pine, also called running cedar, looks as if it may be related to the pines or cedars, but it is actually a primitive plant known as club moss. Its scientific name "Lycopodium" is derived from the Greek word meaning "wolf foot." These plants are known from fossil records to have lived 400 million years ago and perhaps earlier. The plant's long, branching stem lies on or just above the ground. The pale candelabra-like branches jut into the air and bear spores for reproduction. Ground pine was once widely used for Christmas wreaths and decoration.

One of the fastest-growing trees in the area is sweetgum. The tree has star-shaped leaves that turn a spectacular scarlet color in the fall. The resinous sap gives this tree its name. Indians and settlers found hardened clumps of its sap pleasant to chew. Its wood is not strong, but is used for veneers. The prickly seeds and gum balls are eaten by more than a dozen species of songbirds, turkeys, bobwhite quail, chipmunks and gray squirrels.

Biking: Bike riders are welcome on park roads, forest roads and designated bike trail north of Route 655 only. The five-mile biking trail is also open to hikers and wheelchairs. Bikes can be rented from the swimming pool concession stand by the house 10 a.m. - 6 p.m. daily.

The pleasant five-mile Old Mill Bicycle Trail winds through the dense woods and meanders counter-clockwise around the 24-acre Beaver Lake. The trail begins near the park entrance and follows Bottoms Forest Road deep into the multiple-use Pocahontas State Forest. The riding is generally easy and rolling, with wide trails for family rides and riders of all abilities.

In places the trail narrows, often through a tunnel of trees past hardwoods and towering pines. Many the dirt roads in the state forest are open to mountain bikes. These roads criss-cross the forest, forming a well-traveled network where many Richmond bikers ride.

Horseback trails: Trail riders are welcome on forest roads south of Route 655, which is Beach Road. Verification of an EIA (equine encephalitis) test is required.

Day-use areas: There are three reservable picnic shelters available in the area of the pool. Two horseshoe courts, volleyball courts and a small playground are between the pool and the small boat rental.

Swimming pool: Busloads of school children pack the 17,000-square-foot swimming pool at the end of the school year, and during the summer campers and day-users keep the waters churning. The pool, which looks like four tangent circles (much like a four-leaf clover) is one of the biggest outdoor pools in the state. Each of the circular sections has a slightly different depth. The huge parking lots have nearby rest rooms and soft drink machines. A well-used day-use area that has a scattering of picnic tables connects the parking area to the pool complex. The pool is open daily during the summer 10 a.m. - 7 p.m. There is a small fee and lockers are available. The modern gray bathhouse is open during these hours also.

The shady day-use areas along a hillside above the pool are the perfect places for a picnic and view of the pool, nearby paddleboat rental and snack concession. These amenities are connected by hard-surfaced walkways.

Wide cement decks with a few lounge chairs surround the pool and the foot-deep wading pool for youngsters. The wading pool is fenced and separate from the main pool. Two slides and two diving boards are busy with children splashing into the sparkling water.

The food concession serves hot dogs, cheeseburgers, soft drinks, ice cream, chicken sandwiches, nachos, fries and other snacks. The food concession, which has a shady eating area next to it, is open 10 a.m. - 7 p.m. daily during the summer.

Nature: Traditional outdoor education programs are offered at the park. Most programs are limited to Friday and Saturday nights including guided

Fire ring and cabin at the Algonquin Ecology Camp.

hikes, star watch, storytelling and stream walks.

Algonquin Ecology Camp: The popular camp has a lodging capacity from 28 to 112. A clean banquet hall, which is heated and air conditioned, can accommodate up to 150. There are four groups of small cabins with a lodge in four well-spaced areas. Each group of brown cabins has a toilet building, fire ring, and a centrally located showerhouse. The camp kitchen is fully equipped so that groups may do their own cooking or have food catered. The camp, which includes a meeting hall and outdoor recreation fields (court games), is rented by church youth groups, scouts, adult groups for retreats and non profit organizations. The camp is open April to November by reservation.

For three weeks each summer the camp is used by the Chesterfield County Parks and Recreation Department for a day camp. Programs for area youngsters include crafts, environmental education and natural history programming.

Staff says the lodges are a bit like "sleeping in a wooden tent." The facility is named for the Algonquin Indian nation that was once located in the area.

Organized groups can get help with environmental education programs from the state park staff.

Hunting: Generally flat, the hardwood and pine forests of the Pocahontas State Forest and park offer good small game and deer hunting. About 5,500 acres in the area are open to hunting. Turkey, dove, quail and rabbit are popular quarry. Waterfowl hunting on the lake is light.

Insiders tips: This is the biggest state park in the system, with the biggest pool in the system—bring your swimsuit. Tabb Monument is about 10 miles from the park off of Route 360. The Algonquin Camp, a well-maintained group lodging camp, is perfect for all types of groups to escape the urban environment.

24 Sailor's Creek Battlefield Historic State Park

Land: 221 acres

Sailor's Creek Battlefield Historical State Park was the scene of the last major battle in the Civil War in Virginia. Here on April 6, 1865, General Robert E. Lee, commander of all armies of the Confederate States of America, lost more than 8,000 men plus valuable supplies. The battle also left its scars on the Hillsman House, a white clapboard house that still stands at the small, significant historic park.

The park is nestled between tobacco farms, mixed woodlots, pine planta-tions and rocky fields. Hillsman House is the first thing you will see at the small history-based park. It is a simple structure, but rich in craftsmanship and history. It was built in the 1770s by Moses Overton. His relatives and descendants, who included James Moses Hillsman, lived in or near the house until it was designated a battlefield park in 1934. Hillsman's family was living in the residence at the outbreak of the battle.

Complete with thick operable shutters that have wrought-iron latches, the 1.5-story house has small dormer windows and is built from hand-hewn timbers fastened by wooden pegs, anvil wrought-iron nails and a variety of interesting ironwork. Other interesting architectural features include brick nogging daubed in clay, beaded weatherboarding and hard-crafted gutters made from heart pine. Each clapboard on the house has a hand-planed decorative bead.

Certainly the Hillsman House is a terrific handmade colonial structure. The house overlooks the battlefield and served as a Federal field hospital, where the wounded of both northern and southern commands were treated. In fact, blood stains remain on the floor, sad evidence of the fierce battle.

Behind the house is a large painting that depicts the battle lines, booming cannons, shying horses, crying wounded and the men in full charge across fields in the distance. Other information helps you visualize where Ewell's troops were located, the creek and the Hillsman House. Pit toilets and a cannon are also in the side yard of the white house. Try lifting up or pushing down on the cannon's barrel; it will give you an appreciation of how difficult it must have been to transport, aim and shoot the heavy weapon.

The Hillsman House is the eighth stop on the historic driving route called "Lee's Retreat." The route has interpretive signs and a colorful brochure that details those fateful few days as Lee's troops pulled back from Petersburg to Appomattox. Tune your radio to AM 1610 for more information, or call (800) 6-RETREAT for more information about Lee's Retreat. If you notice, the old highway historic marker signs spells Sailor's Creek with an "e," or "Sailer's Creek." I think I like their spelling best.

Information and Activities

Sailor's Creek Battlefield Historic State Park
c/o Twin Lakes State Park
Green Bay, VA 23942
(804) 392-3435

Directions: From State Route 307 (connecting highway between U.S. 360 and 460 at Farmville) to either Route 616 or 617. Sailor's Creek is about 8 miles from Twin Lakes State Park. Tours of the house are irregular; call for an appointment.

April 3, 1865: The days before the bloody battle were filled with tactics, events and challenges. When General Lee departed Petersburg and the Richmond area, he divided his troops into three columns—infantry, cavalry, artillery and wagons. His idea was to eventually regroup his forces several miles north of Blackstone at Amelia Court House.

But the troops had many delays, including the challenges of rain-soaked days, muddy roads and rain-swollen streams. The three weary columns rerouted constantly, winding across the hills and valleys searching for routes that were the easiest to travel. On one such maneuver, most of the wagon trains from Richmond were caught and destroyed by the Union Army.

At Amelia Court House, meanwhile, supplies scheduled to meet the converging troops failed to arrive, and Lee was forced to waste a day while his men foraged throughout the countryside. The unfortunate delay and lack of food gave the Union cavalry of General Phillip Sheridan time to entrench themselves seven miles below Amelia, along the railroad at Jetersville, thereby blocking Lee's route to Danville.

Forced to take his last alternative, Lee ordered his column to detour past the blockade and push westward toward Farmville, a village near the Southside Railroad. Lee thought he could get supplies from Lynchburg from this location.

The Battle of Sailor's Creek, April 6, 1865: The next day, still bearing in a westerly direction while pressed by Union cavalry and the infantry of the Sixth Corps, Lee rearranged his marching order for greater mobility and protect the remaining wagons. His new column alignments consisted of generals Longstreet, Mahone, Anderson and Ewell, the wagons, and finally General Gordon, whose duty it was to protect the supplies and serve as rear guard. The newly formed columns found it difficult to keep up with the marching pace and, as a result, slowed down only to become engulfed in the mire of the soft bottomland at Sailor's Creek. The lines were split without the knowledge of Lee, Longstreet or Mahone, who had marched to Rice, Virginia. Then came the "misunderstandings and confusion, compounded by omissions in communication." While the army (Anderson and Ewell), strung out along roads ankle deep in mud, struggled to keep moving, Union cavalry slashed at its sides and tore into the wagon trains.

In a desperate attempt to save the supplies, the two commanders ordered the wagons on a northerly detour, crossing Sailor's Creek near the Appomattox River. No one told Gordon who, in following General Lee's orders, trailed the wagon tracks and so moved out on the ensuing fight.

Anderson found this route blocked. As he and Ewell conferred on whether to attack or go around the Federals in front, Ewell's column was assaulted from the rear.

Under General Wright, Union troops waiting near the Hillsman House then charged Ewell's men, most of whom were artillery men, sailors and army clerks fighting the infantrymen. The Confederates repelled the attack, and, in return, counter-charged, moving into the sights of the Union artillery batteries. The heavy fire which followed halted the Confederates. Anderson's attack on the Union troops to his front failed, and his men were driven in on Ewell. Surrounded, Anderson and Ewell surrendered.

Meanwhile, downstream, General Gordon had also run into trouble. His cavalry was engaged in a sharp and bloody encounter with Union forces commanded by General George Armstrong Custer. Most of the wagons were abandoned or destroyed in the sloppy terrain of the bottomlands. Gordon and a few of his men managed to escape, but more than three-fourths of his column was captured.

By dusk, the Battle of Sailor's Creek was over. Lee had lost more than half his army, the largest number of men to ever surrender in a single action on this continent. With this drastic reduction in troops and supplies, Lee's situation was critical. His army lacked food and weapons. Seventy-two hours later, General Lee surrendered at Appomattox.

Insiders tips: The driving tour following Lee's retreat from Petersburg to Appomattox is dotted with interpretive signs and rich history. There are 20 stops along the winding route. Call (800) 6-RETREAT for a map and additional information.

25 Shot Tower Historic State Park

Thomas Jackson, builder of the Shot Tower, was born near Appleby, England, in 1762. He immigrated to America in about 1785 to work with Lead Mines in Austinville, Va. After a number of years he became a joint owner of the productive mines, and expanded to the construction of the unique tower and to making shot. The shot was used in guns of the period. Jackson operated the gravity-powered lead mold until his death in 1824.

Historians have wondered why Shot Tower was built here, rather than in Austinville near the mines. One reason often considered was the legal disputes between the co-owners of the mine, Jackson and David Pierce. Its was believed Jackson built Shot Tower here so he could be the sole owner.

However, the site itself has numerous other advantages. There was easy access to the river to cool the shot and later transport it. The steep bluff made digging the tunnel more practical and provided it with walk-in access. Also, proximity to a ferry made it an ideal location for commerce.

Jackson was also a skilled mechanic, a successful farmer and the owner of the main public ferry over the New River. Today, the Shot Tower stands as a monument to Jackson's enterprise and to the industry and creativity of a young and growing nation.

Lead mining began in this area after its discovery by Col. Chiswell in 1756. Daniel Boone, General Andrew Lewis and other famous colonial frontiersmen were known to have stopped at the "Lead Mines," as Austinville was then called. During this early period, the "Fincastle Resolutions," precursors of the Declaration of Independence, were written at the Lead Mines. After the American Revolution, the mines came under the control of Moses Austin, who gave his name to Austinville and, indirectly, to Austin, Texas. Moses' son, Stephen, known as the "Father of Texas," was born in Austinville, Va.

From 1800 to the time of the Civil War in 1861, the mines were involved in a series of legal battles and, finally, consolidation and incorporation. During the war, the mines were the chief domestic supplier of lead to the Confederacy under the name of Wythe Union Lead Mine Company. The company name had little effect in protecting the operation from raids, however; it was attacked twice by Union troops.

Information and Activities

Shot Tower Historical State Park
c/o New River Trail State Park
Route 1, Box 81X
Austinville, VA 24312
(540) 699-6778

Directions: The tower is off of U.S. Route 52, near where the highway crosses the New River in Wythe County. They can be reached by taking exit 24 on Interstate 77.

The tower itself is open 10 a.m. - 6 p.m. weekends during the summer.

Shot Tower: Built by Thomas Jackson in 1807, the technology it employed is as crude, but at the time, simple and effective. The round and oval shot it produced was commonly used by hunters to bag all types of game and to charge their rifles to defend their homesteads.

Shot Tower looks like a fortress. The walls are built of large, finely shaped stones which were quarried from a limestone deposit a mile away. The tower's walls are 2.5 feet thick, and the base of the tower is 20 feet square. The tower, which is on a steep bank of the New River, is 75 feet high. A lower shaft drops 75 feet from the tower floor to the river level.

When the tower was built, there were winding wooden stairs inside by which loads of lead were carried to the top room, containing a fireplace and chimney. Here lead was melted in a large kettle. The molten metal was carefully poured through sieves with meshes of varying size. The size of the mesh controlled the size of the shot produced. These hot droplets of lead fell to a large kettle of water 150 feet below. It was necessary for the shot to fall this distance to properly mold it round. The drop shaft was connected with a tunnel that led to the bank of the river, which provided a constant supply of water for the cooling kettle. After drying and sorting, the shots were ready for market.

Costs involved in this method would be prohibitive today, but this wasn't a consideration at that time because all of the work was done by slaves.

It is believed that the reason for the thick stone walls was to insure a constant temperature inside so that the shot, in its drop from the top to the bottom of the shaft, would not cool too quickly.

Shot Tower was donated to the Commonwealth of Virginia by the Lead Mines Ruritan Club and opened to the public in 1968 after extensive renovation. In 1981, the Shot Tower was designated as a National Historical Mechanical Engineering Landmark by the American Society of Mechanical Engineers.

Insiders tips: The tower is across the street from the New River Trail State Park office and trail access. Horse trailer parking is available at the park office. Foster Falls, a scenic area with historic buildings, is now part of the New River Trail. The property is planned for development. The dream is that some of the building may become a visitor center, bed and breakfast, offices and education centers.

26 Sky Meadows State Park
Land: 1,842 acres   Water: stream/pond

Sky Meadows is one of the best suited names for a state park in the system. Lush pastures, broad valleys and cattle are on each side of the road in to the hilly park. The gentle mountain scenery, intimate farmstead and spectacular spring wildflowers along the Piedmont rise to meet the mountains in northern Virginia. This pastoral park is a charmer.

The park features bridle and hiking trails, pack-in camping, scenic points, a few picnic sites and historic farmstead buildings. You won't find big crowds, a big lake, noisy boats or compact campgrounds at Sky Meadow. Only an hour from Washington, D.C., it is one of the prettiest parks in the state.

In 1713 Captain James Ball purchased from Lord Fairfax a 7,883-acre tract on the east side of the Blue Ridge south of Ashby Gap. When Ball died in 1754, his property was divided among his daughter and five grandsons. James Ball received 1,000 acres on which the present Sky Meadows State Park is located.

In 1780, Revolutionary War officer John Edmonds bought Ball's land. Edmond's son, George Edmonds, was given 250 acres of his father's land in 1798. George and his wife moved to the property, cleared land and built the log house and the wood-frame section of what is now the visitor center.

Isaac Settle, a postmaster, tavern keeper and merchant from nearby Paris, Va., in 1810 purchased a 171-acre part of the property that included the site of the wood-frame house. Soon Isaac built the stone section of the farmhouse of what is now the visitor center. He eventually gave the property to his son Abner as a wedding present in 1835. A typical middle class farmer of his time, he named the house Mount Bleak. The name was probably chosen because the stately building stands exposed on a windy hilltop. But the property transactions weren't over yet.

Abner Settle sold the farm after the Civil War to George Slater, who had been a member of Mosby's Rangers and fell in love with the area during the war. Slater and his son owned the farm for a long time, until 1928. From them the land changed hands several times until 1966, when a housing development was proposed that would have divided the area into 50-acre lots. Thanks to Paul Melon, the scenic park was saved from development. In 1975, Melon donated more than 1,130 acres to the state. More land has been added and the park opened to the public in 1983.

Information and Activities

Sky Meadows State Park
11012 Edmonds Lane
Delaplane, VA 22025-9508
(540) 592-3556

Directions: Two miles south of Paris, seven miles north of I-66 at the intersection of routes 17 and 10. Turn at Route 710 (Edmonds Lane) to enter the park. There is a small parking admission fee.

Visitor center: On a windy hilltop, the beautiful stone antebellum farmhouse with black shutters was built in the early 1800s. The lovely farmhouse features park offices, period furnishings and some educational information. The tan-trimmed house with stone entrance overlooks a rich

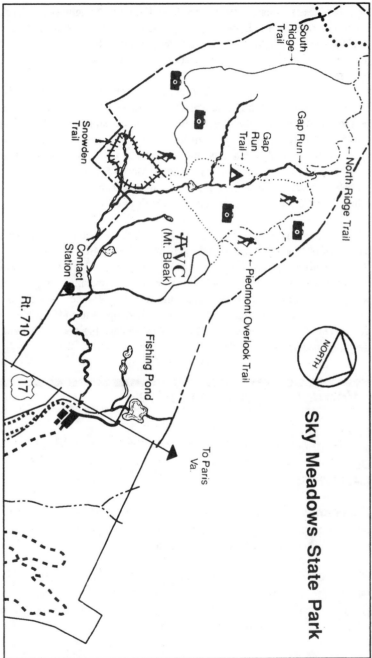

green valley dotted with grazing black cattle and scattered trees.

The stone house, is filled with period furnishings, including lovely wood furniture, a sewing machine, cooking utensils and dishes, rugs, a piano and other artifacts.

Log house: Behind the visitor center, chinked with white material, the tiny cabins has a huge field stone chimney. Planted around the ancient-appearing cabin are plantings of bergamot, lamb's quarter and members of the mint family. Inside are examples of simple log furniture, cast iron cookware, frame bed, sleigh and other period items.

The term log cabin often gives one the feeling of a small rough and ready structure built by people with much to do and little time and materials to do it. The typical Virginia cabin is made of stacked-together round logs with small windows or no windows at all. A "log house," on the other hand, denotes a building made of large well-fashioned logs properly cornered with spaces in between the logs chinked with moss or branches that were well-plastered with clay.

The windows were made of glass. There was a chimney, shingled roof and often more than one door in pioneer cabins. Log houses generally involved a higher degree of workmanship than wilderness log cabins. They tended to be higher, perhaps 10-12 logs tall. The extra logs formed a knee-wall, which meant there would be head room for a loft.

The log house at Sky Meadow was built in 1798 by George Edmonds after receiving 250 acres as a wedding present from his father. The log house demonstrates the influence of German craftsmen who defined the techniques for hewn logs and squared-off corners. They are also considered responsible for the development of Pennsylvania key notches found in this house. Pennsylvania corners provide a good system for shedding water and for locking the logs in place.

If you notice inside, the logs were marked with Roman numerals. If the log house was to be dismantled, it could be easily reassembled at another site. At an unknown time, the chinking at the Sky Meadow log house was replaced, but much of the clay and horse hair mixture can still be seen.

Historic log cabin is one of many buildings on site.

Ice house: Ice houses were part of American life until the early 1900s, when modern refrigeration became available. Ice cut from local ponds in January could last all summer if stored properly. The floors of the typical Virginia ice house were dirt with chestnut logs used to build up the side walls. Straw was laid on the floor, up the sidewalls and between the ice layers for maximum insulation.

To cut ice, the pond was first surveyed and boundary lines were marked with a hand-operated cutter. On large ponds, a horse-drawn cutter (scribe) was used to mark a grid pattern across the surface. Final cutting was accomplished with hand tools including long-bladed saws with jagged teeth, long-handled spades and fork bars. Using an ice hook, ice was moved into wagons and hauled to the ice house. The labor of hardy men in the cold winter enabled their families to enjoy refreshing ice drinks through the summer months.

Camping: Twelve primitive hike-in campsites can accommodate up to six persons each. No reservations are taken. Nonpotable water and pit toilets are available. Each camping site has a fire ring. Only dead wood on the ground can be collected for firewood.

Fishing: Children are welcome to fish in the small pond northeast of the stone visitor center. Lots of small bluegills and perch are easily taken on small jigs or live bait under a bobber.

Hiking: A 3.6-mile section of the Appalachian Trail is accessible in the park. This is one of the few public access points in the area and a popular camping and resting spot for long-distance hikers on the rugged mountain trail. In fact, many backpackers spend a couple of days in the park exploring the pastoral setting before heading back on to the long Appalachian Trail.

The park's highest point is 1,840 feet and the lowest 640 feet.

The Snowden Interpretive Trail has information signs about the area's natural history. The trail winds through a mature oak forest and along a road and fence row.

Gap Run Trail (1.2 miles) serves the camping area. South Ridge Trail (1.6 miles) follows an ascending road through a wooded area, past Snowden Manor and features views of the adjoining farmland. North Ride Trail (1.7 miles) is blazed in blue and tracks along a mountainside that was once a pasture. Areas of this trail can be rugged.

Using the hiking map available at the visitor center, hikers should find their way to the Piedmont Overlook, north of the visitor center. The view of the eastern edge of the Blue Ridge Mountains and the flatter Piedmont stretches for miles before you. It is one of the great state park views in Virginia.

Bridle trails: The park maintains five miles of bridle trails. The Lost Mountain loop (3 miles) is moderately difficult and scenic. Ask about horse stalls and overnight equestrian camping.

Day-use areas: Shade trees cover large areas behind the stone visitor center, offering cool picnic areas that are furnished with pedestal grills and tables. Several other outbuildings on the property house period farming and household implements. Drinking fountains and soft drink vending

Twelve primitive campsites and the Appalachian Trailhead are a short hike away.

machines are near the visitor center.

Although bikes are not allowed on park trails, the back country roads that weave through the valleys and along the green hillsides are terrific scenic routes. Cyclists could make the park their stop for lunch and a tour of the historic buildings. Route 688 is an especially appealing nearby road that takes travelers through a tunnel of trees and along a quiet countryside.

Nature: From the banks of a small stream to mountains and woodlots, Sky Meadow offers excellent birdwatching opportunities. Woodpeckers, ground dwellers and birds that frequent open fields all converge at the park. Look for mockingbirds, red-headed woodpeckers, raptors soaring overhead and tiny songbirds along fence rows and shrub lines.

White-tailed deer are abundant, and easily spotted at dusk. Search the distant edge of fields and you might see a fox or coyote on the hunt.

High meadows offer sprawling crops of sun-tolerant daisies. The rolling woodlands are dotted with fire pink, lady's slippers, columbine, skunk cabbage, yellow violets, wild geranium, ox eye daisies, yellow crownbeard, spotted touch-me-not, mullein, jack-in-the-pulpits, and corydailis and flowering shrubs. Trees around the farmhouse (visitor center) include plum, flowering crabapple, cherry, walnut, forsythia, lilac, dogwood, sourwood, pecan and cherry.

Interpretive programming: Sky Meadow has one of the most advanced outdoor learning and interpretive programs in the system. From farmhouse tours to birding and basket-making, the park has a program for any age or interest. Fun and educational programs include (some require a small fee) strawberry festival (late May), birding, Civil War weekends, orienteering, kid's fishing day, astronomy, spinning and weaving, many historical programs about the Civil War era, crafts (chair caning, rug-hooking, wool felting), owls, full moon hikes, and many interpretive hikes and treks on the Appalachian Trail.

Insiders tips: Cows will approach cautiously if you stand quietly by the fence. While in the area plan a trip to the adjacent G. Richard Thompson Wildlife Management Area. Here, and in the park, are wonderful springtime displays of trilliums and other colorful wildflowers. Fall, when the hillsides turn to a blazing crimson and gold, is also a perfect background to the stonewalls and farm buildings in the hilltop park.

27 Smith Mountain Lake State Park

Land: 1,506 acres   Water: 20,000-acre lake

Smith Mountain Lake State Park opened in 1967. The lake, the second largest freshwater body in the state, was created in 1960 by the Appalachian Power Company when they dammed the Roanoke River in Smith Mountain Gap. The power company donated the first parcel of property for the proposed park soon after the lake was filled. The state purchased the remainder of the property over the next six years and the first stage of development, road construction, began in 1975. Sixteen miles of lake frontage was opened to the public in 1983. The scenic park is best known for trophy sport fishing, boating and a busy white sandy beach.

By placing the park on a cove-lined peninsula, the Commonwealth created a facility with more than 16 miles of shoreline on a mere 1,506 acres. Surrounded by mountains—Smith Mountain is to the southeast—the massive lake is filled with pleasure boaters and fishermen. Also surrounding the lake are more than 25 private marinas, tackle and bait shops, lodging, restaurants and recreation attractions.

Smith Mountain Lake is 40 miles long and has more than 500 miles of shoreline. In the middle of the channel the lake can be more than 165 feet deep. The water is about 200 feet deep by the dam.

Smith Mountain Lake lies in both Bedford and Franklin counties. Each of these names, Smith, Bedford and Franklin, contains a story which reflects the history of the region. Bedford County, for example, was formed by the Virginia House of Burgesses in 1753. It was named in honor of the fourth Duke of Bedford. During the Colonial years the county seat was located in a small bustling town appropriately called New London. In 1779, during the American Revolution, residents of southern Bedford County complained that they were too far away from the county seat and they petitioned the state legislature to form a new county seat south of the Staunton River.

The assembly initially denied the request, but in 1782 the county seat was moved from Tory-infested New London to a more centrally located town patriotically called Liberty, now known as Bedford. Still, residents in the southern part of the county were unhappy. In 1786, the state assembly finally granted their wish and created a new county. They named it Franklin, after Pennsylvania inventor Benjamin Franklin. The name was popular with local residents because many of them had lived in Pennsylvania before settling in Virginia.

As for Smith Mountain, it received its name from the Smith brothers, Daniel and Gideon, pioneer settlers to this part of Virginia. Bedford County was once a top chewing tobacco producer.

Information and Activities

Smith Mountain Lake State Park
Route 1, Box 41
Huddleston, VA 24104
(540) 297-6066

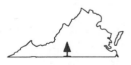

Directions: The sprawling park on the north shore of Smith Mountain Lake in Bedford County, 35 miles from Roanoke. From Roanoke, take State

Route 24 (or U.S. 460 from Lynchburg) to State Route 43 south to County Road 626 south to the park entrance. Many signposts in the park are made from wood, rather than metal.

The angular park office has an outside telephone, wildlife feeding station and newspaper machines near its entrance.

Emergency number: 911 system.

Visitor center: Just before the visitor center is an old log barn that was used to cure tobacco leaves harvested from nearby fields. Inside the small barn are some simple displays about tobacco curing and cultivation. A small plot of tobacco is also growing in a rectangular garden nearby.

The rough-sawn-sided visitor center, open 10 a.m. - 6 p.m. Wednesday - Saturday, is perched on ridge above the shimmering lake. It has a terrific view in three directions of the tree-lined shore and boats plying the water in the distance. A stone retaining wall surrounds the building. Around the building are some demonstration plantings of wildflowers that include purple coneflower, ox-eye daisy, dwarf crested iris, black-eyed Susan's, bergamot, wood sorrel, bloodroot, columbine, cardinal flower, fire pink, miterwort, false Solomon seal, wood poppy, pink turtlehead, spiderwort, bluestar, wild ginger and others.

The visitor center has a soft drink machine and rest rooms that are available when the facility is open.

The bright center features natural and cultural history, with an emphasis on the tobacco farming era. Other displays include the story of moonshining, natural history displays, baskets, quilts, old tools, audio and visual programs, a black bear, a touch table and a spotting scope.

The center has wall-size dioramas and photographs of the cultural and cultivation of tobacco. Large black and white photographs depict farmers wearing big overalls and wide-brimmed hats tending their crops, loading mule-drawn wagons and working on the farm. The exhibits interpret the difficult lifestyles of tobacco growers and their families. A variety of implements of the tobacco farming are displayed including seed planters, horse harnesses, shaving horse and specialized agricultural tools.

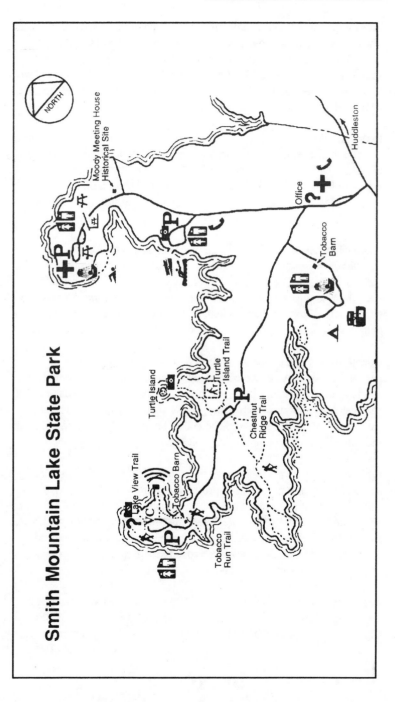

Raising quality tobacco is arduous work and consumes much of the year. The season begins in November when seed beds are prepared. Seeds are planted in these beds in early February, and 10-12 weeks later during the spring rainy season, small seedlings are transplanted into the fields. Over the course of the summer, the plants must be tended carefully and the fields cultivated or hand-hoed.

In the fall, the crop is harvested one leaf at a time, hung in tobacco barns and cured with temperatures ranging from 200-240 degrees. Finally these plants are packed and sent to market. In the 18th and 19th centuries this work was done by hand, first by slave labor and later by tenant farmer. In the 20th century some of the work has been mechanized. Still, the essential steps remain the same and the year long.

Although tobacco farming was almost endless labor, farmers and their families did have some leisure time. In the county people learned to provide their own pleasures in a small-scale society where face-to-face relationships were the rule; visiting became a way of spending free time. Post offices, general stores, parlors, barns, kitchens and sheds were gathering spots for neighbors, especially during the slack winter season.

Country music and dance were also common leisure-time pursuits in this part of Virginia. As in the case of other traditional crafts, the revival of country music and dance in the second half of the 20th century has ensured survival of traditions which many people thought were on the verge of extinction only 50 years ago. The center has several traditional musical instruments on display, including dulcimers.

Religion for tobacco farmers was important. It fulfilled both social and spiritual needs in rural areas and provided opportunities for fellowship and reflection. In this part of Virginia, revivalistic or fundamentalist groups were—and are—well represented. Baptists, Methodists, Disciples of Christ, Dunkards, Wholiness and Pentecostals have been popular in Bedford and Franklin counties. In fact, the remains of an early Baptist meeting house can be found on the grounds of the park.

At the site (a low stone foundation wall) known as the Moody meeting site, a congregation of 32 people met and organized as the Baptist Church of Christ on Staunton in 1790. The 18-foot by 30-foot log church rested on a

An old log tobacco barn is used in educational programs.

stone foundation for many years until it was relocated in 1877 to Pleasant Grove School, and in 1884 to the present site of Staunton Baptist Church.

These sects have many things in common, often stressing simplicity and purity in both secular and religious activities. Their commitment to 18th and 19th century traditional values can be witnessed in small churches and their style, dress and life. The center's display features photographs of church gatherings, simple clapboard churches and a baptismal ceremony in a nearby river.

Campground: Smith Mountain Lake has 50 primitive sites. Cabins and utility hook-ups are proposed for the park and campground over the next few years. Ten to 20 cabins may be built in the park, near the water, in the coming years.

The park has an honor camping system, a one-way gravel road and plenty of shade. Most of the sites have grass and gravel pads that are equipped with ground-mounted fire rings and a picnic table. Sites on the outside of the loop are backed up against a natural area. Site No. 9 is a pull-through site. Many sites have handy brown lantern hanger posts at the corner of the pads. Sites 16-26 are walk-in tent camping sites. They are down a gravel path to shady level spots, where tents can be pitched in the coolness of the woods.

Sites 27-35 are also a group of walk-in sites with plenty of off-road parking. This group of private sites is covered with mature trees offering dense shade. Steep valleys are nearby. Site 38 is a pull-though next to a shallow wooded hollow.

Sites 41 and 48 are next to the rest rooms, which have cold-water rinse showers, outside slop sink and soft drink machine humming near the doorway. Sites 42-47 are walk-in sites along a low ridge above a wooded valley. Sites 48 and 49 are ideal for popup campers.

Fishing: Deep and cool, the lake is a popular and productive striped bass fishery. In fact, each year many citation-size striped bass are taken, making the lake one of the hottest trophy fishing waters in the region. Large bass angling tournaments are regularly held on the lake.

Muskie and walleye are stocked. River techniques take the most walleye. Use lead-head jigs tipped with a minnow jigged gently. Several state record muskie and crappies have been taken from the large lake. Currently the Virginia state record striped bass is from Smith Mountain Lake. The record denizen weighed in excess of 45 pounds. The lake also has good populations of large- and smallmouth bass, catfish, yellow perch, sunfish and large crappies.

Off Turtle Island is a section of the lake along the shore called the S-curve. Fishermen troll with downriggers along the shoreline between peninsulas for muskie and other species. Bass anglers work the coves, fishing along the undercut banks, overhanging trees and near fallen timber. Some bass clubs and the fish commission have placed underwater structures in the lake over the years. A lake map that depicts depths and underwater contours is available from area marinas and bait and tackle shops.

During the summer, night fishing for stripers is the most productive method. Most of the big stripers are taken on shad and alewives. Craddock Creek

The visitor center has a variety of cultural and natural history displays. It interprets the area's tobacco farming era.

---

near the dam is also a hot spot for stripers. Blackwater Channel is known for good muskie fishing.

Shoreline fishing is allowed, but sites are limited to those where you can scramble down the rugged banks to the water's edge. Some of the best shoreline access is near the visitor center.

Boating: On weekends during the summer, the staff offers two hour guided canoe trips. The interpretive trips depart from the boat launching ramp and tour the coves up to Turtle Island and back. Canoes, paddles and life jackets are provided. Make reservations by calling the park office.

The large two-lane launching ramp on a cove is open 24 hours daily. The parking lot can accommodate more than 75 cars and trailers. A few picnic tables are scattered near the gravel parking area and rest room building. A telephone and soft drink machine are at the rest room facility. Many pontoon boats gently cruise the lake, launching from the state park ramp

Pleasure boating and fishing is excellent at the park.

or from private marinas.

Two courtesy docks allow mooring for not longer than one hour.

Paddleboats, floats, canoes and small rafts are rented at the beach during the summer.

Hiking: All of the trails at the park are easy to moderately difficult.

Turtle Island Trail (1.3 miles) is the park's self-guided interpretive trail. The popular trail has six picnic tables and parking for about a dozen cars at its trailhead. A 16-page booklet (small fee) that details 22 learning stations on the trail is available at the trailhead or from the office. The learning stations are marked by four-by-four-inch posts with white numerals on a brown field.

Hikers will learn about how nature is always changing along the trail, and everywhere. Near station No. 1, if you look carefully, you might see faint traces of the last furrows a farmer plowed. When this field was abandoned, the forest reclaimed it through a process known as natural selection. At first, grasses, weeds, bushes and pine trees flourish in the strong, direct sunlight of the open field. In a few years, a thick stand of small pines shaded the land and caused other vegetation to die off.

Along the gentle trail is a demonstration area that was cleared in 1983 and is now going through succession, changing and maturing slightly each year.

At station No. 5 are honeysuckles, a weedy vine that often tangles around small trees and hangs from branches. It was introduced into this country mostly because of its fragrant flowers. In places along the trail, views of the shoreline are abundant. In several places where land and water meet, you can observe large trees lying in the water. Those trees once grew upright and were fed by a sturdy system of roots until wind-whipped waves cut away the soils beneath. These fallen half-floating trees now offer protection for fish.

Hikers will also have a chance to see mature forests near post No. 16. Here grow oak, hickory and beech. Their tree branches are limber and spread out. Tree crowns are wide and shade the land beneath the trees. The understory (low vegetation beneath the trees) is relatively open because of the amount of shade preventing thick growth. Also notice in this area the many dead standing pines that were killed by the lack of sunlight.

Finally, guests to the natural area will learn about soil. American chestnut trees (most have died because of a blight imported from Europe in 1904), roots, rocks, and the history of the lake.

Chestnut Ridge Trail (1.5 miles) meanders along an exposed ridge above the lake. This trailhead is directly across the road from Turtle Island Trail outside the gate to the visitor center west of the park office.

Day-use areas: Much of the day-use picnic area is near the beach, which is near the tip of the peninsula. The main picnic and mowed open spaces are outlined by a hand-laid stone wall. Parking, drinking fountains and other amenities are offered throughout the area.

Beach: The cove-side guarded beach (small fee) is open 10 a.m. - 7 p.m.

daily from Memorial Day to Labor Day. The 250-yard-long beach is the only public beach on Smith Mountain Lake. The colorful changing house has a red roof and yellow canopy that covers part of a large wooden deck, where picnic tables serve concession customers. Yellow picnic tables and trash containers offer splashes of color against the green grass, mountains and lake. The occasional Jet Ski that zooms near the beach adds more color.

The beach concession sells plastic toys, T-shirts, novelties, soft drinks, grill items and snacks. Floating mats and other watercraft can be rented at the beach.

A sand volleyball court is in front of the concession only steps from the beach.

Nature: Red and gray fox (look in the fields) overlap in this part of Virginia. Visitors also might see raccoons, opossums, squirrels, beaver, flocks of turkeys, deer and many songbirds and raptors.

The park offers a variety of public interpretive programs during the summer including guided canoe trips, campfire talks, marshmallow roasts, hay rides, night hikes, bluegrass music (the No Grass bluegrass band is a local favorite!) and guided nature hikes.

Waterfowl viewing is good during many months of the year. Common wildlife, especially deer, can be seen while driving slowly in the park. Hikers may see many songbirds and a variety of spring and summer wildflowers.

Hunting: South Bedford County is one of the top deer harvest areas in the state. Call the park manager for details on deer and turkey hunting. Bedford County is No. 3 in the state for annual turkey harvests.

Electricity from Smith Mountain Lake: The lake was built to make electricity. Operation of the project makes maximum use of two natural resources—water and coal—through a process called pumped storage. Water stored in Smith Mountain Lake drops through turbine generators in the dam powerhouse to produce electricity. Instead of allowing all of the spent water to run away downstream, much is caught and held by Leesville Dam, the lower dam in the project, to be pumped back into Smith Mountain Lake. A portion of the water goes through turbine generators at Leesville, generating additional electricity.

Generation takes place during weekdays, when demand for electricity is at its highest. Water from the lower lake is pumped back into the upper lake when demand for power is low—nights, holidays and portions of weekends. Power for operating the pumps comes from Appalachian Power Company's steam-electric generating plants via transmission lines. The pumped storage concept allows these plants to operate more efficiently since their loads do not have to be reduced to extremely low levels during nights and weekends. Steam-electric generating plants are designed to operate most efficiently at or near their full load levels.

The Smith Mountain dam is 816 feet in length, 235 feet high and is made of 175,000 cubic yards of concrete.

Insiders tips: Paddle to Turtle Island, and explore the jagged shoreline by canoe. Drive the nearby 470-mile-long Blue Ridge Parkway along the crests of the southern Appalachians.

28 Southwest Virginia Museum

The Southwest Museum is housed in a stately mansion built by Rufus Ayers during the years of 1895 to 1899 (the town's heyday) at a cost of $25,000. Ayers paid the craftsmen 17.5 cents per hour to construct the hand-chiseled sandstone building in downtown Big Stone Gap. Skilled carpenters used native red oak throughout the interior of the building, with hand-carved motifs adorning the many tall windows and doors. There are 13 motif patterns above doorways throughout the mansion. Can you find all 13?

Ayers was Virginia's Attorney General in 1885. During this time he and civic leaders John Imboden, Charles Sears, George Carter and John Taggart felt that Big Stone Gap could become the "Pittsburgh of the South" because of its significant iron ore and coal deposits. Ayers was instrumental in helping develop the coal and iron ore industry in southwest Virginia and in bringing railroads to the area. Big Stone Gap, however, didn't become the next Pittsburgh, due to a variety of reasons. Nevertheless, many wealthy families did live in the town and had an influence on its growth.

The mansion was bought by C. Bascom Slemp in 1929. Slemp was a native of Lee County, served many years in Congress and later became the private secretary to President Calvin Coolidge. C. Bascom and his sister, Janie Slemp Newman, had a love of southwest Virginia, its people, history and rich culture. The family traveled extensively collecting artifacts depicting life in the area and beyond, which were originally displayed in the Janie Slemp Newman Museum. Before C. Bascom's death in 1943, he established the Slemp Foundation. It was his wish that the state acquire the Ayers' home for a museum and the Janie Slemp Newman collection be given to the state for its museum.

The Commonwealth acquired the Ayers' house in 1946 and the Slemp Foundation donated the collection. The museum was dedicated in 1948.

In short, the expertly-designed museum tells the story of the men and women who settled in and around the area. The exhibits depict the early "boom and bust" era of the late 1800s. Life at the turn of the century can be seen through professional displays, video programs, interpretive exhibits and collections. Artifacts from the early settlers who developed the area in the late 1700s are also on display. Also in the collection are rare pieces that C. Bascom and Janie acquired during their extensive travels. The collection includes a set of Disraeli china which Queen Victoria had made for her Prime Minister, Benjamin Disraeli. Also on exhibit are fine French paintings, a cassone, which is an Italian hope chest, and antiques from the Orient.

Information and Activities

Southwest Virginia Museum
Box 742
Big Stone Gap, VA 24219
(540) 523-1322

Directions: In Big Stone Gap at the corner of West First Street and Wood Avenue (U.S. Alternate Route 58), just off U.S. Route 23 in Wise County. The museum is 14 miles south of Norton and 35 miles northwest of Kingsport, Tenn. There is a small fee to visit the museum.

Nearby Karlan State Park, which is scheduled for development, is managed by the Southwest Virginia Museum. The 200-acre site includes an old Victorian home that is set for restoration, and a scattering of picnic tables.

Museum: The elegant three story museum is open Memorial Day to Labor Day, Monday - Thursday 10 a.m. - 4 p.m., Friday 9 a.m. 4 p.m., Saturday 10 a.m. - 5 p.m. and Sunday 1-5 p.m. After Labor Day and from March to Memorial Day the facility is closed on Mondays. The museum is closed in January and February.

A short orientation video is the best way to start your visit to the museum. Underfoot in the video room is wonderful one-inch wide oak flooring, cozy fireplace, built-in oak bookshelves and a photo of stern-looking Rufus Ayers.

Big Stone Gap's "booms and bust" era is interpreted in the main gallery on the first floor. Information includes the short-lived quest to turn the town into another Pittsburgh, the railroad's impact, mining and local cultural matters like the newspaper, police force, hotels, banks and schools. The second floor galleries tell the story of the residents of Big Stone Gap at the turn of the century. Many tools and items of everyday life are displayed. Two second floor galleries chronicle the life and times of prominent local citizen and eight-term U.S. Congressman C. Bascom Slemp. Slemp was a graduate of the Virginia Military Institute and attended law school at the University of Virginia.

Details about the first pioneers to this region are also offered. Following Daniel Boone's Wilderness Road in wagons, these adventurist pioneers braved rugged mountain terrain, isolation and the threat of Indian attack in their efforts to homestead the remote region. The axes, firearms, spinning wheels and housewares that were used to transform the region are enlisted to tell the story of exploring and homesteading.

On the main level, one of the more interesting exhibits is about small town medicine. Until the early 1800s scarcely one U.S. physician in 10 had any formal training. West of the Appalachians, a doctor might be anyone calling himself or herself one. Surgery was largely confined to dressing wounds and amputating limbs without using anesthesia. Small town doctors in southwest Virginia were not particularly bound by rigid theories which guided doctors in big cities. So during the 1800s doctors in Virginia and Kentucky often had to improvise using traditional remedies and old fashioned horse sense in treating their patients. The display includes a number of crude surgical instruments.

The only major industry to survive Big Stone Gap's "booms and bust" was coal mining. Since the 1800s locally mined coal has served the needs of steelmakers, power companies, textile mills and other businesses throughout the world. Production tonnage peaked in 1926. Over the years demand has risen and fallen, although mining has been an important source of jobs and regional pride all along. Near the display about coal mining is a timeline that depicts the growth and significant events in the area over the past 150 years.

Big Stone Gap's most famous resident was author John Fox, Jr. the author of *"The Trail of the Lonesome Pine."* John Fox was a Rough Rider with Teddy Roosevelt and a member of the Big Stone Gap's Town Garden. A world-traveling author, Fox's 12 books made Virginia's mountain life well-known to readers around the world. "The Trail of the Lonesome Pine" was made into a motion picture. In 1908, Fox married a famous opera singer, Fritzi Scheff. She arrived in mountainous Big Stone Gap with two personal companions and numerous heavy trunks, including one that held her jewels. John and Fritzi were soon divorced and the episode became a sour subject to Fox.

Also on the main floor of the museum are some labeled hand tools (some of which may have been used to build the house), a large five-foot-tall marble fireplace and several other small displays.

Up the bulky but elegant stairway to the second floor are several galleries that have oak ceilings and considerable decorative woodwork. Upon entering the first gallery, victrola music begins to play, and you are greeted by a collection of baby carriages, treadle sewing machine (which cost $13.05 new), information about suspenders and corsets, family entertainment in the 1800s, walking canes, a lady's fan and information on public schools.

Before the 1900s began, the public school in Big Stone Gap was a tiny two-room structure. As the population increased, leading citizens including Rufus Ayers recognized the need for a bigger, better school. A new school

The classy gift shop offers themed products and souvenoirs.

---

was built in 1903 at a cost of $17,000. It had 15 rooms and could accommodate 450 pupils. In small towns across the country, schools became important social centers. Church and civic groups used the facilities for meetings and other gatherings. Older family members were often invited to join students in spelling bees in those days. The exhibit includes an example of a tiny desk, quill pens, school bell and primer books.

A large collage of photos depicting all types of social groups, workers, teams, families and individuals of Big Stone Gap are also along the walls of the second floor galleries. Some of the people in the photos have terribly grim looks on their faces. Near the photos is a small display about being a policeman in Big Stone Gap. Items displayed include a Billy club, tin whistle, badge, .32-caliber pistol, tarnished handcuffs and a worn Winchester rifle. Part of the story is an exciting tale about the 1892 capture of Doc Taylor, a feared outlaw of the day. He was wanted for 19 murders, and eventually hung for his outrageous crimes.

Some of the most impressive features of the second floor galleries are the wonderful examples of Victorian furniture. Also here are beautiful examples of English Minton bone china, Pillow Patternware and china once owned by Benjamin Disraeli, Prime Minister of Great Britain. Artwork hangs on the walls including works by Charles Daubigny, Diaz, Theodore Rousseau and others. This is all part of the Slemp collection, which was put together during their worldwide collecting trips. In this gallery are examples of ancient pottery, oil bottles, Palestine (circa 2,000 B.C.) jars and other antiques.

A fun exhibit of the sporting life depicts photos of tobacco spitting baseball teams, old leather ball gloves, itchy-looking uniforms, a faded cheerleader outfit, a blue woman's basketball uniform from 1910 and other artifacts of this playful age.

On the third floor, wide creaking floorboards are underfoot and information of the pioneer life is everywhere. The galleries offer examples of pioneer tools including a spiral auger, spoke shaves, wheelwright's mallet, human-powered lathe, leather working tools and examples of their craft. Other items from everyday life are a Kentucky long rifle, spinning wheels, flintlock pistol, as well as information about Native Americans of southwest Virginia.

Prior to the first European contact, Indians of southwest Virginia lived in many primitive villages consisting of 50 to 500 people. The livelihood of this expanding population depended on growing corn, beans, squash and hunting and gathering deer, turkey, fruit, berries and nuts. In 1671, Thomas Batts and Robert Fallam, under commission from General Abraham Wood, were the first Europeans to visit and record an Indian village in southwest Virginia. In this Indian display are fiber fishing lines and crude hooks, stone projectile points, stone celts, gaming disks, a time line and marina shell beads.

The time line depicts the time of the pioneer to the patriots. It shows the early days of forested Virginia to the time of Thomas Walker and Daniel Boone, on to the era when Kentucky and Tennessee became territories. The graphic time line also shows the War of 1812, when the first church was built in Wise County, the United States' two-year war with Mexico over the Southwest Territory, when Rufus Ayers was born, and all the way up to the date of C. Bascom Slemp's birth in Lee County in 1870.

In yet another third floor gallery sits a shingle-shaving horse and tools for making wood shake shingles. Tools include worn-appearing mauls, heavy froes, broad ax, jagged bow saws and pit saw. This exhibit is part of the "Taming the Wilderness" theme. Related displays include farm tools, horse-drawn plows, cider mill, corn sheller, flax breaker, three-foot-in diameter spinning wheel and labor-saving items from the home.

Before electricity and appliances appeared in the home, homesteaders had to make work easier by creating more efficient tools and establishing some new customs. The hand-operated washing machine replaced the washboard, and swinging or rocking churns made butter with less effort than hand-pumped churns. Irons heated on stove tops were replaced by irons with hollow compartments for hot coals or charcoal. To dry apples or other fruit, women hung wooden trays filled with fruit slices near the fireplace. For jobs such as barn or house raising, shucking corn and boiling sorghum cane to make syrup, people often gathered together and made social events out of the hard work.

Many of these labor-saving items are on display along with sausage stuffers, coffee grinder, washboard, children's potty chair, candles, whiskey still, loom, blacksmith's anvil and sample of the iron benders work and leather working tools.

Settlers depended upon leather more than we do today. They wore leather pants and boots, sat on leather saddles and drove horses hitched with leather harnesses. Tanners needed a full year to turn a fresh hide into good leather. They removed the hair, scraped the inside of the skin and then soaked and turned the leather in curing vats of tannic acid extracted from hemlock bark. Finally they cured the leather to make it smooth and soft.

Shoemakers, or cobblers, were important because stores offering ready-made shoes were unknown until well into the 1800s. Cobblers often employed assistants for binding, stitching and sealing shoes. The cobbler either supplied the leather himself or used leather provided by customers. Many carving and stitching tools, shapers, wedges, islets and so forth are displayed in the well-lit gallery.

An impressive display of 12 beautiful quilts is carefully exhibited. Information about the various patterns and the art of quilt-making is posted. You'll

The high-quality museum teaches about the lifestyles of west Virginains.

learn about blocking, stitching in layers, planning and identifying patterns. Patterns include a log cabin, broken dish, aircraft, orange peel, Dutchman's puzzle, friendship ring, box and star, around the world, clam shell, variable star, crazy quilt, Dresden plate, drunkard's path and the flying geese pattern, which contains 18 triangles.

Touring the grounds: The manicured grounds of the museum are almost as diverse and interesting as the interior of the facility. A small booklet is available for a self-guided tour around the cultivated gardens and lawn spaces that are enclosed by an attractive stone wall. Two picnic tables are inside the stone wall.

One of the most interesting outdoor features is the carriage house. The handsome structure was built some time after the mansion. It was probably used by the Ayers to store their carriage. The architecture of the white carriage house is different from that of the museum. It has a slate roof and detailed woodwork along the roof line. In recent years the carriage house has served as a residency for many of the museum's curators and as a storage facility.

Walkers will also see an old buggy chassis and cast iron pot used for boiling seawater to obtain salt. The seawater was boiled off until only pure salt was left in the bottom of the large pot. Cast in Europe before 1776, the pot was brought from France to the U.S. by the Van de Vanter family. After several relocations, the pot became the possession of a family in nearby Jonesville, Va., nearly a century ago.

The mansion's landscaping also includes eastern hemlocks, a member of the pine family. They were once used as a commercial source of tannin used in leather tanning and dyeing. In the spring, thick clumps of rhododendron thrive in the moist, acidic soil. Other plant materials include American holly, the kind used for Christmas decorations; yellow poplar, sometimes called tulip poplar; flowering dogwood, the state flower; and some large Norway spruce, the largest and most ornamental of the spruce tree family. Some of the plant materials are labeled.

Programs: The museum offers a wide menu of public interpretive programs including arts and crafts, wreath making, ghost stories, topiary, applefest, Christmas tours, children's Christmas tree and many others.

Gift shop: Open Tuesday - Thursday, 10 a.m.-4 p.m., Friday 9 a.m. - 4 p.m., Saturday 10 a.m. - 5 p.m. and Sunday 1 -5 p.m. The shop has some of the best merchandise of any gift shop in the state park system. All of the items are related to the museum or the local culture and history of the region. Including ornate reproduction jewelry, books about the pioneer and Victorian eras, locally made crafts, music boxes, caps, T-shirts, post cards, porcelain dolls, hard candy and many other items.

All of the items have terrific interpretive tags that explain the item, its history and so on. Even the T-shirts carry designs found only in the museum. One such design is of the fancy woodwork found through all three floors and the lower level. Other designs are taken from the extensive quilt collection.

Victorian parlor: The meeting room can accommodate 50 and is available for rent by groups. The colorful Victorian decor is a quiet setting, perfect for business meetings, club meetings, seminars, training events, socials and banquets.   The room is available day and night.   Food service can be arranged. The multi-purpose room is located in the basement of the grand old mansion and has many large historic photos on the walls.

Insiders tips: Take the walking and driving tour of Big Stone Gap that includes 14 stops at area museums, parks, library, Poplar Hill, historic streets, buildings and points of interest. One of my favorite points on the tour is the restored Interstate Railroad Private Car #101, which was built in 1870 and now serves as a tourism information office. Natural Tunnel State Park is 18 miles south of the museum.

29 Staunton River Bridge
Battlefield Hist. State Park

Land: 87 acres   Water: River

"The hot summer afternoon of June 25, 1864, would forever change the lives of 700 old men and young boys from Southside, Virginia. They had responded to a call to assist a Confederate volunteer force of 296 men in the defense of an important railroad bridge over the Staunton River, against a Union Cavalry force of more than 5,000. The courage they showed in the trenches that day helped the Confederate soldiers win the battle and maintain an important supply line for the south," says a description in the park's richly appointed visitor center.

Although badly outnumbered, Confederate Captain Farinholt's troops held their ground and saved the bridge, maintaining a vital link for General Robert E. Lee and his besieged Army of Northern Virginia in Petersburg.

In June 1864, Lee and his army were engaged in a desperate defense of the city of Petersburg. Victory for General Lee depended upon a steady flow of supplies from the west and south, via the Southside and Richmond & Danville railroads.

Union General Ulysses S. Grant knew that if these supply lines could be destroyed, Lee would have to abandon Petersburg. To accomplish this, Grant planned a cavalry raid to tear up the tracks and destroy the railroad bridge over the Staunton River.

The raid began on June 22, and was led by Brigadier General James H. Wilson and Brigadier General August V. Kautz. They left Petersburg with more than 5,000 cavalry troops and 16 pieces of artillery. During the first three days of the raid, Wilson's cavalry tore up 60 miles of track and burned two trains and many railroad stations.

At 10 p.m. on June 23, Captain Farinholt received word from General Lee that a large detachment of enemy cavalry was coming to destroy the bridge and that he should "make every possible preparation immediately." Though his numbers were increased by volunteers, Farinholt was still badly outnumbered.

He had only six pieces of artillery, four in the earthwork fort on the hill just east of the bridge and two in a small fortification west of the bridge. Between these artillery positions and the river was a line of trenches, and across the bridge lay a semicircular line of hastily constructed but well-concealed rifle trenches.

Captain Farinholt knew that his activities at the bridge were being watched by Union scouts who had arrived ahead of the main body of troops. To make them think he was receiving reinforcements, Farinholt ordered any empty train to run back and forth between Clover Depot and the bridge, giving the appearance that fresh troops were arriving constantly.

There's lots more to the story. Plan a visit to the museum to learn about the assaults on the bridge and how old men and boys from the area fought gallantly in the face of overwhelming odds, distinguishing themselves on the field of battle.

The colorful visitor center is for all ages.

Information and Activities

Staunton River Bridge Battlefield Historic State Park
Route 1, Box 183
Randolph, VA 23962
(804) 572-4623

Directions: Near Clover, Virginia, on Route 855.

Clover Center at Fort Hill Visitor Center: Opened in 1995, the Old Dominion Electric Cooperative and Virginia Power funded construction of the wood building. The visitor center has wonderful tongue and groove ceilings, gray carpeting and excellent, professionally designed displays. About half of the center interprets the Civil War battle and the other half has information about power generation and the nearby electric plant.

Just inside the center's entrance is a large, three-dimensional, free-standing diorama of the region showing the location of the power plant, river, roads, bridge and battlefield.

The center has some interesting artifacts including a sword pulled from the well at the fort, old banjoes, a model of a train like the ones that crossed the Staunton Bridge, a replica of a six-pound cannon, examples of shot charges, Civil War-era handguns and long rifles, historic photographs, a surgeon's kit, field mess kits, books, painful-looking saddles and examples of clothes and military equipment.

Information about the bridge, battle, Confederate earthworks (fort) and Wilson's retreat are detailed using graphics, photographs and descriptions. The center also has an 18-minute orientation videotape.

The brightly-colored visitor center is open 9 a.m. - 5 p.m. daily. A small sales counter offers mugs, caps, books and T-shirts for sale. Also inside the visitor center are a carpeted conference room, rest rooms and staff offices.

The bridge: The steel framework of the old bridge, which looks like the bones of a skeleton from a distance, was built in 1902. The iron structure spans the murky Staunton River, which once played an important role in the

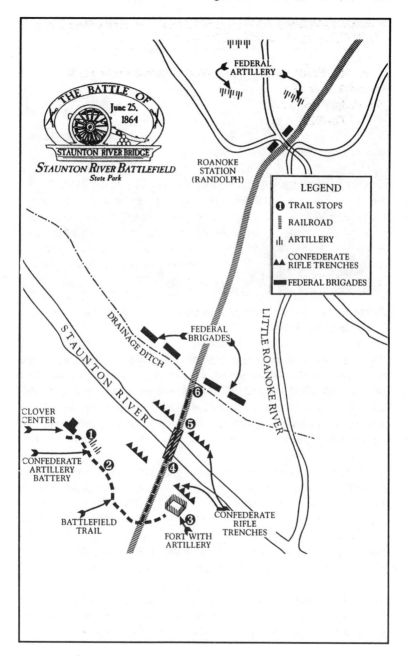

Interesting Civil War strategy is interpreted at the Clover Center.

nation's history. Today, the bridge has been decked with pressure-treated wood and railings to create a short pedestrian walkway. Visitors can walk across the old railroad bridge and take in tree-lined views of the slow-moving river. The brown river is filled with floating branches and a few hardy fish. Birdwatchers like the bridge because it brings them closer to the treetops, where many species forage for seeds or nest during the spring and early summer. The bridge is about 40 feet above the river and 10 feet wide.

The rattle under your foot today, as you walk the bridge, serves as a faint reminder of the clatter and bluster of steam trains ferrying men and supplies back and forth across the river during the Civil War. The history of the bridge and battlefield is a lesson in strategy, courage and low technology warfare. A self-guided trail, called the Battlefield Trail, leads visitors to six numbered stops where various aspects of the battle are interpreted. A four-panel white brochure explaining each stop is available at the visitor center.

Re-enactments: On summer weekends, staff and volunteers erect living history displays, dress in period clothes and conduct a variety of interpretive programs about the fort, Civil War and lifestyles of that era.

30 Staunton River State Park

Land: 1,277 acres
Water: Buggs Island Lake, 48,000 acres

Staunton River is on the shores of Virginia's biggest lake, Kerr Reservoir, also called Buggs Island Lake. It is an excellent place to bring the family. The park, on a peninsula, features a cozy campground, sprawling day-use areas, swimming pool, cabins and tennis courts. Staunton River is about a 45-minute drive from Occoneechee State Park.

Significant tracts of wildlife management lands are scattered around the reservoir, offering excellent hunting, hiking, horse trails and outdoor recreation. Twenty federally owned parcels totaling 40,000 acres are open for use. Many of the tracts are lakeside. The rolling areas are often oak and hickory, pine or upland hardwoods and nestled along small coves and high banks.

One of the primary objectives in management of Kerr Reservoir is the protection and management of wildlife habitat. Many disciplines are involved in this objective, including land management, forestry and wildlife biology. They include establishment of permanent forest openings, planting of wildlife food plots, restoration of native grasses, periodic mowing or burning of old fields, thinning of pine and hardwood stands, erection of artificial nesting structures for wood ducks, gray squirrels, bluebirds and small raptors, and placement of artificial fishing reefs in the reservoir.

The management areas vary from 10 acres to several hundred acres. The U.S. Army Corps of Engineers publishes a Guide to the Wildlife Management Area that is available at the state park office or Corps contact stations.

Information and Activities

Staunton River State Park
Route 2, Box 295
Scottsburg, VA 24589
(804) 572-4623

Directions: 18 miles east of South Boston; take U.S. 360 north, then State Route 344 east 10 miles.

Visitor center: Recently renovated, the center was built in 1936. It has tile floors, a circle driveway and many natural history exhibits inside. Of special interest are the interpretation of tobacco farming, rural lifestyles, a touch table and cultural history. The wood building is surrounded by a flagstone walkway and broad, open fields.

The visitor center sells simple grocery items, camping supplies, hot food, sunscreen, caps, T-shirts and snacks.

A small amphitheater behind the visitor center has eight wood benches that surround a fire pit. A small tobacco shed is next to the amphitheater.

Campground: The 46-site campground has two loops and a centrally located bathhouse. All of the sites have gravel pads, hook-ups, wood picnic tables and steel fire rings. The entire campground is shady, but the trees have been gently thinned to allow good breezes and some sunlight to hit the surface. Twelve sites do not have water hook-ups. Sites on the inside of the loop seem to be higher and drier than sites on the outside. The interior sites also get some midday sunlight.

Sites 1-5 can accommodate medium-sized RV rigs and is next the showerhouse. Sites 43-45 are large, open grassy sites perfect for a big trailer or motor home.

Sites 10, 13 and 28 are pull-throughs and often requested. Site 14 is slightly oversized and is an excellent choice for large RV campers.

Cabins: Staunton River's tan cabins are tidy, well-maintained and air-conditioned. The seven units are strung out along a ridge off a gravel road. Each cabin has parking places outlined by timbers, grills and shady lawns. Most of the cabins have a partial view of the water.

Cabins 3-5 have porches that face toward the lake. Cabin 1 is at the end of the spur and private. It also has a stone chimney and is popular, according to staff. Mowed open spaces around the colony of cabins are ideal for children to engage in informal games and play.

Fishing: Many large catfish are taken by shoreline fishermen, often near the boat launches, using livers, homemade stinkbaits or commercial mixtures. For more information about fishing, turn to Occoneechee State Park, which is also on Buggs Island Lake. Largemouth bass and striper fishing is considered good to very good near the park.

Boating: Lake water levels can dramatically impact the use of the launching ramp. Sometimes, depending on the weather and water level, the ramp can be under water. Nevertheless, when conditions are right, the hard-surfaced ramp with floating wooden dock is busy.

Next to the small gravel parking lot that serves the boat ramp are a small building and soft drink machine. A smaller second launch is near the main day-use area. A boat rental concession may open in the near future.

The park has year-round, indoor boat storage. Check with the office for rates and details. If you rent a storage space, you will receive an annual launching pass.

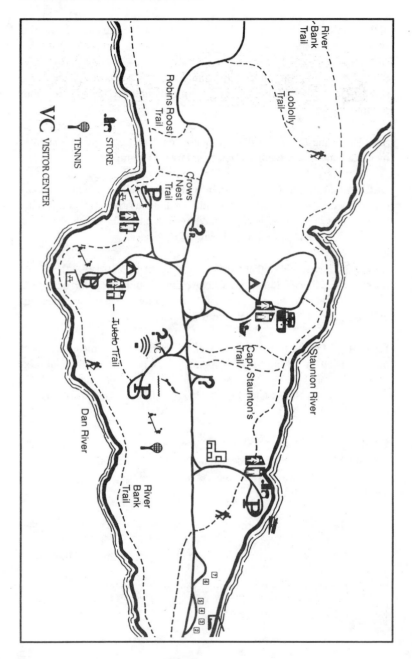

Staunton River has a large amphitheater that is used for programs.

Hiking: The Kerr Reservoir and Dan River surround the peninsula, known locally as "The Fork." The Occoneechee Indians inhabited this area as far back as the 13th century. They maintained a thriving culture based on trade, agriculture and hunting. Evidence of their culture now lies beneath the water of the reservoir. In the 18th and 19th centuries, several plantations dotted the riverbanks upstream from what is now the park. Red Hill, Patrick Henry's last home, and Oak Dale, the home of Mark Twain's father, were located in the surrounding communities.

The park has almost 10 miles of hiking trails. River Bank Trail (7 miles) encompasses most of the park and is mostly easy hiking. Connecting trails to Route 344 provide alternative hiking opportunities and access to the park. Newer directional signs and trail upgrading are under way at the park.

Captain Staunton's Interpretive Trail (.6 mile) is a loop that begins at the visitor center and connects to the office. Signs along the trail mark places of natural and historic importance.

Day-use areas: Wide and flat open fields are a hallmark of the park. The mowed spaces are scattered with picnic tables and newer play apparatus. The park has two reservable picnic shelters.

Two tennis courts enclosed by tall wire fences are used mostly during the summer. Tennis players must pay by the hour to use the blue courts.

Swimming pool: A new pool recently was built, replacing the old large pool. The pool features a small food concession, lifeguard stations and a children's wading pool. The pool is open 11 a.m. - 6 p.m. Memorial Day weekend to Labor Day.

Nature: Seasonal interpretive programs are offered during the summer. Guided hikes are provided to school groups requesting them during the spring and fall. Weekend programs, campfire talks and guided hikes depart from the visitor center and trailheads.

Insiders tip: Plan a day trip to South Boston Museum (open weekends) or to the South Boston Speedway.

31 Twin Lakes State Park
Land: 425 acres   Water: 44-acre lake

In central Virginia, Twin Lakes State Park is in the Piedmont; it's secluded, but well-equipped for meetings or seminars at the conference center, swimming at the sandy beach, fishing, hiking or conducting peaceful family reunions in CCC-built pavilions. Bring your bike or canoe for even more fun at the rolling, super clean park.

The plentiful tract of land was initially purchased from struggling farmers by the federal government during the Great Depression. Two parks, Goodwin Lake and Prince Edward Lake, were founded in 1939. As a result, Twin Lakes has virtually two complete sets of facilities.

For more than 20 years the Prince Edward Lake and Goodwin Lake parks were segregated. Prince Edward Lake was known as Prince Edward Lake State Park For Negroes. Some evidence suggests the segregation began as early as 1939. Unfortunately, segregation was commonplace and understood at the time. During these years both neighboring units had contact station rangers that made sure whites went to Goodwin Lake and blacks to Prince

Edward Lake. The two parks desegregated in 1964, then merged in 1976 and were renamed Twin Lakes State Park in 1986.

Twin Lakes is adjacent to the sprawling 6,950-acre Prince Edward State Forest. The forest is managed for watershed protection, recreation, hiking, cross-country skiing, horseback riding, timber production, applied forest research, hunting and fishing.

Information and Activities

Twin Lakes State Park
Route 2, Box 70
Green Bay, VA 23942
(804) 392-3435
(804) 767-2397 Cedar Crest Conference Center

Directions: Near Farmville, one hour southwest of Richmond and 98 miles east of Roanoke. Take U.S. 360 west of Burkesbille to Route 613, then east on 629 to the park entrance. A topography map of the region clearly shows the two lakes, and history of the park(s). The park office is open in the summer 9 a.m. - 5 p.m. Monday - Thursday, 9 a.m. 9 p.m. Friday and Saturday and 9 a.m. - 7 p.m. Sunday.

Twin Lakes also manages nearby Sailor's Creek State Park.

Emergency numbers: 911 system; police, 392-8101.

Conference center: Recent renovations have further improved the popular lakeside conference center. The conference center can house 44 and feed up to 90 people in the convivial dining hall. The nearby group campground (Hunter Campground) can accommodate up to 100. Up to 54 people can be accommodated at outdoor picnic tables for group barbecues or business meetings. You may use your own caterer, or pick one from the list that the conference center business manager maintains. You can even cook your own food, if you like.

The main building has tile floors, brass lamps, varnished entrance doors, a wooden railing and inviting common deck that connects it to the other

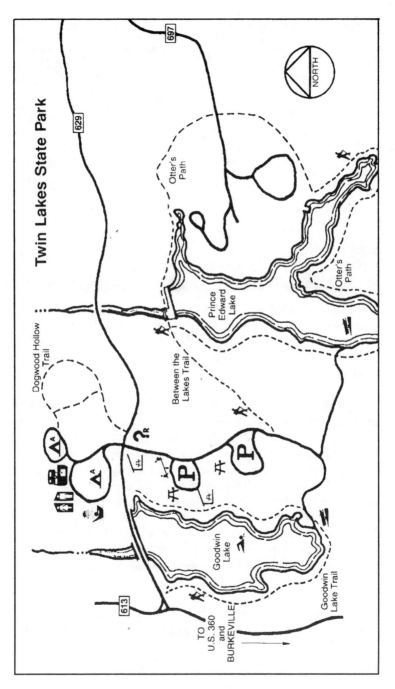

Twin Lakes State Park

Bring your volleyball and sunblock.

buildings. The view from the conference center, through a wall of windows, is onto a small dock with bobbing paddleboats, sandy beach, green lawn, gazebo and glossy lake.

The half-dozen gray-green housekeeping cabins sleep six. The cabins are within an easy walk to the conference center and can be rented by families by advance registration. The cabins have dishes, stove, refrigerator and quiet screened porches with rocking chairs. The lakeside cabins are on a low ridge above the water. Day-use areas and a sandy volleyball court are nearby. Cabins have a Bavarian style. They are air-conditioned and equipped with pedestal grills, designated parking and picnic tables.

Cabins along the lake have an attractive lawn and are set back about 40 yards from the shoreline. The views of the small lake are relaxing. Each cabin has a fireplace, wood kitchen table, polished wood floors and other cozy amenities.

A separate building near the conference center houses a large barbecue grill on wheels. Just above the center on a long ridge is a pavilion (No. 6) with red brick chimneys that offers an excellent view.

The grounds of the cozy conference center are well-maintained, almost resort quality. Near the lakeshore, a bright white gazebo is used for casual purposes and an occasional small outdoor meetings.

The conference center is a terrific site for business meetings, seminars, training events, family reunions, company picnics, retreats, receptions, banquets and weddings.

Campground: All 33 sites have electrical and water hook-ups. They also have gravel and grass pads, picnic tables and ground-mounted grills. A tan block shower building is centrally located. Most sites are best for small- to medium-sized RV rigs. A small spur with sites 6-15 is cramped and best left to tents and tiny popup campers. Site 13 is private and near the Dogwood Hollow Trailhead.

Sites 22, 24 and 26 are against natural areas. Site 26 has a partial view of the lake. The campground is shady and sites are level.

The group campground is near the Cedar Crest Conference Center.

Fishing: Fishing is fair in both lakes. The shallow lakes have grass carp (release upon catching) that help to keep the water clean by eating vast amount of aquatic vegetation. Anglers may not take bass less than 15 inches long; there is a two-fish limit per day. Live bait is the best technique for these small lakes. Anglers may want to travel to Bear Creek Lake State Park, Holliday Lake State Park or Briery Creek Lake on Route 15 for additional fishing.

Boating: A tiny tan boat rental concession is near the beach where rowboats and yellow, red and blue paddleboats are offered for hourly rent.

Cartop boats only can be launched from the gravel one-lane ramp at each lake. Electric and human-powered boats only are allowed on the bantam-sized lakes.

Hiking: Twin Lakes has six miles of multi-purpose trails.

The Otter Trail (4 miles) winds through a mixed hardwood-pine forest and rolling terrain typical of the Piedmont that surrounds the lakes. The mostly easy trail skirts the water's edge and at several points crosses tapering creeks that flow into the lake. While hiking, look for beaver, whitetail deer, cottontail rabbit, bobwhite quail, wild turkey, wood duck, blue and green heron, whippoorwills, red-tailed hawks and a variety of amphibians and reptiles. Look for trails in the soft mud and listen for the loud rapping of crow-size pileated woodpeckers in the distance.

The trees and shrubs that characterize the walk include oak, maple, beech, ironwood, elm, pines and various shrubs such as sassafras, huckleberry, alder and sumac. Wildflower enthusiasts will find spring to be the best season to look for colorful blossoms. You may discover hued wild azalea, Mayapple, trillium, lady's slippers, violets, evening primrose, false Solomon's seal, rattlesnake plantain, daisy pipsissewa, cardinal flower, butterfly weed, pokeweed, lobelia and arrowhead.

The Dogwood Hollow Self-Guided Trail (1 mile) has seven learning stations that are described in a 10-page booklet available at the park office. The trail is accessible from the campground. Hikers will learn about the ever-changing landscape (succession), pileated woodpeckers, man's impact on the land, stream ecology and trees' place in nature. Visitors will also see many dogwoods, whose bark was used by Indians as a remedy for malaria. They also used the dogwood's roots to extract a red dye.

Bikes: Persons 16 years and older can rent bikes by the hour and ride them on designated trails and park roads.

Day-use areas: Near picnic pavilion No. 1 is a playground comprised of swings, uneven bars and climbing apparatus. Picnic tables and grills are scattered throughout the park. Picnic pavilion No. 2 is a peeled log-style structure that can be reserved in advance. Twin Lakes has some of the best equipped day-use areas in the state park system.

Beach: Under a blue umbrella, a lifeguard patrols the small sandy beach that is in view of the dam. On one side of the beach are four benches that face a day-use area and the small lake. A diving platform, changing house with showers, seasonal concession stand and soft drink machines are also at the swimming area. The food concession serves hot dogs, pizza, ice, corn

The popular beach has a concession stand and diving platform.

dogs, ice cream and other snacks. The pleasant and open sandy beach is about 125 yards long.

A popular volleyball court—and horseshoe court—near the swimming beach are heavily used during the summer. So are some old CCC stone grills that dot the area. Twin Lakes has container-like boxes where typically ugly garbage cans are hidden.

Smoky the Bear: A fun display at the park uses Smoky the Bear as narrator. Smoky says, "Money doesn't grow on trees..." Who owns Virginia's forests? 12 percent government; 11 percent the forest industry; and 77 percent by farmers and other landowners.

Virginia's forests generate $3 billion yearly. One out of every six wage earners is employed by the forestry industry. Forests cover 16.4 million acres, which is 65 percent of Virginia. Virginia plants more than 70 million forest tree seedlings each year.

Insiders tip: Bring your group, association or club to the conference center for your next meeting or small conference.

32 Westmoreland State Park
Land: 1,300 acres Water: Potomac River

Westmoreland State Park is on high cliffs above the Potomac River, flanked by the birthplace of George Washington and Robert E. Lee's early home. Covered with cool oak-hickory forests and dotted with green fields, the park is famous for summer outdoor recreation including swimming, camping, cabins, fishing, hiking, boating, fossil hunting, eagle watching, cozy restaurants, concessions and sprawling picnic areas.

The Northern Neck region features many scenic, recreational and historical destinations only minutes from the state park. One of the most popular day-trips from the park is George Washington Birthplace, a national monument. The birthplace evokes the spirit of the 18th-century Virginia tobacco farm complete with farm buildings, groves of trees, livestock, gardens, fields of tobacco and wheat, rivers and creeks—these were the earliest scenes of Washington's childhood and the kind of surroundings in which he reached maturity.

The birthplace includes the Memorial Shaft, a granite obelisk made of Virginia marble. The towering monument is a one-tenth replica of the Washington Monument in the Nation's Capitol. The birthplace also includes a family burial ground, colonial herb and flower garden, memorial house furnished in the 1730-1750 period style, artifacts, birthplace site and much more.

History buffs can also take a day trip to Stratford Hall Plantation (Robert E. Lee's birthplace), one of the great houses of American history. Its magnificent setting on a high bluff above the Potomac River and its bold architectural style set it apart from any other colonial house. But its highest distinction is in the family of patriots who lived there. The plantation is still managed as a farm today on 1,600 acres. Call (804) 493-8038 for information.

The Lee family, distinguished by Robert E.—and Richard and Francis Lee, the only brothers to sign the Declaration of Independence—built Stratford in the late 1730s. Using brick made on the site and timber cut from virgin forests, builders and craftsmen constructed the H-shaped manor house, its four dependencies, coach house and stables. The Great Hall in the center of the house, 29 feet square with an inverted tray ceiling 17 feet high, is one of the most architecturally significant rooms to survive from colonial America.

Visitors can walk through meadows where the young Lees rode their famous horses and followed a trail to the "cool, sweet spring" so fondly remembered by General Lee. Scenic nature trails offer a delightfully varied landscape. A formal garden outlined in boxwood invites a stroll to the east of the Great House. Also at the plantation is a mill (operates seasonally), gardens, log cabin dining room and open spaces.

Information and Activities

Westmoreland State Park
Route 1, Box 600
Montross, VA 22520
(804) 493-8821

Directions: From Montross, take VA PR 3 west four miles to the park entrance on the right. From Fredericksburg, take VA PR 3 east 40 miles to the park entrance. A public telephone is at the park office.

Emergency number: 911 system.

Visitor center: The small wood frame center is open noon to 5 p.m. weekends. From this vantage point, visitors have an elevated view of the Potomac and its marked shipping channels.

Visitors can learn about cultural and natural history at the visitor center in the middle of the park. Displays include caring for the river's resources, bald eagle and osprey information, animal mounts, the settling of the Potomac, fossils and more. Fossils include the tapir, manatee, crocodile, whale, porpoise, rhino, shark-toothed whale, camel, chowder clam, turtle, stingray, limestone catfish, cow shark, six-gill shark, mako shark, a palm-sized white shark tooth and dozens of others. Also on display is a seven-inch long mastodon tooth from 15 million years ago.

Other displays include decoys, waterfowl and fish mounts, bird mounts, a touch table labeled "please touch!," natural history displays, owl pellets, turtle shells, posters, a butterfly collection and lots more interpretive information.

Virginia's first successful colonist was Captain John Smith, who explored the Potomac. As the decades passed the adventurist carved settlements along its shores. From the fertile soil fortunes were made growing tobacco with slave labor. By the mid-1700s rich plantations lined the banks of the Potomac River inland as far as modern-day Washington, D.C.

The Potomac was essential for commerce with ships bringing in sugar, spices, cookware, salt, needles and thread, and luxuries such as silk, china and fine furniture. Ships departed with tobacco, corn, lumber and other raw materials from the land for faraway ports in Europe, England and the West Indies.

When the English first settled in the New World in 1607 at Jamestown, there were about 13,000 Indians occupying the Virginia coastal plain. These Indians were referred to as the Powhatans after their powerful leader, Chief

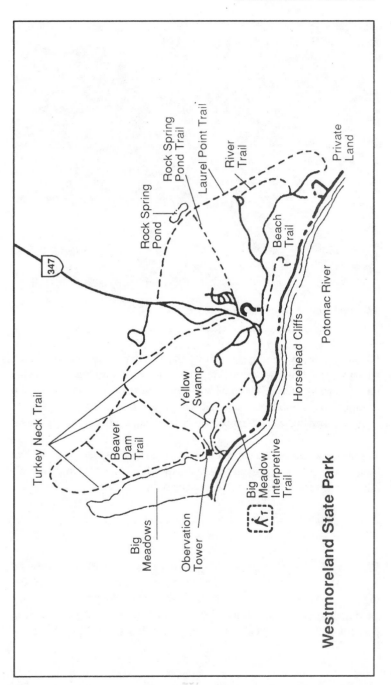

The park has 25 housekeeping cabins.

Powhatan. Many were supported by the Potomac River and its banks, which provided fish, waterfowl for food, water for transportation and clay for pipes and pottery. The Powhatans lived off the land with the women raising corn, squash, peas, potatoes, gourds and tobacco in their gardens. While the men hunted and trapped wild game from the forest and the marsh.

Despite the wealth in the land and water, the Indians did not survive. Settlers brought with them strange diseases and powerful weapons. Only 40 years after the settlers arrived, the Indian society had perished.

A small amphitheater, with lectern, benches and screen is behind the visitor center.

Cabins: Each cozy, rustic-feeling cabin has two car parking spaces and a gravel walkway outlined by landscape timbers. Some of the 25 housekeeping cabins have side yards. Cabins have mini-blinds over the windows, air-conditioning and heat. Many of the cabins have small lawns, screened porches, metal-frame picnic tables and are well separated by vegetation.

Westmoreland has one-and two-bedroom models. Cooking and eating utensils, linens and towels are provided. The cabins are furnished, complete with refrigerator and stove. The cabins are available from early March through early December.

Most cabins are rented by the week or by the night (two nights minimum) and can be reserved in advance. Six of the units (rustic camping cabins) at the park may be rented by the night. Two consecutive weeks is the longest permitted stay. Firewood is offered to cabin guests as supply permits. Cots can be rented from the park.

Cabins 11-14 are up a short gravel road to a hilly, quiet area. Wooden valleys and hills roll through the tract where cabins 1-18 are located. Cabins 15-18 are modern design.

Cabins 1-10 and 15-18 are south of a swimming pool and boat launch along a spur with a dead-end turnaround. Cabins 1-4 are log-style cabins with white chinking and a large overhanging porch. They are notched into the woods and include a picnic table. Cabin 5 has vertical log sides, while log cabins 6 and 7 are notched into the woods near trails that access the beach. Cabins 9 and 10 are at the end of the spur and feature a larger lawn for children to play near the cabins.

Cabins 19-25 are on a spur along a ridge. Some of the units have an obscured views of the river. Cabins 24 and 25 are constructed of cement block. Just a few steps from cabin 25 is a panoramic view of the wide Potomac River from on top of the high bank 100 or more feet above the water's surface. Be careful along the cliff; it does slide and most of the its edge is secured by a protective wire fence.

Campground: The campground has 138 sites in three areas, A, B, and C. Reservations are taken through the central office in Richmond.

Near the park store and restaurant, campground A is one loop and spur with thick woods and many pull-through sites. Each site has a gravel and hard-packed dirt pad, ground-mounted fire box and picnic table. The older style bathhouse has flush toilets, deep laundry sinks and showers. Twenty sites have hookups. Larger RV rigs tend to stay in the A section.

The L-shaped pool has two diving boards.

Sites 19-22 are high and dry, with a view into a wooden ravine. Sites 24 and 25 join each other along a ridge line and would be a good selection for two families camping next to each other. Some of the sites in campground A are somewhat sandy and dry. They are on varying elevations and against natural areas. Site 43 is a terrific site for a medium-sized RV rig.

Also in this loop are six tiny brown cabins with asphalt shingles and shutter-style windows (with no glass). The sparse cabins are like a wooden tent, four walls and a roof, with no furnishings except simple wooden bunks. Many cabin users also pitch a tent next to the small wood-frame structures.

Campground B, the most popular loop according to staff, is shady with a gravel road that traces through the one loop and two spurs. The loop has an access for the Rock Springs and Laurel Point trails. Sites in the loop are smaller than in the A section. They have sandy gravel pads, fire rings, limited electrical hook-ups and picnic tables. Tent and popup campers are the most comfortable in this wooded tract. Sites 31 and 32, near the bathhouse (with exterior slop sink and soft drink machines), are large enough for a medium-sized RV rigs. Some of the sites in the 40s, especially site 43, could accommodate a medium-sized trailer. Sites 50 an 51 are ideal for two families who want to camp adjacent to each other. This loop has a scattering of larger sites; take an inspection trip through the loop before selecting a site.

Campground C is one big loop, and is rolling and mostly shady, much like loop B. Campers are greeted by gravel pads, fire rings and picnic tables. Campground C has no electrical sites and is used mostly for group camping.

Campgrounds, park roads, day-use areas, shelters and buildings in many Virginia state parks were the handiwork of the Civilian Conservation Corps (CCC). The program was one of the means of alleviating hardships prevalent during the Great Depression. President Franklin D. Roosevelt established the CCC in 1933. The public works program put thousands of unemployed men to work planting trees, building dams and creating parks throughout the Commonwealth. The young men were paid $30 per month, with most of the money sent home to their families. The men usually set aside five dollars for pocket money.

Westmoreland was one of the six original state parks built by the CCC in 1936.

Restaurant/store: Cozy and shady, the food is good, too. The small brown wood-frame eatery (The Park Restaurant, open Wednesday - Sunday) has French-style entrance doors and is perched on the shady cliffs overlooking the wide river. It is connected to the campground store, which is open daily during the summer. The family restaurant has a vaulted ceiling with wood floors and seating around 20 tables. The wood paneling, furniture and floors and beam ceiling offer a charming, country-style atmosphere.

The very neat and clean park store features camping necessities, hot dogs and buns, candy, bread, soft drinks, limited grocery items, T-shirts, cooking and cleaning supplies, hats, ice cream treats, sunscreen, propane fuel, coolers, post cards and other small items.

Fishing: Striped bass were once so abundant in the Potomac waters that the Indians and colonists used what they couldn't eat as fertilizer for gardens. But in recent years striped bass numbers have become danger-ously low, probably due to over-fishing, pollution and loss of habitat for the young. Now the future is more promising, fishing is carefully regulated and the waters are getting cleaner. Much of the aquatic habitat is returning. Striped bass are being raised in hatcheries and are planted all along the tidewater region by the millions.

Potomac River anglers have an opportunity to land a variety of saltwater fish species. Among the most common are bluefish, spot, croaker, flounder and perch. Shrimp cutbait, bloodworms and artificial lures fished on the bottom or trolled can catch these species. Stripers, renowned as a fighter, are also tasty and caught using yellow spinners and bucktails.

Bottom fishing in the Potomac starts in June for trout, flounder, spot and croaker.

Other species in the upper Potomac include bowfin, carp, catfish, crappie, trout, large- and smallmouth bass, suckers, sunfish and chain pickerel.

Boating: Use care down the steep, winding road to the single-lane boat launching ramp (small fee) and boat rental concession. The low, tan boat rental sells gasoline, insect repellent, charcoal, nets, ice, limited fishing supplies, bait and more. Pedal boats and rowboats are rented by the hour or longer. Many picnic tables are near the tiny boat rental concession.

Hiking: Seven park trails are designed primarily to deliver visitors from one developed amenity to the next. The interpretive Big Meadow (.6 mile) and Turkey Neck (2.5 miles) trails combine to form a loop pasts come scenic views, Horsehead Cliffs and wetlands. Most of the trails are easy to moderate in difficulty.

About one-quarter-mile from the visitor center is the Big Meadow Trailhead. As you walk down the ridge of this 1890 logging trail, notice markers (there are 11 of them) that correspond with a self-guided trail brochure available at the visitor center, distribution boxes and park office. The trail has an overlook on the Yellows Swamp and crosses boardwalks, taking walkers to views of the beach, fossil-rich Horsehead Cliffs and the river.

Turkey Neck Trail winds by a wetland beside Yellow Swamp, over board

The modest cabins are sometimes called "wooden tents."

walks and back. Laurel Point Trail (1.3 miles) crosses once-farmed fields, past a small pond where you can access Rock Spring Pond Trail, then crosses near the north end of the campground.

Laurel Point Trail (2 miles) is a forested trail passing over land that was farmed before the development of the park in 1936. Hikers can search for evidence of the farmer's plow. The vegetation is in succession, from low grasses to low shrubs and pine to a broadleaf forest. The moderately difficult trail ends at the boat launch and day-use area. The trailhead and small parking area are off the main park road.

Day-use areas: The primary day-use areas are near the swimming pool, along the shoreline near the boat rental west of the park office. Pedestal grills and picnic tables are scattered along the narrow sandy shore. The smell of barbecued chicken can be overwhelming good on most weekends during the summer. A few picnic pavilions with stone chimneys are in the main day-use area.

In the distance, bald-faced cliffs and wide views of boating traffic on the river makes the concentrated area a popular family picnic site. Many day-users here are also using the swimming pool (small fee). A small concession stand with walkup windows serves the entire area and is next to the fenced-in swimming pool. The concession stand serves pizza, sno cones, chicken fillet sandwiches, hamburgers, beverages, onion rings and chips. The concession also sells sunscreen.

Swimming pool: Two diving boards, supervised by lifeguards, keep the action fast in the L-shaped pool. An eight-foot-tall tan wire fence surrounds the noisy pool. The pool ranges from four to 10 feet in depth. Several wooden benches and teal-colored lounge chairs are scattered around the deck. A small blue slide popular with younger children allows them to splash into the cool, shallow water.

Cement-block changing rooms are next to the swimming pool and they have outside drinking fountains. Showers are inside the bathhouse.

From the swimming pool is one of the best river views in the park. Swimming passes and coupon books are available from the pool attendant.

Nature: Westmoreland's tall cliffs contain an abundance of fossils of prehistoric sharks, dolphins and whales. Representing the whale family were early baleen whales that strained zoo plankton from the seas, long- and short-snouted dolphins and carnivorous sperm whales. Sharks common to the Miocene epoch about 22 million to 23 million years ago were the hammerhead and sand sharks, six-gilled shark and giant white shark. Many of the mammals in the sea vanished about the time the first man appeared, roughly two million years ago.

Proof of their existence are their fossilized remains, some of which are buried below the surface throughout the park.

Today the Potomac River attracts a variety of birds, the most majestic of these the bald eagle. The adult bald eagle is easy to identify with its white head and tail. They also have a six-to seven-foot wing span. Plumage depends on age. A complete, all-over dark plumage is characteristic of a first year. In the second and third years, a molted plumage and white belly are evident. At four years the eagle begins its molt to the first adult plumage.

In the first three stages, a small white line is on the underwing, and is not present on the adult eagle. Many bald eagles are seen from the visitor center soaring above the river, looking for a meal. Also examine snags along the river for perching bald eagles.

Osprey are also seen in good numbers cruising the cliff line and river. The osprey is a remarkable bird or prey feeding mostly on fish, with well-adapted and specially textured feet that help the lightning-fast bird hold on to slippery fish. Osprey are capable of hovering briefly, then diving into the water and most often emerging with a flapping fish held firmly in its talons. Once back in the air, the bird deftly aligns the fish so its head faces forward, reducing the air flow against its body.

Also common to Westmoreland and the Potomac River are migrating ducks and geese, cormorants, herons and gulls. Watch for perching birds in the trees along the river's woodland shore. Their high visibility along the river's shore makes bird watching fun and rewarding. White-tailed deer are also abundant in the early morning or late afternoon throughout the year. Look for wild turkey in the grassy clearing. Other mammals that are sometimes seen in the park are river otters, beavers and muskrat.

Insiders tips: Shark teeth collecting is popular below the cliffs. If you want to see more shark's teeth and other zany stuff (crocodile teeth, live iguanas, whale bones, Civil War artifacts, etc.), visit the Historyland Highway General Store (on Route 3) only two miles from the park. Chris Boswell, the owner of the store, collects some huge shark's teeth from the park, donates them to the visitors center and will readily talk about the area's history if you stop by his cluttered, unique store.

33 York River State Park

Land: 2,505 acres
Water: Taskinas Creek/York River

York River has more than three miles of riverfront, 15 miles of trails that span freshwater and saltwater marshes, hardwood forests, gentle bridle trails, canoe rentals, an interpretive visitor center, day-use areas and some of the finest outdoor education programming in the state park system.

The unit takes its name from the river along its border, which is formed from the joining of the Pamunkey and Mattaponi (pronounced mat-a-one-EYE) rivers at West Point, 10 miles upriver from the park. The park was once the site of a 17th and 18th century public tobacco warehouse where local planters stored their crops to be shipped to England. Remnants of wooden "corduroy" roads dating from this period can still be seen along Taskinas Creek at low tide.

The York River has been a well designed highway of commerce for centuries. The Mattaponi and Pamunkey Indians inhabited the area before the 1700s and used the river to carry fur, fish, pottery and other valuables for trade.

In the 1700s and 1800s colonists transported tobacco and farm products on the York. Today recreational and commercial fishermen use the river daily during certain seasons. Pleasure boaters may also be seen on the river— motorboats, sailboats and windsurfers. You may even see tugboats pushing barges of wood chips for paper making from Virginia's east shore and North Carolina to the paper mill in West Point.

The history of the park goes back much farther than human habitation. A few million years ago this land was covered by an ocean full of life. Early whales, porpoises, sharks, clams, scallops and snails all left traces of their existence which we now find as fossils (the word fossil means to dig up). The York River formed 4,000 to 6,000 years ago. Some geological formations are nine million to 10 million years old. These various land forms are filled with fossils that can be found along the York River shore. One of the best places to look for fossils is just off the Mattaponi Trail, parallel to the river at the base of the eroded cliffs. Limit your actual collecting to the beach and take only a few representative pieces.

The park opened in 1980.

Information and Activities

York River State Park
5526 Riverview Road
Williamsburg, VA 23188
(804) 566-3036

Directions: Take exit 231B off I-64, 11 miles north of Williamsburg, near Croaker. The region is gently rolling with mixed agricultural fields interspersed with small woodlots. There is no swimming or camping at York River.

Emergency number: 911 system.

Visitor center: Planting beds outlined by landscape timber line the entrance into the center. Flora specimens in the wildflower planting beds include inkberry, American beautyberry, viburnums, sweet pepper bush, Virginia willow, rose vervain and other plants and low shrubs that attract

York River State Park

butterflies.

The gray center with steel roof is open 9 a.m. - 5 p.m. Tuesday - Friday and 10 a.m. - 6 p.m. Saturday and Sunday. Books, novelties, T-shirts and other small items are sold. The timber-frame-style building houses a number of interesting displays including old wood boats and marina items, free-standing kiosk of York River fishermen, aquariums, decoy displays, brochure rack, Chesapeake Bay history, estuary system model, fossil samples, and archaeological and geological history including the Croakers Lands archaeological site, where many pieces of pottery were recovered.

You will learn that nine million to 10 million years ago the park was under water. The York River is built on what was then the floor of a shallow sea which extends to about where the city of Richmond now stands. As the sea slowly receded, a series of rivers and streams were left in its place. Many fossils on display in the visitor center were found along the stream banks, exposed by erosion.

Snack machines and rest rooms are accessible from the outside and are at one end of the wood-sided visitor center. The park office is in the visitor center.

Natural history displays include a bird identification board, underwater diorama of fish and their habitats, audio/visual presentation and other interpretive displays that detail estuary life and habitats.

A terrific overlook onto meandering Taskinas Creek is near the visitor center.

Fishing: Anglers can fish at three areas in the park. Woodstock Pond (seven acres) offers freshwater anglers a chance to catch bluegill, large-mouth bass and rough fish. The Taskinas Creek is brackish and has catfish, some stripers, croakers and white perch. Saltwater anglers can access the York River at Croaker Landing and fish for catfish, spot, croaker trout and crabs. There are also three fishing piers (courtesy docks) at the landing.

The York River, which at times is heavily fished, is a broad tidal river with a channel that can be more than 50 feet deep where the river meets the bay. Anglers may want to try many locations along the river. Access points are at Gloucester Point, Tide Mill, West Point, Messick, Tanyard and other sites. Species include croaker, gray trout, spot, striped bass, flounder and bluefish.

The croaker, or drum, is plentiful at York River. A large fish, croakers make a croaking sound produced by the muscles adjacent to the swim bladder. The sound increases during mating and after sunset. Croakers live in murky water such as estuaries and use this sound system to navigate. Distinguishing physical features include two dorsal fins, the first with a short base, and the second with a long base and many rays. Their colors are somber, with shades of brownish-green and gray. They have a short anal fin with two spines. They are carnivorous, feeding on mollusks and crustaceans. The croaker is abundant and an important food fish found from Texas to Cape Cod. It is one of the most familiar and easy to catch fish in the York River area.

Boating: A small two-lane boat launching ramp is at the end of Route 605 (Croaker Landing Road). The launch has a nearby rest room and 40-space parking and staging area for small boat trailers and towing vehicles. The ramp accesses the two-mile-wide York River.

Canoes are rented by the hour at Woodstock Pond from May to October. Lifejackets and paddles are provided.

Paddling on the Taskinas Creek is a quiet experience. It's a tidal estuary that winds gracefully through the salt marshes of the York River shoreline. Marshes are among the most productive plant communities on Earth. A dominant and very important salt grass plant is the cordgrass group, Spartina. When the cordgrass dies the dead plant material or detritus serves as a vital food source for microscopic organisms. It is a major part of the food web. The marsh is also important as a habitat for many mammals, fish, reptiles and amphibians.

The salt marsh community you paddle through also prevents erosion by breaking up waves as they approach the shore, and serves as a filtering system for sediment and pollutants before they reach the stream. Taskinas Creek is one of only four sites along the York River that has been designated as a Chesapeake Bay Estuary Research Reserve by the Commonwealth. These reserves provide representative natural areas for long-term research

Visitor Center at York River State Park.

and monitoring in order to improve scientific understanding of the estuary system.

Hiking: The Woodstock Pond Trail (1.3 miles) features exercise stations that include stretching stations, bars and other devices. The Blue Bird Loop Trail is hard-surfaced and accessible to persons with disabilities. The park has 14 trails; many are slightly over a mile long and form concentric loops. A trail map is available at the visitor center.

The Taskanis Creek Trail (trail 1, 1.6 miles) is a self-guided interpretive trail that passes through a number of settings ranging from field to forest to marsh. Numbered markers along the trail correspond with numbered paragraphs in a 20-page brochure that describes points of interest.

The opening paragraph in the handsome booklet with line drawings says that many habitats are along edge areas "where sky meets earth, water meets land, field meets forest. Some edges are as broad as a marsh; others as narrow as a blade of grass. Some are as local as a turtle's mossy back

Equestrians have a large staging area near the trailhead.

others as expansive as the coasts of the world. Clinging to these edges is life."

The free booklet has a map and descriptions of hedges (which are a thin edge where seeds grow and birds flock), Christmas ferns, forests and field edges (a place of goldenrod, daisies, sweet gum and thickets), the forest floor (where the leaves of autumn build soil, and nutrients are stored), forest succession, trees, living creatures large and small, tidal marshes (which is in continuous fluctuation, with rich soil, cordgrass, mink, raccoon and herons), fiddle crabs, mountain lake, biting bugs, cicada (a noisy insect that emerges after four to 17 years underground and buzzes loudly from treetops), animal tracks and lots more. The fine booklet was produced by the senior art class at Lafayette High School in Williamsburg.

Biking: York River has more than 15 miles of easy bike trails that wind from the visitor center to the riverside overlook and beyond. The Backbone, Riverview, White and Woodstock trails are among the most popular for biking. Remember to ride on designated trails. The Riverview Trail is the only challenging trail, with spots of deep sand and a narrow single track.

Many cyclists stop along the trail, scramble up and down the cliffs and look for fossils in the high bank.

Bridle trails: Trail riders have a large, grassy and partly shady staging area where they can park truck and trailer and saddle up. The area has a few picnic tables and modern rest room. The designated area is quiet, with no through traffic. Other day-use areas and the visitor center are nearby. Horses and bikes share the designated trails.

The river trail is the most popular with bikers and equestrians.

Day-use areas: Most day-use amenities are near the visitor center, where the Taskinas Creek meanders by. Volleyball, horseshoe courts, play apparatus and open spaces are dotted with picnic tables near the visitor center. One picnic shelter is near the visitor center.

A small amphitheater, built into a knoll, is near the visitor center and is the launching point for many hikes and other interpretive programs.

Nature: Interpretive programs include fossil hunts, discovery hikes, tree hikes, tiny tots exploring nature, junior rangers, boat safety, marine life, themed nature hikes, water testing, teacher in-service programs, interpretive canoe tours of the Taskinas Creek and many estuarine life study classes. During the summer an ecology lab is complete with a variety of aquarium tanks where native fauna are maintained. Many school groups and other programs start or end in the ecology room in the visitor center. The room also has interpretive posters and materials that teach visitors about brackish water, pond ecology and reptiles and amphibians.

Guided canoe trips (small fee) are on the weekend only and registration is required. Children must be 3 years of age and all children between 3 and 15 years must have a parent or guardian with them on the trip. Bring insect repellent and sunscreen; wear functional shoes and a jug of water. The trip includes life jackets, paddles and an interpreter who is certified by the American Canoe Association and/or the Red Cross.

Birders will be interested to know the park publishes an excellent checklist that details avian species seen, when and where. The handy list talks about many birding habitats (open water, sand and mud flat, marsh, field, hardwood swamp, uplands, etc.) and abundancy by season. Species seen include four species of terns, four types of owls, several swallows, osprey, some hawks, many sparrow types and lots of warblers. The six-panel brochure also has a small map that depicts the areas where certain habitats in the park are located.

Woodland mammals seen include deer, fox, raccoon, river otter near Taskinas Creek and others.

Fiddler crab watching is entertaining and fun. The pancake-like crabs put on a wonderful show defending their territories, mating and lurching about, inspecting the earth for food. A simple pair of low-power binoculars is all you need to watch. Look for the crabs to wave, fight, burrow, grip and fling stuff, tap their claws, lunge and build.

Fiddler crabs play an important role in the ecology of the marsh. Through their feeding activities, fiddlers are regulators of primary production and decomposition. They are also an important link in the food chain. They are eaten by larger animals such as blue crabs, rails, egrets, herons and raccoons. The biomass (numbers) of crabs is huge. In some areas around the region there can be up to 500,000 crabs per 2.5 acres! This number attests to the tremendous productivity of wetlands.

The busy crabs forage for food as soon as the tide recedes from their burrows. At low tide the marsh and sand fiddlers sometimes congregate in large clusters, or droves, on open mud or sand flats. They feed on microorganisms and detritus (disintegrated plant and animal matter). Droving is like schooling in fish and fun to watch. The behavior provides protection, while at high tide the feisty crabs hide in their burrows to avoid swimming predators.

Fiddler crabs love to fiddle about, displaying some zany and interesting behavior patterns that can be easily viewed if you are quiet and patient. Males are territorial and will fight like crazy over burrows. Their combat has a forceful component of pushes, grips or flings and a ritualized component of claw rubs, aggressive stances and lunges. Worked-up males also make sounds by tapping the ground, stomping, rubbing their legs together and chirping like a cricket.

The males also wave their big claw to show off and attract mates.

Females in the Chesapeake Bay region spawn from June to August, carrying 10,000 to 30,000 eggs depending on their size and species. About two weeks after spawning, the eggs hatch as planktonic larvae called zoeae. The zoeal stage larvae are carried by winds and currents into the main streams where they molt many times to become juvenile crabs. After a few more shell molts, they become adults.

Fiddler crabs are avid burrowers. They dig either straight or J-shaped holes and many reach two feet in depth. It can take the little workers several days to build the burrow, but if maintained, it can last forever. Each burrow houses one crab, except during mating season. The park offers guided fiddler crab walks during the summer. Check with the visitor center for a schedule.

Hunting: About one week each year the park is closed for deer hunting. About 40 stands are maintained and hunters are selected through a random lottery.

Special events: Estuary Day is an annual celebration of estuaries, the fertile waterways where rivers meet the sea. The event is usually held in mid-September and features naturalist hikes and tours, exhibits, a pontoon cruise, canoe trips, food, bayscaping (learn how proper landscaping can save energy, lower pollution, etc.) and lots more.

Insiders tips: Some vistas over the York River are worth checking out. Bring your horse or try some fiddler crab watching along the flats.

Other great books available:

Indiana State Parks Guidebook:

A Hoosier's Guide to Parks, Recreation Areas and Reservoirs
by John Goll

Indiana's only comprehensive guide to the great state parks! All the details about camping, hiking, scenic areas, lodges, fishing and family recreation opportunities. Maps, photos, directions, 268 pages, $14.95.

Michigan State Parks Guidebook:

A complete recreation guide for campers, boaters, anglers, hikers and skiers by Jim DuFresne

Complete information on Michigan's 92 diverse state parks. Welcome to Michigan's playground! Wilderness retreats, great fishing and the nation's longest freshwater shoreline. Maps, photos, 287 pages, $12.95.

Ohio State Parks Guidebook:

A complete outdoor recreation guide to the Buckeye state.
by Art Weber and Bill Bailey

With 65 maps and 90 photographs. Complete park descriptions, camping, hiking trails, handicapped accessibilities, boating, fishing, rent-a-camps, rentals, lodges, beaches and nature notes. Everything you need to know to enjoy Ohio's terrific state parks! 384 pages, directions, phone numbers, $14.95.

Illinois State Parks Guidebook:

A complete Outdoor Recreation Guide
by Bill Bailey

Detailed guide to the natural features and facilities of the great Illinois state park system. Where to camp, fishing tips and hot spots, trails, watersports, historical and educational attractions, lodging, beaches, cabins, day-use areas, natural history, skiing and more. Photos, maps, 352 pages, $14.95.

Pennsylvania State Parks Guidebook:

A Complete Outdoor Recreation Guide, by Bill Bailey

Your total guidebook to the state parks and natural areas of the Keystone state. Pennsylvania has more state parks than any other state east of the Mississippi River. A thoughful and detailed guide to mountain parks, campgrounds, fishing, hiking, boating, swimming, cabins, natural areas and lots more. Photos, maps, 400 pages, $15.95.

Ask for these fine books at your bookstore,
or order direct from
Glovebox Guidebooks of America.

To order call (800) 289-4843, or send a check or money order, plus $2 shipping for the first book and .50 cents for each additional book, to: **Glovebox Guidebooks of America**
1112 Washburn East
Saginaw, Michigan 48602-2977
24-hour fax order: (517) 792-8363.

About the Author

Bill Bailey is America's foremost experts on outdoor recreation, environmental education, parks and communications.

He is the author of *Pennsylvania State Parks, Kentucky State Parks, Ohio State Parks, Ilinois State Parks, Thrill Sports* (editor of the *Indiana State Parks* guidebook) and six other books.

Bill is a former director of a large environmental eduction center; chief naturalist, communication consultant, publisher and senior public administrator. Bill has been an active member of the Outdoor Writers Assocation of America (OWAA) since 1980. He lives with his wife and two sons, "Buster" and Mike.